# FIGHTERS
# O V E R
# I S R A E L

# FIGHTERS OVER ISRAEL

## LON NORDEEN

### ILLUSTRATIONS BY KEN KOTIK

ORION BOOKS/NEW YORK

Published by Orion Books, a division of Crown Publishers, Inc.,
201 East 50th Street, New York, New York 10022.
Member of the Crown Publishing Group.

ORION and colophon are trademarks of Crown Publishers, Inc.

Manufactured in the United States of America

Library of Congress Cataloging-in-Publication Data
Nordeen, Lon O.
    Fighters over Israel: the story of the Israeli Air Force from the
War of Independence to the Bekaa Valley/by Lon Nordeen: with
illustrations by Ken Kotik.—1st ed.
      p.  cm.
    1. Israel. Hel ha-avir—History.  2. Israel—History, Military.
I. Title.
UG635.I75N67  1990                                    90-34675
358.4' 0095694—dc20                                        CIP
              ISBN 0-517-56603-6

Design by Jake Victor Thomas

10 9 8 7 6 5 4 3 2 1

First Edition

# Contents

# Acknowledgments

I would like to thank the following people who provided research material, photographs, and other assistance: Keith Schirmer; Michael Manahan and Priut Design; Rudy Augerten; Col. Elizer Cohen (Ret.); Lt. Col. S. Gilboa (Ret.); Lt. Col. Nori Harel (Ret.); Aharon Lapidot, editor, *Israel Air Force Magazine*; Lou Lenard; Col. N. Merchavi (Ret.); Lt. Col. Y. Offer (Ret.); Maj. Gen. Benjamin Peled (Ret.); Brig. Gen. Joshua Shani (Ret.); Col. Yallo Shavit (Ret.); Lt. Hila Yafat; Col. Aharon Yoeli (Ret.); Amir Yoeli; and many other Israel Air Force personnel who cannot be named.

Yigal and Nurit Berman were very kind and helpful, while Shirley King deserves special mention for her assistance.

Most of all, Suzy and Brad, thank you for being so patient and understanding.

Lon Nordeen

I would like to thank Dot and Erin for their sacrifice and understanding; my mother and father for teaching through example and value of hard work; and Bob Pukala, John Brooks, and Robert (Beaver) Blake for research materials used in the preparation of the illustrations.

Ken Kotik

# Israel's Changing Borders

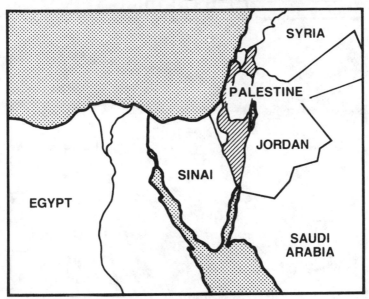

**1947 U.N. PARTITION**

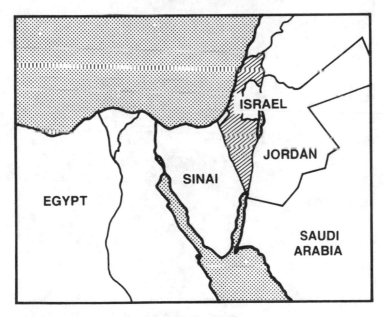

**1949 ISRAELI–ARAB
ARMISTICE LINES**

# Operation Kadesh
# 1956 Conflict

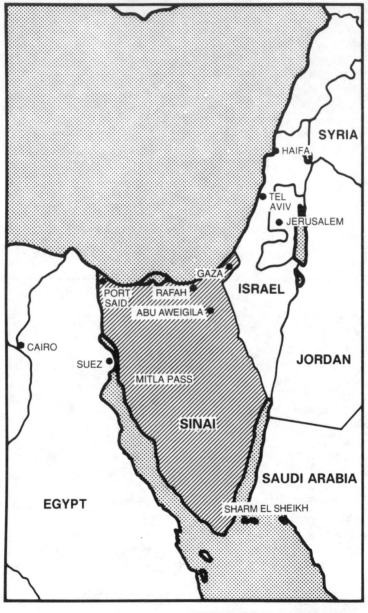

SYRIA

HAIFA

TEL AVIV

JERUSALEM

GAZA

PORT SAID

RAFAH

ABU AWEIGILA

ISRAEL

CAIRO

SUEZ

MITLA PASS

JORDAN

SINAI

SAUDI ARABIA

EGYPT

SHARM EL SHEIKH

////// TERRITORY CAPTURED
////// DURING THE 1956 CONFLICT

# 1967 Arab Israeli War

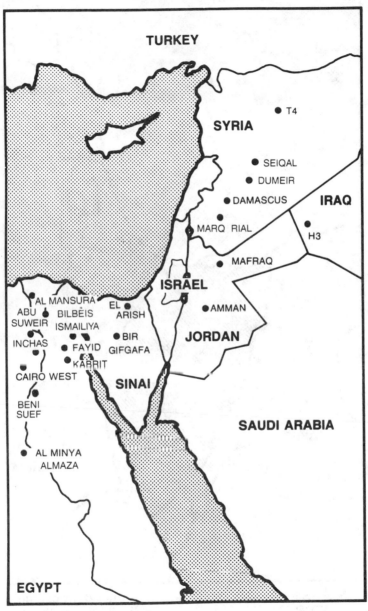

TURKEY

SYRIA

● T4

● SEIQAL

● DUMEIR

● DAMASCUS

IRAQ

● MARQ RIAL

● H3

● MAFRAQ

ISRAEL

● AMMAN

AL MANSURA    EL
ABU           BILBEIS   ARISH
SUWEIR        ISMAILIYA

INCHAS        ● BIR
        FAYID   GIFGAFA
        KABRIT

JORDAN

CAIRO WEST    SINAI

BENI
SUEF

● AL MINYA
ALMAZA

SAUDI ARABIA

EGYPT

● AIR BASES ATTACKED
BY IAF IN 1967

# Israel and Occupied Lands

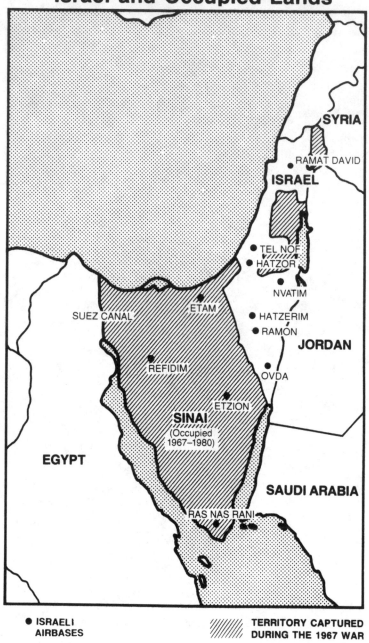

# The Entebbe Rescue Mission

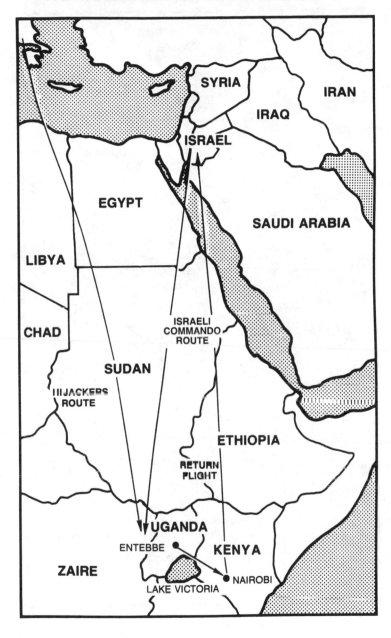

# IAF Operations in Lebanon

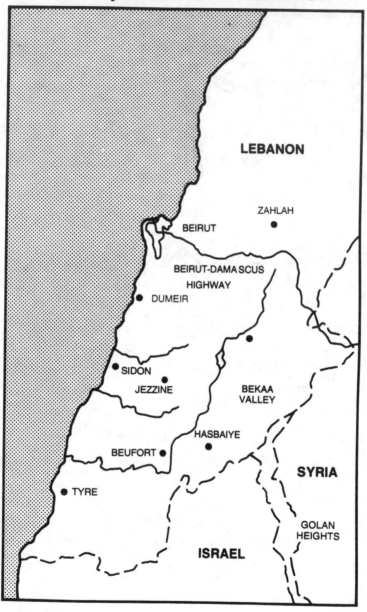

# Introduction

*I*srael is a small nation surrounded by neighbors who have tried to destroy it since its birth on May 15, 1948. Arab neighbors regard the land on which Israel stands as theirs, unjustly taken from them by the British. Arab forces have repeatedly tried to undermine the Jewish state through overt hostile actions as well as through more subtle efforts. During the four plus decades that have elapsed since the creation of Israel, its citizens have fought four major wars (1948, 1956, 1967, 1973), several significant conflicts (including the War of Attrition, Operation Litani, and Operation Peace for Galilee in Lebanon), and thousands of local battles and terrorist engagements. The Israeli Air Force has played a major role in most of these military actions.

Outnumbered and surrounded by hostile Arab nations, Israel has from its inception had a critical need to develop its air force. The very day Israel's independence was declared, Arab planes bombed Tel Aviv. Even in the days of propeller-driven aircraft, Tel Aviv and other major Israeli cities were less than fifteen minutes flying time from airfields in Egypt, Jordan, and Syria. In early 1948 Israel's air fleet consisted of only two dozen light, civilian planes. Shortly after it became a nation, the air force was upgraded and by 1949 grew to over one hundred transports, fighters, and bombers. The founders of the Israeli Air Force (IAF) did not have a defensive mentality: the first fighter missions flown by the air arm on May 29, 1948, attacked an advancing Egyptian column.

Since Israel must fight outnumbered, it relies on the IAF and reserve forces to even the odds. In a conflict, the IAF is charged with defending the skies so reserve forces can mobilize. Destruction of enemy air forces on the ground, as in the 1967 war, is one way to achieve air superiority. Once air superiority is achieved, the IAF concentrates on providing support for Israeli ground and naval forces with fighter sweeps, close air support, strikes against enemy troops well behind the battle area, supply drops, casualty evacuation, scouting, air defense, and many other missions.

From its humble beginning in 1947 when the air arm comprised less than twenty worn-out light aircraft, the IAF has developed into one of the most experienced and respected air forces in the world. Israel, a country with a population of only four million, today fields an air force comparable in size to that of such major powers as Britain, France, and West Germany. In terms of experience, the IAF can match even the much larger air forces of the United States and the Soviet Union. During the past twenty-five years the IAF has claimed more than five hundred air-to-air victories against first-line Soviet-built jet fighters, flown hundreds of thousands of combat sorties, and successfully battled the densest collection of air defense weaponry ever deployed.

To upgrade the effectiveness of their forces, many countries have sought to learn the IAF's secrets of success. Israel in general and the IAF in particular are among the most security-conscious groups in the world. Despite mountains of press, accurate information on the IAF's history, structure, development, doctrine, tactics, and equipment is limited. More than a decade of research has gone into the production of this work. The author and illustrator have reviewed volumes of information on the IAF and interviewed dozens of people—including those who have served with the force and its former opponents—in search of historical information.

Our research has led us to the conclusion that people are the real secret weapon of the IAF. Recruiting concepts, such as The Good Ones Fly, have attracted the best and brightest Israeli youth to the IAF. Screening, testing, and training procedures developed over several decades along with the rigors of almost continuous combat have produced pilots, navigators, and other aircrew who are second to none. The Israelis fly their planes aggressively, and training standards are high. During the past four decades, dozens of IAF aircraft and numerous aircrew have been lost in operational accidents during realistic training. Despite these losses the IAF has continued to train aggressively following the old Roman proverb which states that, "The more you sweat in peace, the less you will bleed in war." The same tough screening and training standards have been applied to the mechanics, weapons loaders, air defense gunners, intelligence staffs, and other personnel who make up the IAF. *Fighters Over Israel* tells the story of this dynamic air force and how it accomplished the task that needed to be done.

# 1

# *War of Independence*

*T*he creation of the Israeli Air Force was a natural outgrowth of Jewish efforts to form self-defense military organizations. An air service equipped with light civilian airplanes was formed in late 1947. With the birth of Israel in 1948, this air service became part of the new Israeli military.

In 1917, the year the British took control of Palestine, approximately 85,000 Jews lived in the area. In exchange for Jewish support during World War I, Britian backed the creation of a Jewish homeland, thus opening the way for the immigration of Jews to Palestine.[1]

As Jewish immigration increased, so did the anxieties of Palestinian Arabs. The Palestinans thought the influx of Jews would threaten their rights to the land. The popular Muslim Mufti of Jerusalem, Haj Amin el Husseini, called for Arabs to resist the Jews. Disturbances between the two cultures increased and large-scale anti-Jewish riots occurred in Palestine in 1922, 1929, and 1936.

To protect themselves from persecution, Jewish community leaders established a number of defense organizations. In the 1920s the Jews established militia units collectively known as the *Haganah* (Defense) to protect Jewish settlements. In the face of continued violence, some Jews favored a more aggressive approach. The Irgun Zvai Leumi (National Military Organization), headed by Menachem Begin and Lohamei Herut Yisrael (Fighters For Israel and Freedom) struck back against the Arabs and attacked British targets.[2]

The British government attempted to smooth relations in Palestine and moved toward a policy designed to separate Arabs and Jews. The 1937 Peel Commission report concluded that it would be advisable to partition Palestine along ethnic lines: Transjordan for the Arabs, a new Jewish state, and an independent Jerusalem.

The MacDonald White Paper, released by the British government in May 1939, set tight limits on Jewish immigration. These restrictions angered the Jews and prompted members of some of the more violent Jewish military groups to strike out against the British. However, the five hundred thousands Jews in Palestine supported the British once World War II broke out in September 1939. More than forty thousand Jewish volunteers from Palestine served with British and Commonwealth forces during the war. Many Jews fought in combat, some served as members of ground crews in aviation support units, and a small number flew as pilots with the Royal Air Force (RAF) or Commonwealth air arms.

In November 1945, Ernest Bevin, the foreign secretary, announced that Britain planned to continue to follow the Jewish immigration limits established in 1939. Despite worldwide pressure to allow Holocaust victims to settle in Palestine after World War II, British forces turned back refugee ships. In response to these policies, the Jews united in action against the British. The Haganah and other military groups openly clashed with the British troops that garrisoned Palestine, while the Jewish community smuggled in thousands of illegal immigrants.

The British declared martial law and fought back against Jewish terrorism, but their determination soon faded. In February 1947, Bevin referred the "Palestine problem" to the United Nations.[3] He also announced that Britain would withdraw its forces from Palestine by mid-1948. Expecting to have to fight, Jewish community leaders began importing arms and organizing a military force for self defense.

The first Jewish effort to organize an air force took place on November 10, 1947, when military leaders formed the Haganah Sherut-Avir (Air Service). Yehoshua Eshel was named head of this new unit and Aharon Remez appointed chief of operations. A fighter pilot who flew with the RAF during World War II, Remez controlled the day-to-day operations and worked hard to expand the capabilities of the air service.

The Jews faced two major challenges in establishing an air force: finding planes and recruiting pilots. The air service initially had a complement of eleven single-engine light aircraft of the following types: Tiger Moth, R.W.D.-13, Zlin, Taylorcraft, Auster, Seabee, and Rapide.[4] Soon two Taylorcraft and six Auster Autocraft light airplanes were added to this fleet.

In January 1948, Aviron, a Jewish-owned, import company purchased the scrapped hulks of twenty-five Auster light observation aircraft from the British. The Auster was the standard British army artillery observation and liaison aircraft during World War II. The three-seat, high-wing craft could take off from short strips and carry a payload in excess of five hundred pounds.[5] By combining the parts of these surplus hulks, air service maintenance personnel produced six serviceable aircraft. These ex–British Army Austers and civilian light planes constituted the bulk of Israel's air arm until well into 1948. These aircraft were frequently the only link to outlying Jewish villages. In addition to undertaking resupply and reconnaissance missions, air service pilots fired rifles and machine guns and dropped homemade bombs on Arab forces.

Finding pilots to fly the air service planes was difficult; about forty Jewish pilots served initially. Some of these pilots had earned their wings through civilian flying clubs, while others had been trained to fly military aircraft by the RAF and Commonwealth air forces during World War II. The Haganah also used its worldwide network of contacts to recruit foreign pilots.

In November 1947, a UN commission recommended the establishment of separate Arab and Jewish states in Palestine with Jerusalem governed by a UN-sponsored international trusteeship. The plan was ratified by a UN vote on November 29, 1947.

In Palestine, fighting began almost immediately as Arabs and Jews struggled over important settlements, rail centers, and roads. During the first six months of the War of Independence (November 1947–April 1948), Jewish forces were on the defensive. The Haganah was busy organizing combat units and acquiring weapons from British depots and sources overseas. Jewish forces incurred heavy losses while trying to resupply outlying settlements. It was not until the second phase of the war (April–May 1948) that Jewish units conducted several successful offensives. The State of Israel was established on May 15, 1948.

Struggling to establish a homeland, the Jews faced powerful Arab armies. King Farouk's Egyptian Army totaled fifty-five thousand men, plus armor and artillery. The Royal Egyptian Air Force (REAF) included about forty Spitfire fighters, ten C-47 Dakota aircraft modified to carry bombs, twenty Dakota transports, and an assortment of trainer and liaison aircraft.

King Abdullah of Transjordan had one of the most effective armies in the Middle East. This Arab Legion consisted of approximately eight thousand men trained and led by British officers, with armor and artillery support, but no air force.

The eight-thousand strong Syrian army had been trained by the French and included a small element of tanks and self-propelled artillery. The Syrian air component included Harvard trainers that could carry light bombs and machine guns. The smaller four-thousand-man Lebanese army, which shared a heritage of French training and equipment, was also poised to attack Israel.

Iraq was likewise committed to preventing the creation of an independent Jewish State of Israel. The country's twenty-one-thousand-man, British-trained army was well equipped with tanks, armored cars, artillery, and aircraft. The Arab Liberation Army and Arab Home Guard troops were already fighting Jewish forces in Palestine and looked forward to support from neighboring armies.[6]

Arab invasion forces totaled about thirty thousand men with limited armor, artillery, and air support. These forces had significant advantages over Israel in both manpower and equipment, and they could attack the new nation from several directions simultaneously. However, poor communications and rivalries among Arab leaders and army commanders made it difficult to coordinate the actions of the various Arab armies. Morale was another Arab weakness; while Egyptian, Syrian, Lebanese, and other Arab troops were invading Palestine, Jewish soldiers were defending their homes. The Jews could field a force of nearly forty thousand but had weapons for less than half that number and no tanks, fighter aircraft, artillery, or heavy ordinance.[7]

David Ben Gurion, chairman of the Jewish Agency, predicted a long and bloody war would be waged to establish the state of Israel. He believed that Israel would have to fight back several Arab invasions. At a meeting of the Napoi (Labor) party in Tel Aviv in August 1947, Ben Gurion stated that the Haganah would have to "obtain heavy arms: tanks, artillery, halftracks and heavy munitions for the ground units, fighter planes for the foundation of an air force, torpedo boats and even submarines for the Navy."[8] Jewish military leaders were slow to respond, but Ben Gurion began sending agents overseas to buy weapons. In 1945 Ben Gurion had visited the United States and opened communications with Jewish leaders to raise money and secure the necessary equipment.

Yehuda Arazi was sent to New York late in 1947 to acquire aircraft and heavy weapons for the Haganah. Arazi and his associates had a difficult task: Although public opinion favored the Jewish cause, on December 5, 1947, the U.S. government announced a total embargo on arms shipments to the Middle East. Despite intense lobbying by the Jewish agency and pro-Zionist groups, the embargo was maintained.

In late 1947 Adolf (Al) W. Schwimmer, an experienced U.S. Army Air Corps crewman and TWA flight engineer, contacted Shlomo Shamir, the Haganah officer in New York, about a plan to airlift Jewish refugees into Palestine. Arazi agreed to support Schwimmer's plan, provided that aircraft could be acquired quickly. The Schwimmer Aviation Company was hastily established and a maintenance base set up at the Burbank, California, airport. The company bought ten C-46 Commando twin-engine transports and three four-engine Constellation long-range transports from war surplus stocks and reconditioned them at Burbank.[9] Schwimmer also recruited aircrews and maintenance technicians with valuable wartime experience to maintain and fly these aircraft.

The first C-46 left Teterboro, New Jersey, on March 6, 1948, for the long flight to Palestine. Flying the same route traveled by thousands of World War II transports, the C-46 stopped at Labrador, Greenland, Iceland, Ireland, and then Geneva, where the discovery of several pistols by Swiss customs led to long delays. The transport finally arrived in Palestine on May 3, 1948.

Because of U.S. restrictions on exports of aircraft, all of Schwimmer's aircraft were given Panamanian civil registration certificates. Five transports left Panama on May 8, 1948, and headed across South America, the Atlantic, and Africa to the Middle East. It was not until May 16 that the aircraft reached Israel.

Czechoslovakia was looking for foreign currency and was willing to sell arms to any country that could pay in secure Western money. The Czechs had sold rifles, machine guns, and ammunition to Syria, and arranged transport by ship. When Jewish agents reproached Czech officials for the Syrian arms deal, they were told that the sale was simply a commercial transaction and that the Czechs were also willing to sell to the Haganah.

In early 1948, Jewish leaders took the Czechs up on their offer. A DC-4 transport of Overseas Airways, a U.S. firm, left Czechoslovakia on March 31, 1948, bound for an abandoned British air base in Palestine. The aircraft carried a cargo of two hundred rifles, forty machine guns, and ammunition, all of which were distributed to Jewish troops. Although several other supply runs were completed, U.S. authorities in Prague soon put a stop to the airlift, which used U.S.-licensed carriers.

On April 23, 1948, Czechoslovakia agreed to sell ten Avia S199 fighters and provide pilot training to the Jews.[10] Disassembled and in crates, the first Avia was flown out of Zatec, Czechoslovakia, on May 20, only five days after the establishment of the State of Israel. Al Schwimmer's C-46 transports flew a relay between Czechoslovakia and Israel carrying disassembled fighter aircraft and other weapons.

The Avia S199 was not a popular aircraft, but at least it was a fighter that could counter the Egyptian Spitfires on more or less equal terms. At the end of World War II, the Avia aircraft works in Czechoslovakia was producing Messerschmitt bf 109 fighters. When the plane's Daimler Benz 605 engines were no longer available from Germany, Czech engineers substituted the 1350-horsepower Junkers Jumo 211F.

This engine was not an ideal replacement, but it was the only power plant available. The Czechs fitted this engine to the rapidly expanding backlog of airframes coming off their assembly line. The Jumo engine, with its high torque, accentuated the bf 109 fighter's poor takeoff and landing characteristics. The S199 was nicknamed the Mezec, or mule, by Czech pilots.[11]

Czech, Israeli, and Jewish volunteer mechanics reassembled the Avias upon their arrival in Israel. On May 29, 1948, the first four were turned over to the newly commissioned 101st Fighter Squadron, which was based at Eqron near Tel Aviv.[12] Of the five pilots who could fly the Avias, two were Israelis—squadron commander Modi Alon and Ezer Weizman—and three were foreign volunteers, Eddie Cohen from South Africa, and Cy Rubenfield and Lou Lenart, both from the United States.

With the establishment of the State of Israel, the war predicted by Ben Gurion became a reality. Syria and Iraq advanced from the north, Egypt attached from the south, and the Arab Legion invaded Jerusalem. Checking these attacks came at considerable cost to the Israelis, who suffered hundreds of casualties and had to evacuate a number of kibbutzim and towns, including the old city of Jerusalem. Egyptian Spitfires attacked the new nation on its first day as an independent state. In the ensuing weeks, Dakota bombers, escorted by Spitfires, roamed over Israel at will. During one raid, Egyptian bombers hit the central Tel Aviv bus station, killing more than forty people and wounding more than one hundred.

With the founding of Israel, Yisrael Amiv took over the IAF, which was composed of three squadrons, some twenty operational planes and thirty-eight pilots. Amiv's tenure lasted only several weeks and, in late May, Aharon Remez was promoted to commander in chief of the IAF.

Israel's small fleet of light aircraft did what it could to help in the fighting. The existing force had been divided into three squadrons: the Galilee stationed at Yavnell, the Tel Aviv located at Sde Dov, and the Negev based at Dorot and Niram. Often the light planes performed attack missions using hand-dropped bombs and machine guns. One Jewish pilot, known simply as Pinchas, described how he readied his Auster for an attack:

> I asked the settlers to get me a machine gunner. One of
> the boys of the village offered to be my machine gunner.
> I took on a load of grenades. Then I ripped off both
> doors of my plane to give my gunner, whom I strapped
> into his seat, room to maneuver. I set up the gun so the
> propellers would not interfere with its action. Then we
> took off. A few minutes later we were flying over the
> Nvatim region where the Arab bands were attacking. We
> opened fire with great success; before long the enemy
> was in flight.[13]

These nuisance raiders had little impact on the course of battle but continued to chip away at the morale of the enemy.

Lou Lenart, an American pilot who flew some of the first fighter missions of the Israel Air Force, described the events:

We knew the Egyptians had over forty aircraft, mostly Spitfire fighters. We also knew that at the beginning we had only four aircraft . . . what could we do to have an impact?

We got to Israel along with the aircraft, and the mechanics worked to reassemble the fighters inside two hangars. As luck would have it, one day the Egyptians bombed the other hangar, the one which did not contain our planes, but several people were killed. We worked feverishly to get the planes together to commit them as soon as possible. The plan was to attack El Arish at first light as soon as we were ready. The first flight was to be a test flight and a combat mission at the same time. However, at about five o'clock in the evening on May twenty-ninth the commander of the Givati Brigade came up. They had blown the bridge at Isdud—and they were desperate because between the Egyptian army of ten thousand men with several hundred vehicles and Tel Aviv stood only about 250 Israeli soldiers. The Egyptians were so confident of victory that they were lined up bumper to bumper behind the bridge. We were told that it was a matter of life and death that we fly *right now*. I wasn't sure where Isdud was—I had only been in the country a few days, but I knew it was very close.

So we climbed into the airplanes and there was a great amount of excitement—it was the culmination of all we had worked for and a chance for us to strike back.

At a signal the doors opened, engines started, and we did a fast taxi out to the head of the runway. It was a runway heading west toward the sea. I looked back and saw the other aircraft taxiing behind me. At the head of the runway I pushed the throttle and kept my fingers crossed. Would it take off? You never knew. I took off and did a pass around the field at 30 or 40 feet. Eddie Cohen was still on the ground with engine trouble. I did

two circuits with Modi Alon and we took off since we
couldn't wait. We climbed up to about 6,000 feet over
the sea and I looked down and saw, like ants, the
Egyptian column. By that time Eddie Cohen and Ezer
Weizman were catching up with us.

I couldn't wait since the ack-ack had started and
hanging around just invited fire, so I pushed the nose
down and attacked with Modi on my left. I dropped my
two bombs in the square of this village (Isdud). The
surprising thing for me was the amount of ack-ack. I saw
a lot of ground fire over Japan, but never like this. I
don't know how we got out of it. So I made four or five
passes and then flew around looking for everybody. It
turned out I was the first to take off and the last to land.

I don't know how much damage we caused, but the
psychological shock of attack by fighter planes shook
them up. It was an exhilarating moment and also a sad
time because we lost one aircraft, 25 percent of our air
force, but worse than that, Eddie Cohen was killed. We
were like brothers and I felt very bad that he was lost on
that first mission.[14]

The fighter flown by Lou Lenart and the other pilots was the
Avia S199. As a result of the British arms embargo, the
Czechoslovakian-built derivative of the Messershmitt bf 109 was
the only aircraft that Israel was able to acquire.

At 5:30 A.M. on May 30, Ezer Weizman, later to become commander of the IAF, and Cy Rubenfield, an American volunteer,
bombed the Tulkarm railway station and strafed a column of
Iraqi and Jordanian troops advancing into Israel. Rubenfield's
Avia was hit by antiaircraft fire, but he successfully bailed out
and came down near a Jewish village.

Flying alone, Modi Alon, commander of the 101st Fighter
Squadron—the first Israeli fighter squadron and the only one
ever officially identified—attacked an advancing Arab column
near Latrun the following day.

Since the outbreak of widespread fighting on May 15, 1948,
Egyptian Spitfire fighters and C-47 Dakota transports that had
been converted into bombers had made repeated attacks against
Israeli targets. On the afternoon of June 3, two Egyptian C-47

Dakota bombers, escorted by several Spitfires, swept in from the sea to bomb Tel Aviv. Modi Alon, piloting the only serviceable Avia fighter, attacked one of the Egyptian C-47s. Damaged by cannon and machine-gun fire, the Dakota crashed into the sea south of Tel Aviv. A head-on pass against the second Dakota sent it, too, hurtling to earth. Ignoring the air raid sirens, many inhabitants of Tel Aviv ran out into the streets to watch the battle. The twenty-seven-year-old former RAF flight lieutenant chalked up the first air combat victories of the Israel Air Force.

The sizable South African Jewish community included a number of experienced pilots, aircrew, and technicians who were sympathetic to the Israeli cause. Boris Senior, a former lieutenant in the South African Air Force, acquired nearly a squadron of surplus P-40 fighters, which had been sold as scrap in South Africa, with the intent of supplying them to the Haganah in Palestine. When he was not able to secure export rights for these fighters, he set up the Pan African Air Charter Company. Senior used this company to acquire aircraft and hire aircrew to transport civilian aircraft to Palestine. Senior and his associates flew a Beechcraft, Rapide, and several other aircraft to Israel.

On June 4, 1948, Israeli light planes, including Senior's Beechcraft and Rapide and a Fairchild, bombed and strafed an Egyptian ship convoy that was ferrying troops north from Gaza. The aircraft repeatedly attacked the Egyptian convoy, using hand-held bombs and machine guns. Although the Israeli planes scored only a single hit and the Egyptian shot down the Fairchild, the convoy retreated.

Additional aircraft from Piper Cubs to large transports and Avia fighters were beginning to arrive in Israel in a steady stream, thanks to both legal and clandestine purchasing efforts by Jews in Europe, the United States, and other countries. The C-47 Dakota transports that arrived in May were quickly pressed into service. While most transports carried cargo and troops to outlying settlements, some were converted into makeshift bombers. On June 10 three C-47s dumped over 4,500 pounds of bombs on the Transjordan capital of Amman during a nocturnal attack.[15]

While the arms and aircraft-buying efforts of the worldwide Haganah organization made newspaper headlines, this same network was busy collecting funds, disseminating information about events in Palestine, and recruiting volunteers. The Haganah especially sought World War II veterans who could contribute their military knowledge and experience. Pilots, aircrew, and skilled mechanics were very much sought after. Some were Jewish and wanted to help Israel, many were bored with their postwar life and wanted to see action, while others joined for the money. Salaries for a pilot with combat experience were as high as $600 per month. Volunteers from the United States, Canada, South Africa, Great Britain, and other countries numbered in the hundreds. Named the *Mahal* (volunteers from abroad) by the Israelis, this group formed the backbone of the air force during the War of Independence. Because of the large representation of English-speaking volunteers, English became the main language of the Israel Air Force.

A UN-sponsored cease-fire began on June 11, 1948. During this period, both sides rearmed and reorganized. It was a critical break for Israel; although the new nation had managed to hold off the combined Arab armies, it had suffered over fifteen hundred men killed and several thousand wounded and had to give up considerable territory.

By late June the C-46 flights from Czechoslovakia, which were known as Operation Bolak, had transported nearly a dozen Avia fighters to Israel, where they were assembled by technicians. After a successful attack by Egyptian aircraft, the 101st Fighter Squadron was moved to a strip in Herzalia, where the aircraft could be camouflaged among the trees of an orange grove. The squadron settled into its new facilities and continued training activities for its pilots.

In June, the Israeli purchasing team in Czechoslovakia concluded an important agreement. The Czech government wished to dispose of some seventy-five Spitfires that had been flown home from England by Czech pilots at the end of World War II. Israel agreed to purchase fifty of the aircraft, all Spitfire Mk 9 models, and the spares and equipment necessary to maintain them.[16] The sale of Spitfires was a great step forward for the Israelis. However, almost three months would pass before any of the fighters reached Israel, because the planes had to be overhauled, payment terms arranged, and transportation worked out.

Back in the United States, Al Schwimmer's export of C-46s

and Constellations had aroused considerable consternation. The FBI was examining Schwimmer's activities, and customs officials limited the export of transport and surplus military aircraft. However, Schwimmer found four B-17 four-engine heavy bombers, and four A-20 twin-engine medium bombers and purchased them through a dummy corporation.

Only three of the B-17s could be quickly overhauled and put into shape for shipment to Israel. The three B-17s left Miami airport for Puerto Rico on June 12, 1948. The next day they flew across the Atlantic to the Azores. After filing flight plans listing Corsica as their final destination, the B-17s flew across the Mediterranean. Following a brief refueling stop in Corsica, the B-17s flew on to Zatec, Czechoslovakia. Here the B-17s were armed with machine guns and bombs.

Once U.S. authorities discovered that the B-17s had flown to Czechoslovakia, a country allied with the Soviet Union, the crackdown on arms exports to Israel was intensified. Despite efforts to stop them, aircraft and volunteer pilots continued to make their way to Israel, often by very circuitous paths.

In early July the cease-fire broke down and widespread fighting started in the north of Israel, around Jerusalem, and on the Egyptian front. On July 9, four Avia of the 101st Fighter Squadron were assigned to attack the Egyptian airfield at El Arish. One Avia crashed on takeoff and the others, after failing to locate El Arish because of dense clouds, bombed and strafed Egyptian troops near Gaza. During the attacks, one of the Avias piloted by Robert Vickerman, a volunteer from the United States, was lost. That night IAF Dakota bombers and light aircraft flew bombing and harassment raids against several Arab targets.

Syrian infantry, supported by artillery and tanks, staged a major counterattack on July 10 against the Israelis, who had achieved gains the previous night. Harvard trainers, armed with machine guns and light bombs, supported the Syrian offensive by attacking Israeli troops. Few Israeli Avias were serviceable and those available were engaged on the Egyptian front. The Syrian pilots made the most of their air superiority, chasing Israeli vehicles up and down roads and harassing them with machine-gun fire. Later in the day, two Israeli Avias engaged the Syrian planes. One Harvard was shot down by Maurice Mann.

Lionel Bloch, a South African who piloted the other Avia, chased a fleeing Harvard as it withdrew over the Golan Heights. His aircraft failed to return.

Because of the heavy fighting, the Israelis intensified the airlift of weapons and supplies from Czechoslovakia. Transports also flew night attack sorties but not always with positive results. Some aircraft attacked friendly territory while others hit empty fields or dumped their bombs into the sea. A night attack of Syrian positions on July 13 by a Dakota nearly ended in disaster. The crew successfully pushed six bombs out the side cargo door, but a seventh caught on the door as it was released, ripping off the door, and damaging the Dakota's tail assembly. The pilot was able to fly back to Ramat David airfield, but the C-47 was out of service for a considerable period of time.

The three B-17s that had been smuggled out of the United States to Czechoslovakia in June left Zatec airfield on July 14 for Israel. On the way, the three delivered calling cards—500-pound bombs dropped on Cairo, Gaza, and El Arish. These aircraft were immediately pressed into service. C-47s and light planes flew night bombing raids against Arab targets while the B-17s conducted both daylight and nocturnal attacks. The pace of operations was intense and the arrival of the B-17s added considerably to the available firepower. Although the number of attack sorties flown by the IAF from July 8 to 14 nearly equaled those performed July 15 to 18, the weight of the bombs delivered during the latter period was five times greater.[17]

The Arab air forces reacted vigorously to these attacks. On July 11, Jerusalem suffered its first air attack. Before it was driven off by antiaircraft fire, an Iraqi trainer dropped several small bombs on Ramat David airfield. The loss of a Harvard to an Israeli Avia sharply curtailed Syrian air attacks.

Egyptian fighters repeatedly attacked Israeli settlements near the battle zone, using hit-and-run tactics in order to minimize the possibility of interception by Israeli fighters. One Jewish settlement suffered seven air attacks on a single day. In retaliation for Israeli B-17 raids, Egyptian fighters also bombed and strafed Tel Aviv on several occasions.

In the spring of 1948, Rudolph Augarten, an American pilot who had flown fighters with the U.S. Army Air Corps in Europe during World War II, volunteered to fly for Israel. He trained on finally had a fighter plane that allowed the volunteer pilots to engage the enemy confidently.

In late September the IAF fighter force received another boost. Four disassembled and crated P-51 Mustang fighters arrived in Israel from the United States. It was several weeks before these aircraft became operational with the 101st Fighter Squadron because they had to be reassembled and fitted with weapons.

By the fall of 1948, the IAF had grown to nearly one hundred aircraft, including about ten bombers, twenty-five fighters, fifteen multiengined transports, and nearly fifty light planes of various types. However, at any one time a lack of spare parts kept perhaps a third of these aircraft out of service.[22]

On October 15 Israeli forces began a new offensive in the south. Aerial operations started in the evening with an attack on the Egyptian air base at El Arish and strikes against targets near the towns of Gaza and Majdal. Israeli B-17 bombers and C-46 and C-47 transports armed with bombs flew nocturnal attacks against Egyptian targets.

Despite Israeli efforts, the Royal Egyptian Air Force (REAF) continued to fly attack missions over the battle area. Most Egyptian fighter sorties were flown from the air base at El Arish, which was home for a Spitfire squadron that was supported by a detachment of Italian-built Fiat G55 fighters. The IAF specifically targeted Egyptian frontline positions and the El Arish air base for attack during the October 15 offensive. During seven days of intense operations, IAF aircraft flew several hundred sorties, dropped more than two hundred tons of bombs, and downed three Egyptian fighters in air combat. Rudolph Augarten later described his experiences flying during this period:

first kill I had was on a patrol mission over Faluja October 16. I ran into a couple of Spitfires. I went e and shot him down and he crashed just north I was flying a Messerschmitt that had a profile a Spitfire. Usually we went on patrols with three aircraft so if you saw a plane, you t be assured that it was the enemy. So you to hesitate—if you used aggressive tactics d chance of knocking someone down

Arrado trainers and Avia fighters in Czechoslovakia and arrived in Israel in July 1948. He served as a pilot, director of operations of the 101st Fighter Squadron, and a base commander with the IAF.

Augarten commented on his first mission:

My turn to fly came up on July 18 and a truce was to take effect that evening at 6:00 P.M. Our flight took off at about 5:30 and we were to fly down to a town just south of Beersheba named Beerasluge to bomb and strafe an Egyptian column. Modi Alon led the flight. The second pilot was Sid Anteim from Boston and I was the third pilot to take off. We found the convoy and they bombed, but I only had guns so I ran up and down strafing. Then I joined the other two and we headed back to base. Modi was in the lead, I was on the left and Sid Anteim was on the right. Sid radioed, "Hey Rudy, there is something on your left." I gave it gas and came up right behind two Spits with Egyptian Roundels. I put my gunsight on one, pulled the trigger, and nothing happened. I said, on the radio, "For Christ sake, I'm out of ammunition," so I put my nose down to get out of the way and Modi came in and shot down one Spit.[18]

After ten days of heavy fighting, a cease-fire came into effect on July 18, providing an opportunity for the IAF to repair and overhaul aircraft and to resupply. The many volunteer pilots, aircrews, maintenance personnel, and Israeli conscripts who made up the air force intensified their training efforts.

With fighting expected to resume at any time, collecting additional aircraft weapons and spare parts was vital. American pressure and a change in attitude in Prague led to the announcement in late July that Israeli facilities at Zatec airfield in Czechoslovakia were to be closed, shutting off the aerial pipeline that had provided Israel with its only fighters and tons of other weapons. Transport crews flew to the point of exhaustion to move spare parts, weapons, and equipment to Israel before the base was closed. Between August 6 and 12 they lifted out forty tons of supplies.

Secret procurement efforts by Jewish agents in other coun-

tries continued to bear fruit. In early 1948 a dummy film production company was established in England and four Bristol
Beaufighters were purchased, allegedly for use in a film about
the exploits of New Zealand fliers during World War II. The four
Beaufighters were flown to Israel. One of them was cannibalized
for spare parts and the remaining three flew operational missions from Ramat David airfield throughout the summer.

The IAF's first Spitfire did not come from Czechoslovakia but
from Egypt and England! On the new nation's first day, Israeli
machine gunners hit an attacking Egyptian Spitfire. Its pilot
crash-landed on the beach near Tel Aviv and was captured.
Parts of the damaged Spitfire were used along with other plane
parts taken from dumps at several former RAF air bases to
produce a serviceable aircraft. This Spitfire first flew on July 23,
1948, containing the fuselage of a photo reconnaissance model
and the wing of an Mk 9 fighter. Later a second Spitfire was
constructed using parts obtained from the various abandoned
RAF bases.[19]

Having decided to focus its efforts on defeating Egyptian
forces in the south, the Israeli high command prepared to move
men and supplies into position for the offensive. Since truck
convoys would be easily detected and subject to attack, Prime
Minister Ben Gurion asked the Air Transport Command, the
logistics arm of the air force, to transfer the necessary men and
supplies. Using a tractor and a bulldozer, Jewish settlers and
Israeli troops created a 4,000-foot dirt runway on a relatively
flat section of the Negev Desert. To maintain secrecy and escape
marauding Egyptian Spitfires, the transports flew at night, un-
loaded their cargo, and flew out by dawn. Finding the single
poorly lit strip was a challenge since the Israelis had no navigation aids. Takeoffs and landings created large dust clouds,
which gave the resupply effort its name—Operation Dust.

Between August 18 and September 9, C-46s of the Air Transport Command flew hundreds of sorties to the Negev airstrip.
Fewer than ten aircraft were available, and usually only five to
eight planes were serviceable. Pilots, maintenance crews, and
logistics personnel pushed themselves to the limit. On the night
of September 7, transport aircrews flew thirteen trips to the
airstrip, delivering eighty-one tons of supplies. By September 9,

the transport crews had flown 170 sorties, delivering more than
one thousand tons of supplies and moving nearly twenty-four
hundred people.

The combination of pressure by Israeli officials to maintain
the dangerous missions, the punishing pace of operations, and
the poor condition of the aircraft, led to morale problems among
the foreign volunteers. Many transport crews were made up of
foreign volunteers who had come to Israel expecting to help
form a new Israeli airline. When the transport crews learned
that the semi-independent Air Transport Command was to be
integrated into the air force, they went on strike, grounding all
aircraft. Although flying operations resumed after a few days, a
few disgruntled individuals quit and left Israel. In spite of these
problems the remaining aircrews resumed Operation Dust in
early October and additional supplies and troops were flown
into the Negev.[20]

Since July, when Czechoslovakia agreed to supply Spitfi
fighters, a group of Israeli agents had been busy coordina
the selection, overhaul, and delivery of the aircraft. By the
1948 the changing political climate in Czechoslovakia
chill in its relations with the new state of Israel. As
increasing number of obstacles slowed the delivery
the Spitfires. Because the fighters were neede
Israeli officials decided that the Spitfires w
Israel. Weaponry and support equipment f
be shipped to Israel in transport aircraft
Spitfires had a ferry range of only ab
engineers had to modify the fuel syste
new internal fuel tanks and a 90-
the 1,300-mile flight to Israel.[21]

On September 22, six modi
for the Yugoslav airfield at F
Podgorica but one was
Blou, a South African v
landing because his

The remaining f
September 27. T
had to land at Mar
they were interned. Th
flew on to Israel. With t.

because they generally did not show very much willingness to fight.[23]

During the summer and fall of 1948, accidents and Egyptian antiaircraft fire claimed the lives of more than a dozen Israeli and volunteer pilots and crewmen. Modi Alon, commander of the 101st Fighter Squadron who had three air combat victories to this credit, was killed on October 16 when his damaged aircraft crashed while approaching Herzalia. During an attack on the Egyptian fort at Iraq Suqeiden on October 20, Arab antiaircraft fire downed a Beaufighter, killing three crew members. On October 24, an engine fire caused a C-47 to crash while approaching Eqron airfield, killing the crew of four.

While Egyptian forces at El Arish suffered many casualties and lost several aircraft to Israel air attacks, the airfield was never put out of action. Egyptian aircraft based at El Arish and at other Sinai airfields continued to strike back against the Israelis. Egyptian Spitfires bombed and strafed Israeli ground troops on numerous occasions and on October 19 they attacked and heavily damaged two Israeli ships in the Mediterranean.

While Israel was beginning to seize the initiative from the Arabs, losses had been heavy. Hoping to buy time to gather more arms and prepare for a new offensive, Israeli military commanders supported a cease-fire. On October 22, a UN-arranged cease-fire came into effect on the southern front, yet sniping, artillery fire, raids, and attacks continued. The pace of Israeli air operations slowed, but transport and reconnaissance missions continued to be flown.

Rudolph Augarten described the events of November 4, 1948:

We flew down over El Arish to see what was happening, Boris Senior and I. We saw this Dakota. Boris went after the plane. He pulled up and didn't hit it. On an impulse I decided to go after it, so I went down and really shot up that plane and it crashed on the runway. . . . By the fall our squadron had ME109s (Avias), Spitfires, and two P-51s and I flew all three. The Spitfire was the plane I preferred because of its handling qualities. The big advantage of the P-51 was its armament (six 0.5-inch machine guns) and better range. I was able to get kills

with the ME109 (Avia), the Spitfire, and the P-51. This
was very typical of what we were doing then—everybody
flew whatever aircraft that was available.[24]

Despite the cease-fire, Israeli fighters and bombers repeatedly
attacked the Faluja pocket, a salient that contained four thousand Egyptian troops that had been surrounded by Israeli
ground forces. During the day Israeli B-17s and fighters struck
and at night bomb-armed transports dumped bombs on the
defenders. But the defenders held on and fought back with
heavy antiaircraft fire. The Egyptians held these strong defensive positions until the armistice in 1949.[25]

Although heavy ground combat operations had ceased tempo-
rarily in the south, fighting between Syrian, Lebanese, and
Israeli forces continued on the northern front. IAF aircraft
struck at Arab convoys and staging bases behind the front lines.

During the fall of 1948, the RAF flew reconnaissance sorties
over Israel with high-flying Mosquito aircraft. Israeli Air Force
pilots often attempted to intercept the Mosquitos, but were
unable to climb quickly enough to catch them. On November 20,
the pilots of the 101st Fighter Squadron were alerted to one of
the RAF snoopers. Wayne Peake, a non-Jewish volunteer from
the United States, rushed to one of the squadron's few P-51
Mustang fighters and took off. Climbing as rapidly as possible,
Peake closed on the Mosquito. But a fault in his oxygen system
blurred his vision at the higher altitude. Recovering his senses,
Peake flew into firing position behind the Mosquito and opened
fire. Almost immediately his 0.5-inch machine guns stopped
firing because he had exhausted his ammunition supply. De-
jected by his failure, Peake spiraled down and returned to the
base. However, it turned out that his machine-gun fire had hit
home. Observers on the ground saw the Mosquito catch fire and
explode over the Mediterranean. British forces conducted an
air-and-sea search after the Mosquito did not return, but they
never found a trace of the aircraft. As a result of the loss, RAF
reconnaissance flights over Israel were suspended.[26]

During the fall, the REAF stepped up its efforts against Israel.
Egyptian pilot training was intensified and several alternative
airfields were established in the Sinai. The air force had received additional aircraft, including Spitfires, and Sterling four-

engine bombers from England, and several dozen Fiat G55 and Aeromacchi C205 Veltro fighters from Italy.

The IAF continued to receive reinforcements through its international network of agents. Harvard trainers, bought and shipped in crates from Canada and the United States, entered service. This was the same aircraft used successfully by Syrian forces against Israeli troops early in the war. These trainer aircraft were armed with machine guns and light bombs and served as dive bombers.

Twelve more Czech Spitfires set out on December 18, but two crashed when they encountered a severe snowstorm in Czechoslovakia. The pilots were killed. The remaining Spitfires arrived in Israel on December 22.

On December 22, Israeli troops launched Operation Horev, an all-out offensive against Egyptian forces. The objective of the Israeli offensive was to cut off the supply route to Gaza. To weaken Egyptian forces southwest of Gaza, Israeli troops made a diversionary attack against the city itself. Israeli aircraft attacked the El Arish airfield southwest of Gaza on December 22, and also bombed and strafed Egyptian troops in the area.

Rudy Augerten described a mission he flew over the Egyptian airfield:

> Although I didn't claim it as a kill, I shot and damaged
> a Fiat that had his wheels down and was in the landing
> pattern at El Arish. That was our first encounter with
> the Fiat. I was flying a reconnaissance mission in a
> Spitfire with Doyle over El Arish and I saw this plane in
> the landing pattern. By the time I caught him he had his
> wheels down and was on final approach. I shot him and
> he crashed off the runway. There was a tremendous
> amount of flak coming up so I stayed close to the ground
> until I was five or six miles away from the airfield.[27]

Egyptian armed forces, reacting to the threat to their rear, counterattacked vigorously, but Israeli troops tightened their grip on Gaza. The REAF strongly defended El Arish and struck at the Israeli columns advancing into the Sinai near Gaza. Angered by the Israelis' success, Egyptian pilots bombed targets in Israel including the Mishmar Haemak kibbutz, Allenbay bridge, and the town of Jericho. Air combat was also heavy: On December 28, Israeli Spitfires downed three Egyptian Fiat fighters. On December 31 and January 5, 1949, volunteer pilots flying for Israel shot down additional Egyptian fighters.

With Gaza surrounded and Egyptian forces in retreat, Egypt asked England to intercede. Evoking the 1936 Anglo-Egyptian Treaty, the British called for an Israeli withdrawal from Egyptian territory. The British government made it clear that it was prepared to enter the conflict to support Egyptian sovereignty.

On January 6, Egypt indicated that it would like to initiate a cease-fire leading to discussions for an armistice agreement. The fighting was to end the following day at 2:00 P.M.

Royal Air Force aircraft stationed near the Suez Canal flew early morning reconnaissance sorties near the Israeli border to monitor the situation. The first flight consisted of a Mosquito escorted by four Tempest fighters. A second group of four Spitfires overflew an Israeli roadblock in Egyptian territory and was greeted by antiaircraft fire. One Spitfire was hit and its pilot bailed out. The three remaining RAF Spitfires circled and watched their comrade as he parachuted to earth.

Two IAF Spitfires, piloted by 101st Fighter Squadron volunteers Slick Goodlin and John McElroy, attacked the circling RAF fighters and shot down all three. One of the RAF pilots was killed while the other two parachuted to safety.[28] Goodlin and McElroy stated that they did not notice the RAF markings on the Spitfires.

When the four RAF Spitfires did not return, the British sent Spitfire reconnaissance planes, with an escort of Tempest fighters, to search for the missing aircraft. A patrol of Israeli Spitfires engaged and shot down several of these RAF aircraft.[29] However, Britain protested its losses through diplomatic channels and threatened to retaliate against further Israeli aggression.

The fighting between Israel and the Arabs ended at 2:00 P.M. on January 7, 1949. With the cease-fire between Egypt and Israel, Transjordan, Lebanon, and Iraq decided to suspend military operations. Israel's first and bloodiest war was over. The new nation had suffered six thousand men and women killed and twelve thousand wounded, but it had established a Jewish homeland.

From a small group of light planes, the IAF had grown to over one hundred aircraft, including more than fifty fighters and bombers, by the end of the War of Independence. Aircraft acquired from around the world, including the fighters from Czechoslovakia, were forged into a fighting force that wrestled the initiative from the REAF and contributed significantly to the outcome of the war. The IAF had downed twenty-three Egyptian, Syrian, and British aircraft in air combat. Israeli aircraft losses totaled about fifteen aircraft but many of these were lost in accidents rather than in combat.

The 660 volunteer pilots, aircrew members, and skilled maintenance personnel who fought during the war formed the backbone of the air force. Twenty Mahal foreign volunteers died in the fighting. After the war, Prime Minister David Ben Gurion paid tribute to these men: "In spite of the contribution made by Israeli boys, Israel would not have been able to build up an air force and operate it without the assistance extended by the volunteers from abroad, who had acquired their experience in the service of the allied power during World War II."[30]

# 2

# *The Early Years*

*T*he fighting between Israel and its Arab neighbors ended early in 1949. Protracted negotations led to armistice agreements between Israel and Egypt—February 24, Lebanon—March 23, Transjordan—April 3, and Syria—July 20. No agreement was reached with Iraq. These agreements ended the fighting but were not formal peace treaties because the Arab countries refused to recognize the State of Israel. Following the Israeli victory, thousands of Palestinian Arabs who had not fled the country during the fighting packed up and left. Many left with little more than the clothes on their backs. These refugees were placed in large camps established by Egypt, Transjordan (now called simply Jordan), Syria, and Lebanon near the Israeli border. They rarely were able to obtain jobs and had little opportunity to integrate into the social and economic hierarchy of their new land. The refugee camps became filled with disenchanted people who saw little hope for the future. Egypt, Syria, and Jordan recruited many young men from these camps and sent them to special commando training camps to continue the war against Israel. These commandos became known as the *fedayeen* (those who sacrifice themselves). Terrorist groups organized during this period later became a major factor in the continuing Arab opposition to Israel.

Arab countries also employed all the economic and diplomatic means at their disposal to isolate Israel. By 1950 Israel had demobilized most of the troops who had fought in the War of Independence and was struggling to organize its infrastructure, establish a stable political system, and deal with serious economic problems. It was an austere time.

With the armistice, the air force faced many problems. Most of the foreign volunteers returned to their home countries, leaving the service short of pilots and skilled ground crews. Although the air force had more than one hundred aircraft, many

26

were damaged or worn out. Many planes were cannibalized to keep others in flyable condition.

Aharon Remez, commander of the IAF, set up a pilot-training course and set about upgrading the air force. He wanted to create a powerful, independent air force that could defeat the enemy in any future war. Remez's plans and ambitions did not sit well with Prime Minister Ben Gurion and the senior officers of the Israeli high command, who were concentrating on strengthening the ground forces.

The IAF received the remainder of the fifty Spitfires purchased from Czechoslovakia in early 1949. These Spitfires and a few P-51 Mustangs served to protect Israeli airspace. The attack element of the air force included the B-17s that had been spirited out of the United States by Al Schwimmer's organization. More than twenty-five types of transport, liaison, and utility aircraft were in service including Curtis C-46, Douglas C-47, Douglas C-54/DC-5, Lockheed Hudson, Lockheed Constellation, de Havilland Rapide, Norduyn Norseman, and a diversity of smaller aircraft.

As pilot-training efforts expanded, so did the IAF trainer force. Israel purchased twenty surplus Boeing PT-17 biplane trainers from the United States, forty Fokker S.11 trainers from the Netherlands, and twenty-five Harvard (T-6) advanced trainer aircraft from France. Following 40–60 hours of flying in the PT-17 or S.11 primary trainers, Israeli cadets flew an additional 150 hours in the Harvard. Students training to fly fighters were assigned to Spitfires or P-51s at an operational training unit. Transport and bomber pilot candidates continued their instruction in twin-engine Anson or Consul aircraft.

In 1950, Maj. Gen. Aharon Remez resigned his commission and retired from military service. Although Remez had made improvements during his two years as commander, he was disappointed at the low priority and limited funding the Israel Defense Force High Command afforded the air force. Shlomo Shamir, a naval officer, took over the top position in the air force. His tenure as commander was short and within less than a year he was succeeded by Maj. Gen. Chaim Laskov, an infantry officer. During Laskov's administration, the IAF acquired a large number of secondhand and war surplus piston-engined fighters and fighter-bombers. Contacts in the United States purchased two PBY Catalina amphibious patrol aircraft. Through extensive lobbying, Israel acquired an export license for these aircraft plus their spare parts and support equipment.

In 1950 France agreed to supply Israel with surplus Mosquito fighter-bombers. The twin-engine aircraft had a fine record. During and after World War II, it had served as a night fighter, fighter-bomber, and reconnaissance aircraft with the RAF. The Mosquito was built primarily of pressure-bonded plywood, a material that was easy to obtain. Most of the French Mosquitos were in poor shape, but were available at very low prices. Between June 1951 and May 1952, sixty Mosquitos were reconditioned by Israeli technicians with the help of Nord Aviation personnel and flown to Israel.[1] These aircraft served as the backbone of the IAF attack force into the mid-1950s.

Italian authorities indicated a willingness to supply Israel with surplus Spitfire fighters, extra engines, and spare parts. Following a prolonged series of negotiations, in early 1953 Italy sold Israel thirty aircraft. Sweden, which likewise was modernizing its fighter fleet with jets, had a supply of P-51 Mustangs available. These Mustangs were in first-class condition. The Swedish government responded favorably to an Israeli inquiry concerning purchase of the aircraft. During the winter and spring of 1953, Swedish Air Force pilots flew twenty-five P-51s to Israel.[2] Israel also purchased a dozen P-51 fighters from Italian arms dealers, and these were delivered in 1955.

An intensified pilot-training program continued to produce results. Israeli students began attending RAF flying schools to complete their intermediate and advanced training or to acquire instructor pilot status. These candidates often encountered pilot trainees from Arab countries who were also attending the RAF programs. Egypt, Iraq, Syria, Jordan, and several other Arab countries were building up their air arms by expanding their pilot-training efforts and acquiring advanced equipment.

Although the acquisition of Spitfires, Mosquitos, and Mustangs along with the increased number of pilots considerably expanded the IAF, the Israelis faced a new problem: Piston engine fighters were becoming obsolete. The Royal Egyptian Air Force had received its first British-built jet fighter, the Gloster

Meteor, in late 1949. Shortly thereafter, Egypt acquired twenty single-engine Vampire FB5 fighter-bombers.

The Korean conflict, which was raging at this time, demonstrated that piston engine aircraft were no match for the latest jet fighters in air combat. While Mosquitos, Spitfires, and Mustangs were useful for ground attack, the IAF needed jets to protect its skies.

In 1950 Israeli representatives approached U.S. and British officials about the possibility of acquiring jet fighters to counter Egypt's, but were turned down. France was supplying the Mosquitos and was willing to consider the Israeli request for the Ouragon, its first indigenously designed and built jet fighter. However, approval was stymied by political wrangling. Dassault in France and Macchi in Italy were producing versions of the British Vampire fighter under license and Israeli representatives contacted these firms. But the British government would not allow export of these aircraft.

Eventually, however, as a way to maintain the balance of power in the Middle East, Britain agreed to supply Israel with Meteor jet fighters and resumed deliveries of jets to Arab countries; Egypt received Meteors and Vampires, Syria was supplied with Meteors, while Jordan was given Vampire fighters. On February 10, 1953, Israel ordered eleven Meteor F Mk 8 fighters and four T.7 trainers from Gloster Aircraft, Ltd. The IAF joined the jet age on June 17, 1953, with the delivery of the first two T.7 Meteor trainers. Meteor deliveries continued into 1954.

In 1953 Dan Tolkovsky, a South African and former RAF officer, was given command of the IAF. Tolkovsky instituted many reforms that improved the air force. Since Israel could not hope to match its neighbors numerically, quality, efficiency, and professionalism became the new goals. People were the key. Highly motivated, superbly trained pilots, ground crew, and support personnel equipped with good multipurpose aircraft, Tolkovsky believed, could defeat a numerically superior adversary. He established high standards for dress, behavior, training, maintenance, flying skills, and many other areas. Pilot-training standards were set extremely high and a majority of those who started flight training did not complete it. Only the best graduated. Officers were sent overseas to France and Britain to attend command and staff schools, test pilot training, and other top military courses. Air force personnel at all levels examined their functions, established new standards of performance, and set up training schedules to maintain their proficiency.

Tolkovsky maintained that the air force could have a significant impact on the outcome of the ground battle. Fighters would be used first to destroy enemy aircraft in the air and on the ground. Once air superiority was achieved, aircraft could then concentrate on providing support for ground forces.

Tolkovsky knew that Israel could not afford to purchase and maintain a large air force; aircraft must be capable of performing multiple missions. The small size of Israel itself and its armed forces required that the battles be fought over and on enemy territory.[3]

To help the air force maintain its new jet fighters and keep all aircraft in peak condition, Israeli officials formed Bedek Aircraft, Ltd. The company was headed by Al Schwimmer, the American engineer who had led the team that acquired C-46, Constellation transports, and B-17s for Israel. Bedek maintenance personnel and technicians overhauled IAF aircraft and modified and upgraded them to improve their performance. Over the years Bedek developed into Israel Aircraft Industries, which by the 1980s had produced hundreds of combat aircraft, transports, and executive jets and employed over five thousand people.[4]

The armistice agreements signed in 1949 were considered only a temporary truce by the Arab countries. Raids against civilian targets and artillery attacks continued on a limited scale along Israel's borders. In late 1954 and early 1955 Israeli troops repeatedly attacked targets in the Gaza Strip and the Sinai in retaliation against guerrilla activity. In response, Egyptian President Nasser increased the strength of his forces along the Israeli border and set out to expand his military force structure. Nasser sought to obtain more weapons, including Meteor and Vampire jet fighters from Great Britain. When additional arms were not immediately delivered, Nasser began negotiations with a new source of weaponry—Czechoslovakia. A mere seven years before, this country had provided Israel with its first fighter aircraft. Soviet leaders gave Czechoslovakia permission to supply Egypt with the latest military hardware—including MiG-15 fighters and IL-28 jet bombers.

To match this threat, Israel needed a new supply of up-to-date combat aircraft. Air combat in Korea had demonstrated that the Meteor was no match for the MiG-15. The F-86 Sabre was the only Western fighter aircraft that had proven itself capable of countering the MiG-15. While the United States would not sell the F-86 to Israel, Canada indicated a willingness to consider the sale of the Canadian-built Sabre Mk 6. This aircraft combined a late-model Sabre airframe with the high-thrust Orenda jet engine. Israel ordered twenty-four Sabres and Canada produced the aircraft, but U.S. intervention prevented delivery of the jets.[5]

Sweden at this time was introducing a new jet fighter into its inventory, the SAAB J-29. Israel approached SAAB and the Swedish government, which agreed to sell its planes to the new nation. The J-29 was evaluated and judged to be a good fighter, but its limited ground attack capability was a disadvantage.[6]

For the first time, the French government indicated a willingness to supply advanced fighter aircraft to Israel. France was deeply involved in the civil war in Algeria and President Nasser had supplied arms, training, and political assistance to Algerian resistance fighters. French leaders felt that a strong Israel would keep Nasser's attention focused on the Middle East. The French firm Dassault was developing the Mystere II, an advanced, swept-wing interceptor. Israeli test pilots flew both the J-29 and Mystere II and judged the French aircraft to be superior. In late 1954 France agreed to supply Israel with thirty Dassault Ouragon and twenty-four Mystere II fighters. The first French-designed jet fighter, the Ouragon, was rapidly approaching obsolescence, but it was a better combat aircraft than the Meteor. Highly maneuverable and easy to fly, the 35-foot-long Ouragon could reach a speed of over 550 miles per hour. The 15,000-pound fighter-bomber was armed with four 20-mm cannons and could carry an underwing load of bombs or rockets.[7]

When the Mystere II encountered development problems, Israel canceled its order for the aircraft and chose instead the much improved Mystere IVA. The IAF would have to wait a year for delivery of the advanced fighter and to bridge the gap Israel ordered an additional supply of Ouragons. The first Dassault

Ouragon fighters were delivered to Israel in November 1955. Eventually Israel received seventy-five Ouragons—twenty-four of these were new jets and fifty-one were refurbished aircraft that had seen service with the French Air Force (Armee de l'Air).

The Dassault Mystere IVA was the French Air Force's premier fighter during the mid-1950s. Powered by a 7,710-pound-thrust Hispano Suiza Verdon turbojet engine, the Mystere IVA had a length of 42.1 feet, a 36.5-foot wingspan, and a maximum takeoff weight of 20,000 pounds.[8] Capable of performing both fighter and attack missions, the aircraft was armed with two 30-mm DEFA cannons and a variety of external ordinance including bombs, rocket pods, and fuel tanks. Faster, better armed, and more advanced than the Ouragon, the Mystere IVA ideally fulfilled Israeli requirements; it could beat the MiG-15 in air combat and effectively attack ground targets with cannon fire, bombs, and rockets.

During the mid-1950s tensions were heightened in the Middle East. Egypt, Syria, Jordan, Iraq, and Israel strengthened their arsenals and *fedayeen* guerrillas based in Egypt stepped up their raids into Israel. As casualties mounted, Israeli army units struck back. Eventually the air arms became involved. Israeli and Arab aircraft flew regular reconnaissance missions along each others' borders. Occasionally these planes flew past their respective borders to gather information and test their adversary's response time. On August 31, 1955, IAF Meteor fighters and Egyptian Vampires fought the first jet air battle in the Middle East.

Retired IAF Col. Aharon Yoeli recalled the event:

At seven o'clock in the morning, a standby of four airplanes, Meteor 8s, were ready. I was not a standby pilot, but I am an early riser and bang—the siren goes off. The two duty guys are brushing their eyes and by that time Sedan and I are in the aircraft and we made contact with the controller who said, "Take off heading southwest, fly to 7,000 feet." It was a cloudy day and the sun was only ten to fifteen degrees above the horizon. We took off headed south and were told that there was a bogey consisting of two airplanes flying southbound below us at two to three o'clock. I made a left turn so they couldn't see me because I would be in the sun and two minutes later my number two said, "I see them," and I turned my head and I saw them.

We simply pulled up and started to come down behind them. The closing speed was, say, 150 miles per hour. Number two was behind me. My sight was on night brightness, and since I was slowly closing in, I had no time to mess with it. I saw one aircraft at about five hundred yards range, opened the safety cover, and slowly closed line astern behind the Vampire. At 200 to 250 yards, I opened fire. My tracers moved from the left to the wing, and I simply shifted them to the center and I didn't finish until I saw the bubble explode. We were at about 3,000 feet and I was flying at about 460 knots. Bang, the airplane broke up but didn't explode and I pulled up to the left.

Number two was following; he warned me that the Egyptian number two was behind me. Then I saw him. The second Vampire turned southbound and started to dive toward a sandy area at 1,000 feet. When I was straight behind him, he started to roll with his nose down, and I thought that damn son of a gun will hit the ground before I can shoot him. So I missed a chance to shoot him. He made another roll and I closed in. I headed the gun sight up front as I used to do when shooting targets in training, and I said, "This is the right deflection angle and the right range." I pulled the trigger and hit the cockpit—bang—unbelievable—the airplane exploded right there! That was that! The two other bogeys had already crossed the border so I went back, made two victory rolls over the base, and I landed.[9]

In August 1955, President Nasser signed a major arms deal with Czechoslovakia. By early 1956 large numbers of Soviet-built MiG-15s had entered service with the EAF. The Egyptian army and navy were also receiving a significant quantity of new weaponry. The new arms and support enhanced Nasser's position. He ordered the withdrawal of British troops who were protecting the Suez Canal, increased the forces along the Israeli border, and pressured King Hussein of Jordan into expanding the number of *fedayeen* guerrilla bases in his country. Guerrilla raids, artillery duels, and attacks intensified along the Egyptian border and occurred with increasing frequency along the borders with Syria and Jordan. On April 12, 1956, an Egyptian Vampire was shot down over Israeli territory by an IAF Ouragon, marking the first victory for the French-built fighter.[10]

Israel was compelled to procure new, up-to-date weaponry in order to meet the Arab buildup, and France was one of the only countries willing to supply Israel with advanced weaponry, especially jet fighter aircraft. In April 1956 the first French-built Mystere IVA fighters arrived in Israel. The IAF intensified its training efforts in order to increase the number of combat-ready pilots and support personnel and to bring the new Ouragon and Mystere IVA squadrons to full operational status.

Low-scale conflict with Israel continued during the summer of 1956 and Egypt's relations with Britain, France, and the United States were severely strained. Nasser made a fateful decision on July 26, 1956, when he announced his intention to nationalize the Suez Canal. This was the first step toward a coalition war involving Israel, Great Britain, and France against Egypt.

# 3

# The
# Sinai
# Conflict

*T*he sixteen C-47 Dakota transports, each carrying some two dozen paratroops of the Israeli 890 Airborne Battalion, sped above the sand and rock of the Sinai Desert, flying at only 500 feet to evade radar detection. Ten Meteor fighters flew at low altitude with the Dakotas in order to protect them against interception by Egyptian fighters. Mystere fighters took turns patrolling along the Suez Canal and Great Bitter Lake, a position from which they could detect any Egyptian fighters taking off from their bases. Although the Mystere pilots could observe fighters being towed around on the taxiways, they were under strict orders not to take action unless the MiGs rose to engage.

The IAF plan called for its transport aircraft to drop paratroops near Mitla Pass and then keep this force and other advancing units resupplied. Fighters were to provide air cover for Israeli forces and refrain from engaging Egyptian aircraft unless they struck first. The IAF planners hoped that if Israel refrained from striking Egyptian cities or airfields, then the Egyptians might also select not to attack Israel.

At 4:30 P.M. on October 29, 1956, the sixteen Israeli C-47s ascended to 1,500 feet and the paratroopers began to jump.[1] The 395 paratroopers landed several miles east of the entrance to Mitla Pass and marched to the mouth of the pass where they set up defensive fortifications. This assault interdicted the major transit route from the Suez Canal to Egyptian positions in the central Sinai. Mitla Pass is only 45 miles from the canal and 155 miles from Israel. The Egyptians were surprised by the paratroop assault and the full-scale invasion of the Sinai, which began the following day. The Israeli campaign was timed to coincide with the British and French offensive against Egypt.

In Israel the conflict was known as Operation Kadesh. Israel's intention was threefold: (1) to eliminate *fedayeen* bases in the Sinai and the area surrounding Gaza, (2) to disrupt the Egyptian war-making capability in order to prevent an attack on Israel, and (3) to open the Gulf of Eilat to Israeli shipping.

The fighting between Israel and Egypt continued for eight days. The action was divided into three phases: the opening assault (October 29–30), heavy fighting (October 31–November 1), and exploitation (November 2–5), during which Israel took control of the Sinai. The action ended with the cease-fire.

The two primary causes that led to the 1956 conflict were the alignment of Egypt with the Soviet Union and the nationalization of the Suez Canal. Israel sought to acquire a reliable supply of weapons to balance the Soviet equipment provided to Egypt, while France saw Israel as a potential ally in efforts to regain control of the Suez Canal and reduce President Nasser's influence in the ongoing conflict in Algeria. Initial discussions between France and Israel led to the sale of French tanks, plus Ouragon and Mystere IVA fighters, to Israel.

In September 1956, Israeli representatives met with French officials in Paris to initiate plans for coordinated military action.[2] Britain and France were already beginning to move forces into position for Operation Musketeer, an effort to regain control of the Suez Canal. On October 24, after a series of meetings, Israeli Prime Minister Ben Gurion agreed to initiate limited military actions in the Sinai if British and French forces would strike at Egyptian airfields no later than thirty-six hours after the start of the Israeli incursion. Ben Gurion was particularly worried about the threat of attack by Egyptian IL-28 medium bombers against Tel Aviv, Jerusalem, and other Israeli cities. The French agreed to provide French Air Force fighters and pilots to help protect Israel from air attack. If Egypt struck Israeli targets, the IAF planned to begin immediately an all-out air offensive against the EAF and expected to rely on the French for air defense. After several days of fighting, Anglo-French attacks against Egyptian airfields were expected to eliminate the air threat to Israel. Then the IAF could apply the full weight of its aerial firepower against Egyptian ground forces in the Sinai in order to assist advancing Israeli units.

The French also flew a last-minute supply of weapons and ammunition to Israel and provided transport aircraft to help move material to the Sinai battlefield. Moshe Dayan later commented on the importance of this cooperation: "If it were not for the Anglo-French operation, it is doubtful whether Israel would have launched her campaign; and if she had, its character, both militarily and politically, would have been different."[3]

The 1956 conflict between Israeli and Egyptian forces took place in the Sinai Peninsula, a parched piece of land shaped like an inverted triangle. The southern part of the Sinai is hilly, with mountains reaching as high as 8,000 feet. A force of about two thousand Egyptian troops was stationed in the Sharm el Sheikh region at the southern tip of the Sinai. Armed with coastal artillery and a sizable number of antiaircraft guns and supported by several Egyptian naval vessels, this garrison interdicted shipping bound for the Israeli port of Eilat.[4]

The northern Sinai is a relatively flat coastal plain along the Mediterranean but south of this is a region of desert and mountainous terrain. Only three major roads cross the central Sinai: one parallels a rail line along the coast, a second skirts the mountains from Abu Awergila to Bir Gifgafa, and the final road is located south of the central hilly region cutting through Mitla Pass.

Most of Egypt's thirty-thousand-man force in the Sinai was located in the north, parallel to the Israeli border, and in the Gaza Strip. Egyptian troops were deployed in well-fortified defensive positions and supported by a considerable amount of artillery, tanks, and antitank guns.

Until 1955 the EAF had a close relationship with the RAF. As a result, the EAF was organized into wings like the RAF, relied upon British training concepts, and flew mostly English aircraft, including the Meteor and Vampire fighters and Lancaster bombers. In late 1955 the first Soviet-built MiG-15s began arriving in Egypt and with them came a large number of Czech and Soviet advisors and technicians. These foreign advisors reassembled the crated MiGs, trained Egyptians to fly and maintain the aircraft, and initiated programs to instill Soviet tactical philosophy and organization. The EAF could not easily absorb the more than eighty MiG-15 fighters, thirty to forty IL-28 bombers, and twenty IL-14 transports, MiG-15 UTI, and Yak-11 trainers that were delivered over a ten-month period. The Czech and Russian advisors hurriedly conducted training courses and assisted with maintenance, but it would take time to develop an experienced, capable cadre of support personnel.[5]

A shortage of skilled pilots and aircrews compounded the Egyptians' plight. The Egyptian Air Force Academy, located at Bilbeis, expanded its program, adding Yak-11s to its fleet of Gomhoria and Harvard trainers. However, as with skilled maintenance personnel, it took time to train combat-capable pilots. While the EAF had some five hundred pilots in October 1956, only about three hundred were capable of flying operationally, and the number rated on MiG-15s and IL-28s must have been less than one hundred.[6]

On the eve of the 1956 conflict, the EAF had a total strength of about sixty-four hundred, comprising four hundred officers, three thousand enlisted personnel, and three thousand civilians. Air Vice-Marshall Mohamed Sodky had at his disposal a force of about 255 aircraft organized into the following squadrons: three MiG-15s (fighters), three Vampires (fighter-bombers), two Meteors (fighters), three IL-28s (bombers), plus two transports and one liaison. Israeli intelligence sources identified as fully operational only two squadrons of MiG-15s, two of transports, and one squadron each of Vampires, Meteors, and IL-28s.[7]

Egypt had at its disposal over two dozen airfields. Many of these had been built by the British during World War II, although several had been recently upgraded by Egypt to accommodate the new Russian-built jets. Most of the major Egyptian airfields were located in the Cairo–Suez Canal area. These included Abu Suweir, Fayid, Inchas, Almaza, Cairo West, and Bilbeis. In the Sinai the EAF had operational airfields at El Arish, Bir Hamma, and Bir Gifgafa.

Normal peacetime strength of the IAF was about three thousand men, including over three hundred pilots. However, wartime mobilization expanded the force to more than ten thousand.[8] The IAF was commanded by Brig. Gen. Dan Tolkovsky. A former pilot with the RAF, General Tolkovsky considerably upgraded the capability of the IAF after he assumed command three years earlier.

At the outbreak of hostilities, the IAF had three operational jet fighter squadrons, which included some sixty Mystere IVA, Ouragon, and Meteor jets. Three fighter-bomber squadrons operated about sixteen Mosquito and thirty P-51 aircraft, while two B-17 bombers and twenty-one Harvard trainers could also be used on attack missions. The IAF transport force included sixteen C-47 Dakota and four Noratlas transports.[9] This considerable force was supported by French fighter squadrons whose mission was to protect Israeli cities from Egyptian attack. On October 23 more than two dozen French Air Force Mystere IVA fighters, including most of the 2 Escadre based at St. Dizier, left for Israel's Ramat David air base. Among these aircraft were Mystere IVA fighters from both 1/2 Cigonge and 3/2 Alsace units. Two days later the French deployed eighteen F-84F fighter-bombers of 1 Escadre from the 1/1 Corse, 2/1 Morvan, and 3/1 Argonne units, along with their maintenance personnel, from Dijon to Lod, the civil airport near Tel Aviv. The French also loaned several C-47 Dakota transports to the IAF for the conflict.[10]

Israel had eight major airfields available for use, with Ramat David, Hatzor, and Eqron being the most important. In addition, Lod could be used.

To conquer the Sinai, Israel deployed nine brigades totaling nearly forty-five thousand men along its southern border.[11] The largest force was to engage and defeat the Egyptian forces in the northern Sinai, which were concentrated in the triangle formed by Rafah, El Arish, and Abu Aweigila. Following the defeat of this Egyptian concentration, Israeli units planned to follow the coastal and central roads across the Sinai. The Israeli 202nd Airborne Brigade was assigned the mission of seizing Mitla Pass. Elements of the brigade not used in the paratroop assault were reinforced with artillery, half-tracks, and light tanks and given the task of linking up with the troops in Mitla Pass under the command of Col. Ariel Sharon. Another brigade was assigned the task of defeating Egyptian forces in the southern Sinai and capturing the fortifications at Sharm el Sheikh.

The conflict began with the paratroop drop into Mitla Pass. While the paratroopers dug in to prepare for an Egyptian counterattack, Sharon's convoy of airborne troops began their drive toward Mitla Pass. Sharon's paratroopers quickly captured an Egyptian frontier outpost at Kuntilla and, after a night march, engaged and defeated an Egyptian force entrenched near the town of Thamed. Israeli Piper Cubs landed in the desert to fly out the wounded and, at 7:00 A.M., several IAF transports delivered supplies and ammunition via parachute to the column. Suddenly six Egyptian MiGs swept in from the east at low

altitude and caught Sharon's column by surprise. The Egyptian
fighters bombed and strafed the Israeli convoy, destroying several vehicles and wounding six soldiers. Seeing that his men
were tired and demoralized by the surprise air attack, Sharon
ordered a rest. However, his force was again subjected to air
attack at 11:00 A.M. by four Vampire fighters.

Entrenched at the north of Mitla Pass, Colonel Eiton's paratroopers were attacked by Egyptian troops at dawn on October
30. At about 7:30 A.M. two MiG-15 fighters strafed the entrenched paratroopers and destroyed a Piper Cub aircraft that
was parked nearby in the desert. Within an hour four more
Egyptian Vampire fighter-bombers strafed the Israeli paratroopers. The Vampires, which had flown from nearby Fayid
airfield, were escorted by two MiG-15 fighters. Lieutenant Colonel Eiton, the Israeli paratroop commander, put in an urgent
call for air cover.[12]

In the afternoon, the IAF began to fly patrols over the battle
area and started attacking Egyptian convoys that were moving
into the Sinai with reinforcements. Portions of the Egyptian 2nd
Brigade, which was moving up from the Suez Canal to the
western entrance of Mitla Pass, were repeatedly bombed, rocketed, and strafed by Israeli aircraft. In the late afternoon on
October 30, six Israeli Mystere IVA fighters battled with six
MiG-15 jets over Kabrit, an Egyptian air base near the Suez
Canal. Lieutenant Yosef Tsuk, an Israeli Mystere pilot, shot
down one of the MiG-15s. The surviving MiGs counterattacked.
Tsuk's Mystere was hit by cannon fire, but he was able to return
safely to his base.[13] This was the first air combat victory credited to the recently delivered Mystere IVA jet fighter. The dogfight proved that an aggressive pilot in the larger and heavier
French-built fighter could engage and defeat the MiG-15, which
had earned a reputation for its agility during combat in the skies
over North Korea.

While Sharon's and Eiton's paratroopers were engaged in
operations in the central Sinai, other Israeli units went into
action in the north. Early on October 30, an infantry brigade led
by Col. Joseph Harpaz advanced on foot across desert terrain
that was impassable to vehicles and seized Egyptian fortifications surrounding the road junction of Queisima. Israeli forces

converged on the heavily fortified Egyptian positions at Abu Aweigila.

The Israeli invasion of the Sinai began in earnest on the morning of October 30, and by late in the day Colonel Sharon's column had linked up with Lieutenant Colonel Eiton's paratroops at Mitla Pass.

On the first full day of the Sinai conflict, October 30, Israeli aircraft flew several hundred sorties. IAF fighters downed one Egyptian MiG-15 over Kabrit air base and performed over one hundred successful ground attack missions. It took time for Egypt to react to the Mitla Pass assault, and as a result, the EAF aircraft flew only about fifty combat sorties on October 30. However, the EAF conducted several effective ground attack missions against Israeli forces.

Late on October 30, British and French authorities issued an ultimatum calling for Israel and Egypt to stay ten miles away from the Suez Canal and to end the fighting in the Sinai within twelve hours. If these conditions were not met, Britain and France threatened to assault the Suez Canal and occupy its key positions.[14] Israel accepted the ultimatum, but Egypt rejected it.

The residents of Haifa, Israel, were awakened at 3:30 A.M. the following morning by gunfire from an Egyptian destroyer. The *Ibrahim Al Awwal* fired more than two hundred shells into the town before it was attacked and driven off by the French destroyer *Crescent*. About two hours later, two Israeli destroyers, the *Eilat* and the *Jaffa*, intercepted the *Ibrahim Al Awwat* and engaged her with gunfire. At dawn, two Israeli Ouragon fighters attacked and damaged the Egyptian vessel with rockets.[15]

With no hope of escaping—thanks to the air attack damage and continuing gunfire from the nearby Israeli destroyers—the captain of the ship ran up the white flag at 7:10 A.M. The ship was boarded, captured, and towed into Haifa harbor.

In the early morning hours, Israeli transports air-dropped supplies to the 202nd Paratroop Brigade near Mitla Pass. Colonel Sharon awakened suddenly with a 600-pound bundle of supplies landed within three feet of his head.[16]

The paratroopers received a wake-up call at 5:45 A.M. from four Egyptian Vampire fighter-bombers. Yallo Shavit, an IAF

pilot who was patrolling over Mitla Pass in a Mystere fighter
that morning, described his battle with these Egyptian jets:

> We got a panic call from the ground controller who
> gave the microphone to Colonel Eiton, who knew me
> personally. He said. "We are not well protected so try to
> be here as soon as possible. I know that you are short of
> fuel, but try to do whatever you can." When we heard
> his call, immediately we went into a split S and dived
> 90 degrees down to get over the area in the shortest
> time. While we were doing this, I saw four points
> glittering like mirrors from the sun. Four Egyptian
> Vampires had taken off from a base near the Suez Canal
> and were flying at 1,500 feet, which was above the
> morning clouds. I saw them and said to number one,
> "You be number two because once I lose eyesight, we
> are going to lose them." So we changed positions and I
> kept my eyes on these points. We crossed the speed of
> sound and we put the engines on idle and put the speed
> brakes out. We leveled off at about 2,000 feet and I recall
> to this day our speed was about 550 knots, which with a
> Mystere is a very high speed.
>   They were flying like 250 knots so the closing speed,
> wow, it was like a missile. . . . I picked up one and put
> the cross on him and he was flying into the sun, but it
> was not too bright yet. I saw the cross on him and saw
> the bullets miss him. So I took a deflection, fired a short
> burst and one or two bullets hit him. Immediately he got
> inverted with smoke. I pulled up and went up to 10,000
> feet with my speed. Number two did an S turn and got
> one and then I saw him shooting at another. The fourth
> one ran away, and I got him with a short burst as he
> ran toward the Suez Canal and he exploded in the air.
> Meanwhile number one started shouting fuel, fuel. . . .
> We climbed up to 36,000 feet in order to save fuel and
> headed back to base. We were so short of fuel. . . . I
> landed first and cleared the runway and he landed and
> his engine cut off at the end of the landing. . . . Both of
> us landed with zero fuel—just a miracle.
>   The main point was that we were well trained to look

around to find aircraft. Secondly, we learned how to use the cannons in air-to-air by doing many dogfights: Mystere against Ouragon, Mystere against Meteor, Mystere against Mustang. Even though we were pilots young in age, we had a lot of experience.[17]

Shortly after noon, a heavy task force of Israeli paratroopers, reinforced with armor, moved into Mitla Pass. This task force was trapped when heavy fire destroyed the lead vehicles. The remainder of the paratroop force was drawn into the action. Egyptian fighter-bombers supported their troops in the pass with several attacks. A particularly effective air strike occurred at about 4:00 P.M. when four Meteor fighter-bombers and six MiG-15s strafed the Israeli vehicles that were stalled on the road and then with rockets attacked the troops encamped at the east end of the pass. Two Israeli Ouragon fighters engaged and drove off the MiGs, but the Meteors returned again to strafe the paratroopers. These attacks destroyed several vehicles and caused over a dozen casualties.[18]

A night assault by the paratroopers resulted in the capture of the Egyptian positions in Mitla Pass. However, the hand-to-hand combat required to dislodge the well-entrenched Egyptian defenders cost Israel 34 killed and 102 wounded. Israeli transports landed in the desert during the night to bring in additional supplies and to carry out casualties.

Israeli forces assaulted Abu Aweigila and outflanked Egyptian defensive positions in the central Sinai. Determined Egyptian resistance slowed Israeli forces and IAF fighter-bombers were called in to blast the defenders and restrict the flow of Egyptian reinforcements. Propeller-driven Mustang and Mosquito fighter-bombers and Ouragon jets set upon Egyptian convoys and blasted positions with bombs, rockets, and machine-gun fire.

Eliezer (Cheetah) Cohen, a P-51 pilot who later retired with the rank of colonel, described his attacks against Egyptian forces:

In 1956 my first mission was to attack a convoy of Egyptian tanks that was strolling along the Sinai. We met them with six P-51s and we destroyed twelve tanks

and twenty-five to thirty vehicles. We hit this convoy
badly and as we left, we sent the Ouragons and
Mosquitos in and they hit this convoy more and more.

We would put the tank on the centerline of our nose,
fly very low at the level of the tank, and at the last
moment, when you felt you had to pull up to not hit the
tank, you released the napalm bomb and then pulled up,
and the bomb hit the tank. We always attacked from 90
degrees and dropped only one bomb at a time so each
Mustang, which carried two napalm bombs, six 5-inch
rockets, and several hundred 0.5 rounds for the six
machine guns, could do a hell of a job. The rockets were
huge but not very accurate. But when they hit a tank,
they destroyed it. On my second mission, I was attacking
Egyptians near Aba Aweigila. On my first run, I attacked
a self-propelled gun, like a tank but with a big cannon,
and as I ran in, I saw an Egyptian soldier sitting on the
tank shooting a machine gun at me. My angle of attack
toward him made me a steady target, no angle of
deflection. He hit me. You could really hear it and here
comes all the oil from my engine radiator and it covered
my windscreen. I was blacked out. I told myself, "Oh my
god, I am in trouble. I will have to parachute over
enemy positions." The engine slipped, but I made 4,000
feet before the propeller stopped. . . . I decided to fly
south to open the space between Abu Aweigila before I
went down. I knew from briefings that an Israeli
armored division was coming behind the Egyptians. I
could force land near these forces, which were coming
from the south. I manually threw off the napalm and the
rockets and landed. It was really easy. I was in the
middle of the desert. Now I had to walk. I saw many
retreating Egyptian soldiers and at first I hid, but my
coveralls looked like theirs and, because my skin is dark
since my parents were from Turkey, I fit right in. After
hours of walking, I reached a road, and I saw Egyptian
vehicles. I though, "Jesus Christ, now I am in big trouble
because I am still behind enemy lines and our forces are
not in yet." I found a small bridge, covered myself with
stones so no one could see me and waited. Then I heard

someone speaking Hebrew. He said, "Moshe, give me a Coca Cola." And then I understood that Israeli soldiers were using Egyptian vehicles. I came out, but they though I was an Egyptian and they ran off. They came back with a tank and you can't imagine who commanded this tank—my cousin! He recognized me and he yelled, "What are you doing here?" I got a car and drove back to my plane and took my parachute, radio, maps, and everything. When I got back to my base, they were very surprised.[19]

Late in the afternoon, Mystere fighters, patrolling along the northern coast road over El Arish, engaged a flight of Egyptian MiGs. The brief dogfight that ensued saw the destruction of two MiG-15 fighters.

On October 31 there was intense air and ground action in the Sinai. The IAF flew several hundred ground attack and interdiction missions in support of advancing Israeli troops and these missions destroyed or disabled many Egyptian vehicles. French F-84F fighter-bombers also flew attack sorties against targets in the Sinai with considerable success.[20] Mystere patrols fought air engagements with several Egyptian aircraft and downed four Vampire fighter-bombers and two MiG-15s.[21] Israeli transports flew dozens of resupply missions in support of advancing Israeli units. The EAF flew more than one hundred sorties over the Sinai during the day. Egyptian pilots conducted a number of successful air strikes against Israeli forces and top-cover MiGs intercepted and drove off several flights of Israel fighter-bombers. IAF fighters, however, were beginning to win the air-superiority battle over the Sinai.

British and French forces entered the war against Egypt during the night on October 31. Starting at about 10:30 P.M. Canberra and Valiant bombers of the RAF began bombing Egyptian airfields. Because of the threat of interception by EAF MiG-15, Meteor, and Vampire fighters, the RAF aircraft bombed their targets at night, from an altitude of 40,000 feet. EAF airfields at Almaza, Inchas, Abu Suweir, Kabrit, and Cairo International were struck by RAF bombers, which dropped both contact and delayed-action bombs. These initial raids damaged the airfields but destroyed only fourteen aircraft.[22] In response to these attacks, Egyptian, Czech, and Soviet pilots immediately began ferrying EAF aircraft to remote airfields or to locations out of the country. At first, light Royal Navy fighter-bombers from the aircraft carriers HMS *Albion*, HMS *Bulwork*, and HMS *Eagle* plus land-based French and British fighters operating from Cyprus continued to pound Egyptian airfields. During the first twenty-four hours of their involvement, British and French aircraft flew over five hundred sorties, attacked over a dozen Egyptian airfields, and destroyed more than one hundred Egyptian aircraft.[23]

On November 1, Israeli forces began their assault on Rafah, the heavily fortified Egyptian town at the end of the Gaza Strip. When concentrated Egyptian fire stalled the initial assault, Israeli artillery and aircraft were called in. Mosquito fighter-bombers struck with rockets, bombs, and cannons, while artillery and naval gunfire from Israeli destroyers and a French cruiser pounded the Egyptian defenses.[24] Intense fighting continued until mid-morning, when the Egyptian forces began to withdraw. Retreating Egyptian forces fought back vigorously despite being harried by Israeli armor and repeatedly attacked by IAF fighter-bombers.

Egyptian troops fought stubbornly in the defense of the Sinai but Israeli forces were gaining the upper hand through rapid maneuvers, surprise, and heavy close air support. Interdiction attacks by the IAF inhibited the movement of Egyptian forces. The British and French attacks against Egyptian airfields contributed to the defeat of the Sinai defenders by eliminating their air cover and bringing the focus of the conflict back to the Suez Canal.

President Nasser, on November 1, urged his troops in the Sinai to disengage from Israeli units and fall back to the Suez Canal to protect it from attack by an expected Anglo-French invasion force. By late afternoon, many EAF aircraft had been dispersed to airfields in Saudi Arabia, Syria, or southern Egypt. Those that remained in Egypt were under concentrated attack by British and French fighter-bombers. As a result, the IAF had complete air superiority over the Sinai, and, with some assistance from three French squadrons stationed in Israel, provided unhindered close air support, resupply, and reconnaissance efforts for advancing Israeli columns.

On November 2, Israeli troops drove into El Arish; Egyptian troops had evacuated the airfield and supply depot during the previous night. The fall of Rafah and El Arish cut off the two brigades of Egyptian and Palestinian troops in the Gaza Strip. While the Egyptians held strong defensive positions, the city of Gaza was rapidly taken by Israeli forces. After several hours of fighting, General Digany, the Egyptian commander, surrendered the city to minimize civilian casualties.

The final phase of the war in the Sinai began on November 2 as Israeli units began to close on the Suez Canal and Sharm el Sheikh. Egyptian troops fortified at the southern end of the Sinai were able to halt ships traveling through the Gulf of Aqaba toward the Israeli port of Eilat. After crossing the border on October 30, Col. Avraham Yoffe's 9th Israeli Brigade began to move south along the Gulf of Aqaba early on the morning of November 2. The going was slow because the desert road was uphill and covered with drifting sand.

Israeli Chief of Staff Gen. Moshe Dayan was concerned about the 9th Brigade's capability to move rapidly south across the rugged Sinai terrain and seize Sharm el Sheikh. The United Nations was calling for an end of the fighting between Israel and Egypt and an immediate suspension of the Anglo-French attacks against Egyptian targets.

To increase the force in the southern Sinai, Dayan ordered Colonel Sharon, whose paratroopers were still holding Mitla Pass, to send a detachment south along the Gulf of Suez road toward Sharm el Sheikh.[25] Two companies of paratroopers were also dropped near the town of El Tur in order to secure the western route to Sharm el Sheikh. Following the capture of the airfield at El Tur, IAF transports flew in an additional battalion of troops, vehicles, ammunition, and supplies. Israeli fighter-bombers bombed and strafed the Egyptian positions at Sharm el Sheikh and one of the Mysteres was shot down by antiaircraft fire. Major Benjamin Peled, commander of a Mystere squadron, ejected successfully but landed near the Egyptian position. Despite an injured leg, he was able to take refuge in hilly terrain near the outpost. A Piper Cub pilot spotted Major Peled, landed on a flat stretch of ground, and picked him up, right under the noses of the Egyptian defenders.

By the end of November 2 those Egyptian forces that had not

been cut off had largely withdrawn from the Sinai to positions along the Suez Canal. British and French aircraft from Cyprus, Malta, and aircraft carriers in the Mediterranean continued to strike at Egyptian airfields and began to hit army positions near Port Said and adjacent to the Suez Canal. Eight French Air Force F-84F fighter-bombers, flown from an Israeli airfield, attacked and destroyed about twenty IL-28 bombers located at Luxor air base in central Egypt.[26]

Israeli troops assaulted the remaining Egyptian defensive positions in the Gaza Strip and central Sinai on November 3. With assistance from artillery and IAF close support strikes, Israeli troops forced the surrender of the last Egyptian defensive positions in the Gaza Strip and northern Sinai by late in the day.

Israeli aircraft intensified their assault against fortifications near Sharm el Sheikh beginning at dawn on November 3.[27] Egyptian troops at Sharm el Sheikh were without air cover but fought back courageously. Their antiaircraft fire continued to claim victims; many IAF aircraft were damaged and several Mustangs were shot down in the course of these air attacks.

The final Israeli assault against Sharm el Sheikh began about 3:30 A.M. on November 5. The heavy Egyptian fire initially stalled the assault and caused dozens of casualties. At the first light, with the assistance of heavy mortar fire plus repeated air strikes by IAF aircraft using napalm, rockets, and gunfire, the Israelis regained the initiative. They overran Egyptian positions one by one, and by 9:00 A.M. the fighting in the Sinai was over.

On the same day that Egyptian forces were defeated at Sharm el Sheikh (November 5), British paratroops were assaulting Egyptian positions on the Suez Canal near Port Said and French troops were landing near Port Fuad. The following morning British and French troops landed on the beach at Port Said. Royal Marine Commando Unit No. 45 was flown into action from the assault carriers HMS *Theseus* and HMS *Ocean* via helicopters, marking the first time in warfare that a large-scale amphibious assault was conducted using helicopters.

British and French forces moved south along the Suez Canal and made significant gains against the defending Egyptian troops with assistance from tanks and fighter-bombers. Following Egypt's request on November 2 for a cease-fire, the United States, Soviet Union, and other UN members pressured Britain and France until the two nations finally agreed to end their invasion in the early hours of November 7.

In a little more than one hundred hours of fighting, Israel had achieved Operation Kadesh's objectives: almost the whole Sinai Peninsula had been captured, Egyptian forces defeated, guerrilla bases in the Gaza Strip destroyed, and the blockade of the Strait of Tiran broken. Israeli forces, in the process, suffered 181 killed, 800 wounded, and 4 captured. Egyptian combat losses in the Sinai included about 1,000 killed, 4,000 wounded, and 6,000 captured. Egyptian war material captured by Israeli forces included 100 tanks, 1,000 vehicles, and 200 artillery pieces. Fewer than 100 Israeli tanks, half-tracks, and other pieces of heavy equipment were destroyed in the fighting.[28]

It is important to place in perspective the Anglo-French involvement in the 1956 conflict. After the war, Moshe Dayan admitted that Israel might not have agreed to invade the Sinai at all in the absence of English and French assistance. Britain and France committed 90,000 men, 130 warships and support vessels including two French and five British aircraft carriers, plus 500 aircraft to the operation. Combat aircraft, transports, and helicopters of the RAF, Royal Navy, French Air Force, and French Naval air arm units flew several thousand sorties during their seven-day involvement. Britain and France claimed to have destroyed about 200 Egyptian aircraft on the ground and provided effective support for their ground forces. Anglo/French troops seized Port Said, Port Fuad, and the northern portion of the Suez Canal. In the process, British forces suffered 16 dead, 96 wounded, and lost 8 aircraft (one Canberra bomber, one Venom, two Sea Hawks, two Wyvern fighter-bombers, and two Whirlwind helicopters), while French losses included 10 dead, 33 wounded, and 2 aircraft (one Corsair and one F-84F fighter-bomber). Egyptian losses in combat with British and French forces are estimated to be 650 dead, 900 wounded, and included more than 200 aircraft of all types.[29] The English and French took few risks in their battles with the Egyptians. The slow pace of military action and the intensity of political opposition were disastrous for Britain and France. Any hopes the two nations had of regaining control of the Suez Canal were dashed when the United Nations forced their troops to withdraw following the cease-fire.

After the war the United States and the Soviet Union exerted tremendous pressure on Israel to evacuate its forces from the Sinai. Reluctantly Israel agreed to withdraw and, in exchange, the United Nations created a peacekeeping force that took control of Sharm el Sheikh and the Gaza Strip. Although the Gaza Strip quickly came under Egyptian domination, guerrilla activity did not begin again for many years.

The IAF began the Suez conflict bound by its own tight restrictions. Initially Israeli aircraft did not strike at airfields for two reasons: Israel did not want to be viewed as the aggressor and it hoped the Egyptians would think along the same lines. When Egyptian fighter-bombers struck at advancing Israeli columns and paratroop positions near Mitla Pass on October 30, the IAF stepped up its air cover over the ground forces and began attacking Egyptian units. The IAF was able to defend its units in the Sinai from air attack and simultaneously perform ground attack missions because three squadrons of French fighters were on hand to defend Israeli airspace against Egyptian air attacks. In addition, the IAF did not have to allocate attack sorties against Egyptian air bases because the British and French performed this mission.

The IAF relied on its small force of recently introduced Mystere IVA fighters to achieve superiority in the air over the Sinai. Of seven Egyptian aircraft downed by the Israelis, all fell to Mystere IVA pilots, many of whom had little experience with their new aircraft. Ouragon and Meteor fighters also flew fighter patrol missions but were used more often in the ground attack role.[30]

The air superiority contest over the Sinai only lasted five days. Egypt did not react to the October 29 paratroop assault on Mitla Pass, but it did strike back beginning at dawn the following day. Egyptian MiG-15s, Meteors, and Vampires flew effective ground attack missions and clashed with Israeli aircraft on more than a dozen occasions. Although Egyptian pilots damaged several Israeli planes, their only air combat victory during the 1956 conflict was to down a Piper Cub. British and

One of the first aircraft to serve with the Air Service of the Haganah, the foundation of the Israeli Air Force, was the British-built Auster.

The Czech-built Avia S199 combined the Messerschmit Bf 109G airframe and the Jumo bomber engine. It was an unpleasant aircraft to take off and land because of the high torque of the engine and its narrow-track landing gear. While it was not a popular aircraft, in the hands of a capable pilot it could counter the Spitfire, its principal adversary.

An Israeli photographer captured the image of the first air battle over the new state of
Israel on June 3, 1948. Modi Alon, commander of the first IAF fighter squadron,
intercepted and shot down two Egyptian C-47 Dakota transports that were dropping
bombs on Tel Aviv.

IAF transports, such as this C-47, were sometimes used as bombers at night. However, bringing arms to Israel and moving troops and weaponry to the battlefield were their primary missions.

On June 17, 1953, the IAF joined the jet age with the delivery of two Meteor T.7 trainers. Israeli Prime Minister David Ben Gurion, who addressed the crowd at the delivery ceremony, named the aircraft *Gale* and *Tempest*.

The IAF acquired the Mystere IVA fighter in 1956 and the aircraft served until the early 1970s. This swept-wing jet performed both fighter and attack missions. During the 1956 conflict, Israeli Mystere IVA pilots downed seven Egyptian MiGs and Vampires over the Sinai while French-flown Mystere IVAs patrolled over Israel to protect against Arab attacks.

Israeli C-47 and Noratlas unloading supplies in the Sinai. IAF transports delivered Israeli paratroops to Mitla Pass and moved fuel and ammunition into the Sinai to help maintain the advance of armored columns during the 1956 Sinai Conflict.

The Dassault Supere Mystere B2 was the first European combat aircraft capable of supersonic speed in level flight. Israel procured a squadron-sized force of these highly capable aircraft, the first of which was delivered in 1959.

To modernize the pilot training program and upgrade the capabilities of the Israeli aviation industry, Israel put into service the Fouga Magister jet trainer.

An IAF Mirage IIIC prepares to take off with a heavy load of bombs and external fuel tanks. Almost the entire IAF fighter force was committed to the initial series of strikes against Arab airfields on the morning of June 5, 1967.

The Arab air forces were not totally out of action in 1967. A pair of Egyptian MiG-17 fighter-bombers strafed an Israeli supply convoy, destroying several vehicles and causing numerous casualties.

An IAF Mirage on a reconnaissance mission captures the image of the remains of five MiG-21 fighters at an Arab airfield.

The A-4 was an ideal replacement for the IAF's aging inventory of French-built aircraft. The Skyhawk could carry a heavy weapons load, was easy to fly, and was relatively cheap to buy and operate. The A-4 was the first new American-built aircraft to serve with the IAF.

Israeli commandos jump from a UH-1D transport helicopter. These light, turbine-powered helicopters were used extensively in the anti-terrorist role.

French air strikes, which began on the night of October 31, eliminated the EAF as a factor in the Sinai fighting.

Ground attack was the focus of the IAF during the last five days of the Sinai campaign. The harsh desert terrain kept the Egyptian convoys on the few main roads, with little or no cover for escape. Beginning on October 30, IAF aircraft harassed Egyptian columns that were moving across the Sinai to engage Israeli forces. The fighter-bombers also attacked Egyptian fortifications to weaken them for armor and infantry assault. Close air support missions helped Israeli combat troops overcome strong Egyptian fortifications in several Sinai battles.

During the conflict, all IAF combat aircraft were pressed into service to fly ground attack missions, including the Mystere IVA, Ouragon, and Meteor jet fighters, and Mustang, Mosquito, and even Harvard (trainer) propeller-driven aircraft. Antiquated B-17 bombers also flew operational missions, striking the Egyptians at Sharm el Sheikh and flying maritime patrol sorties over the Mediterranean and Gulf of Aqaba. Ground attack aircraft blasted Egyptian targets with bombs, rockets, and napalm, plus cannon and machine-gun fire. Egyptian antiaircraft fire was frequently intense. Thirteen of the fifteen Israeli losses were to antiaircraft fire, including ten P-51 Mustangs.[31] On the plus side, IAF attack sorties disabled an Egyptian destroyer, blasted dozens of defensive positions, and destroyed more than two hundred tanks and vehicles in the Sinai. Israeli ground commanders stated after the conflict that interdiction and close air support operations hastened the Israeli advance, reduced casualties, and shortened the campaign. While the outcome would probably have been the same, the conflict would have taken a few days longer without support from Israeli air strikes, and more casualties would have been suffered to defeat Egyptian forces in the Sinai.

Beginning on October 31, Israeli-based French F-84F fighter-bombers flew attack missions against Egyptian forces in the Sinai. One aircraft was lost in the course of operations, but the pilot successfully ejected and landed in the Sinai Desert.[32]

IAF scout planes and transports helped ensure the Israeli victory in the Sinai campaign. Piper Cubs performed vital scouting and liaison missions, which aided the ground commanders in understanding the situation on the battlefield. The pilots of these small aircraft frequently landed on rough desert terrain to evacuate casualties and rescue downed IAF pilots. One Piper Cub was destroyed in an air attack and another was shot down by EAF fighters. The IAF transport force made possible the opening move of the Sinai campaign—the interdiction of Mitla Pass by Israeli paratroopers. This innovative strike into the Egyptian-held Sinai came as a complete surprise. Israeli Dakota and Noratlas transports delivered supplies to advancing Israeli columns, resupplied the paratroops at the Mitla Pass, and aided in the capture of Sharm el Sheikh through the rapid deployment of additional forces into the Sinai.

The forces involved in the Sinai fighting were fairly evenly matched in numbers of aircraft, troops, tanks, armored vehicles, and artillery. It was the confidence, initiative, spirit, and leadership of Israeli personnel in the air and on the ground, along with Anglo-French intervention that overcame the Egyptian forces. Aggressive maneuvers on the ground were supported by initiatives in the air. Brig. Gen. Dan Tolkovsky, commander of the air force, stated after the conflict that peacetime training and preparations were the biggest contributors to the efficiency of the IAF in battle. Intense training, the calling up of the reserves, and good maintenance enabled the IAF to fly four missions a day with their Mystere and Ouragon jets and more than two sorties a day with their older Mustangs and Mosquitos. Combat-damaged aircraft were quickly repaired and Israel had almost two pilots available to fly each aircraft. All of these factors combined to enable the IAF to support a rigorous flying schedule. During the war, the IAF flew 1,986 sorties, almost 500 of which were ground attack missions in support of advancing troops in the Sinai.[33] The successful Sinai campaign prompted senior Israeli leaders to reorganize their military force and strengthen the armor and the jet fighter components.

# 4

# *Modernization*

Within weeks of the end of the 1956 Sinai conflict, political pressure from the United Nations forced Israel to pull its troops out of the Sinai. Israeli political and military leaders vowed that this would not happen again. During the next decade the Israeli army, navy, and air force were strengthened. In the event of a future conflict, Israel planned to strike a powerful opening blow, carry the fight to the enemy, and quickly achieve victory. This doctrine would allow Israel to maximize the effectiveness of its mostly reserve army, reduce losses to a minimum, and force the conclusion of the conflict before significant enemy reinforcements and political intervention could affect the outcome of the war.

Israeli leaders understood that, in the event of war, they could not rely on external assistance like that provided by France and Great Britain in the 1956 conflict. The security of the country required a powerful army and an air force composed of fighters capable of performing both air-to-air and attack missions.

The Israelis developed an offensive doctrine that called for fast-moving armored columns (composed primarily of tanks) and a strong air force to spearhead a preemptive attack. Since areas where the fighting was most likely to occur—the Sinai Desert, the Golan Heights, and the Jordan River Valley—afforded little or no cover from air attack, Israeli air superiority was vital to the success of this concept of war. The doctrine called for the destruction of enemy air forces early in the war. Direct attacks against enemy airfields would destroy aircraft on the ground, before they could get into battle. Once enemy air forces had been eliminated and air superiority achieved, the IAF would concentrate on providing support for advancing Israeli ground forces.

Even though Egypt lost the 1956 war in the eyes of the world, the Arab nations considered the "Suez War" a victory because they perceived that President Nasser had overcome Britain, France, and Israel in a political sense. Following the 1956 war, the Soviet Union rapidly resupplied Egypt with new aircraft and weapons to replace those destroyed during the conflict. Scores of advisors were sent to Egypt to train the EAF and large numbers of Egyptian pilots and support personnel traveled to the Soviet Union for military training. By late 1957, the EAF had been rearmed with new Soviet-built aircraft and the air forces of Syria, Jordan, and Iraq had been considerably strengthened.

To meet this threat and support the new offensive doctrine, Israel expanded the IAF. The piston-engined Mustang, Mosquito, and B-17 combat aircraft and Harvard trainers were phased out as quickly as possible and replaced by modern jets. Since the relationship between Israel and France remained strong after the 1956 conflict, the IAF turned to France for these new aircraft.

While not equal in performance to the Soviet-built MiG-15/17, the Ouragon jet fighter had proven itself in action during the 1956 conflict and was immediately available. Israel placed an order in late 1956 for an additional supply of Ouragon jets and France delivered the first of these in 1957. Forty-five ex–French Air Force Ouragon fighters were supplied to Israel. With this second purchase, the Israeli Ouragon force grew to two squadrons and more than seventy aircraft.

Israel also procured additional Mystere IVA fighters from France to make up for combat and operational losses and to expand the frontline fighter force. By the late 1950s, the IAF had received in excess of sixty Mystere IVA fighters. During the late 1950s and early 1960s, the two Mystere IVA squadrons were responsible for the air defense of Israel.

In 1957 Israel purchased eighteen Vautour IIA aircraft to form a fighter-bomber squadron to replace aging Mosquito and B-17 bombers. A large, twin-engine, swept-wing aircraft, the Vautour IIA was armed with four 30-mm cannons. The aircraft could also carry more than 4,000 pounds of weaponry in its internal bomb bay and on underwing pylons. Produced by the French firm Sud Aviation, the French Air Force operated several versions of the Vautour, including fighter-bomber, reconnaissance, and radar-equipped fighter models. The Vautour could fly at nearly 700 miles per hour and had a radius of action in excess of 750 miles.

Satisfied with the performance of the attack version, the IAF purchased seven two-seat Vautour IIN all-weather fighters. These specialized jets served with the remaining NF-13 Meteors in the single IAF night/all-weather fighter squadron. This special unit had the responsibility for night and bad weather air defense of Israeli airspace. Later the IAF purchased four two-seat Vautour IIBR aircraft with a glazed nose and internally mounted sensor pallet in the weapons bay. These planes were used on reconnaissance missions. About thirty Vautour aircraft were eventually delivered to the IAF. Until mid-1958 their existence in Israel was a matter of utmost secrecy.[1]

After purchasing all of these planes and upgrading the role of the air force, Brig. Gen. Dan Tolkovsky had achieved his goal of priority status for the air force. The air arm was first in line for the allocation of defense funds and also received the best Israeli manpower.

Becoming a fighter pilot became the ultimate goal of young Israeli males. The IAF pilot-training pilot program was the most rigorous in the world—nearly 90 percent of the applicants selected for the program were eventually rejected. Extremely high standards were established because the Israelis knew that only an air force with top-quality pilots could fight outnumbered and win.

Israeli youth seeking to be pilots first had to pass a demanding series of preliminary tests and character analyses. Pilot candidates began their training immediately after secondary school. This contrasts with most air forces, which require pilot trainees first to complete their college education. The twenty-month course began with about ten hours of flight training on Piper Super Cub aircraft. This first course was intended more to identify those with flight aptitude than to be a real instructional phase. Students who successfully completed this part of the training then attended intensified classes on applied mathematics, physics, aeronautics, meterology, electronics, navigation, and other subjects. Following the classroom phase, pilot candidates took a demanding infantry-training course to test their physical abilities and become familiar with the missions of the ground forces.

General and aerobatic flight instruction comprised the next part of the IAF pilot-training course. In the late 1950s, pilot trainees flew the Boeing PT-17 biplane and then graduated to the T-6 Harvard training aircraft. Advanced flight training used piston-engined Mustang and jet-powered Meteor fighters. In the early 1960s the Israelis changed the training syllabus so that pilot trainees proceeded from the Piper Super Cub directly into a new jet trainer, the Air Fouga Magister. The new training cycle introduced Israeli pilot candidates to jet aircraft at an earlier stage, better preparing them for the advanced jet fighters that were entering service with the IAF in large numbers.[2]

This new generation of jet aircraft and weaponry demanded skilled aircraft mechanics and electronics technicians. The IAF considerably expanded its maintenance and support staff to ensure that the new jet aircraft were always ready to fly. Conscripts received intense training while skilled personnel were encouraged to reenlist or serve in civilian positions with the air force or aviation firms.

In July 1958, Ezer Weizman became the new commander of the IAF. The thirty-four-year-old brigadier general was determined to expand the capability and effectiveness of the air force. A former pilot with the RAF, Weizman had served with the first IAF fighter squadron in the 1948 War of Independence and held high-ranking positions, including deputy to Dan Tolkovsky.

Weizman continued to strengthen the air force and worked to give it greater independence and esprit de corps. Weizman is best characterized by his statement "Israel's best defense is in the skies of Cairo."[3] Air force personnel focused on his operational plan to attack enemy aircraft on the ground and destroy any aircraft that made it into the air.

Massive Soviet resupply and training efforts strengthened the air arms of Egypt, Syria, and Iraq. Jordan, Lebanon, and Iraq received Hawker Hunter fighters and training assistance from the United Kingdom. The EAF, in particular, worried Israeli planners. In the late 1950s, the EAF received hundreds of MiG-15 and MiG-17 fighters and IL-28 jet bombers. In addition to Soviet assistance, Egypt enlisted the support of German scientists and technicians in an attempt to provide a domestic aircraft and guided missile industrial base. A team of designers was hard at work developing the lightweight HA-300 supersonic fighter, while a group of engineers worked to produce advanced guided missiles.[4]

In 1958 the IAF ordered the supersonic Super Mystere B2 fighter from France. The first European fighter capable of sustained supersonic flight, the aircraft was an evolutionary improvement of the Dassault Mystere IVA. The Super Mystere featured new systems, a thinner wing, and a more powerful SNECMA Atar 101G afterburning turbojet engine that produced a maximum thrust of 9,800 pounds. The aircraft had a maximum takeoff weight of 22,000 pounds, was armed with two 30-mm DEFA cannons and could carry up to 2,000 pounds of external ordnance. Since it could perform both fighter and attack missions, the Super Mystere fulfilled IAF multirole requirements. The first Super Mysteres entered service with the IAF in 1959, and the new fighter squadron was operational within less than a year.[5]

In the late 1950s the Israeli firm Bedek Aircraft, Ltd. (now Israel Aircraft Industries) entered into an agreement with the French company Air Fouga to produce the Magister jet trainer in Israel. The 6,500-pound aircraft was propelled by two 880-pound-thrust Turbomecca Marbore turbojet engines, and was capable of full aerobatics. The Magister could be used as a trainer and as a light strike aircraft, using rockets, light bombs, and two internal machine guns. Israel purchased a small number of these trainers from Air Fouga, the parent company, but most IAF models were assembled by Bedek using a mixture of Israeli-built and imported components. The Israeli version of the aircraft differed from the standard Magister in having larger, unpowered ailerons and strengthened wings that could accommodate external weaponry.

To upgrade the IAF further, Israel again turned to France. Dassault, producer of the Ouragon, Mystere IVA, and Super Mystere, began the design of a small delta-wing fighter in the early 1950s in response to NATO and French Air Force requirements. Promising test results with several prototypes prompted the French Air Force to order ten Mirage IIIA preproduction models and place an option for one hundred production versions in 1958. The Mirage IIIC fighter was developed to defend French airspace from attack by Soviet nuclear-armed bombers. With its Mach 2 speed and ability to climb to over 50,000 feet in less than five minutes, the 20,000-pound Mirage IIIC was expected to make quick work of high-flying enemy bombers. Normal armament for the high-altitude intercept mission was a single radar-guided Matra 511 or 530 air-to-air missile. The Mirage IIIC's Cyrano 1 radar and semiactive radar-homing air-to-air missile allowed the pilot to intercept targets at night and in poor weather. For daytime air combat the aircraft could be armed with two 30-mm DEFA cannons and two American-built AIM-9B Sidewinder infrared-homing air-to-air missiles. Most French air force Mirage IIICs carried only missile armament, since the fuel tanks for the rocket used to boost rate of climb displaced the cannons and their supply of ammunition. For ground attack missions, the Mirage IIIC could accommodate bombs, air-to-surface guided missiles, and fuel tanks in addition to the aircraft's internal cannons.

IAF officials closely followed the development of the Mirage fighter. In 1959 Ezer Weizman, commander of the IAF, traveled to France with Danny Shapira, the IAF's chief test pilot, to evaluate the fighter. Shapira put one of the early Mirages through a demanding flight evaluation, including supersonic flight. At a time when Mach 2 flight was the realm of an exclusive group, Shapira became only the twelfth pilot in France to reach that speed. The IAF's command was very impressed with the aircraft. Following discussions with the ministry of defense, Israeli officials placed an order for twenty-four of the fighters. Like the French fighters, IAF Mirages were equipped with the Cyrano 1 radar. Even though Israel later purchased a limited supply of Matra 530 air-to-air missiles, the IAF continued to rely on the potent DEFA 30-mm cannon as the primary air combat weapon of the Mirage IIIC fighter.

The Mirage IIIC fighter entered service with the IAF on April 7, 1962, and by 1967 the Mirage fleet had expanded to seventy-two aircraft, which comprised three fighter squadrons. Three Mirage IIIB two-seat trainers were also purchased to ease pilot-training efforts.[6]

Air operations in the 1956 conflict underscored the importance of the IAF transport fleet. The C-47 Dakota contributed significantly to Israel's 1956 victory, and, even in the 1960s, a dozen of these aircraft remained in service. Worn and tired C-47s that were acquired during the 1948 War of Independence were retired and replaced by later models purchased from civilian sources and the French air force.

The only Israeli transport that could deliver the large loads needed to support the ground forces during the 1956 conflict was the Noratlas. Satisfied with its performance, the IAF bought more of these capable aircraft and by the mid-1960s about twenty Noratlases were in service. Half of these aircraft were purchased from France and the remainder were supplied by West Germany.

To transport heavy loads beyond the capacity of the Noratlas, the IAF purchased several four-engined Boeing Stratocruisers secondhand from civilian and military sources during the 1960s. Israel Aircraft Industries engineers and technicians combined the airframes of several former Pan American Airways Stratocruisers with the aft fuselages of ex-USAF C-97 aircraft to come up with aircraft that could air-drop heavy payloads, haul cargo, transport troops, and refuel in the air. At least five of these transports were available on the eve of the 1967 war.[7]

After a several-year flight evaluation of helicopters, IAF planners decided to purchase a substantial force of vertical-lift aircraft. In late 1956, the first of six Sikorsky S-55 utility transport helicopters entered service with the IAF. Used for air and sea rescue and coastal patrol, as well as for airborne ambulances, these relatively low-powered helicopters were limited by the high temperatures common in Israel. Israel had better luck with the five-seat, turbine-powered Sud Aviation Alouette II helicopter. Developed to be used in hot, high-altitude environments, these helicopters operated with considerable success. Larger Sikorsky S-58 helicopters purchased from the United States in 1958 performed successfully and an additional supply of these aircraft were bought from West Germany. Slightly larger than the S-55, the S-58 had nearly twice the horsepower of its predecessor, which resulted in a dramatic performance improvement in the heat. The S-58 could carry eighteen troops, a ton of cargo, or eight stretchers to a range of more than 200 miles. The IAF force of more than thirty S-58 medium-lift helicopters was used to transport airborne troops on border patrol and to perform commando operations.

The lift capability of the helicopter force was considerably expanded in the mid-1960s with the introduction of the French-built Super Frelon helicopter. Nine of these aircraft had entered service by the 1967 war. The Super Frelon made possible new combat tactics because it was capable of carrying thirty troops, or jeeps, light artillery, or heavy equipment. Super Frelon and S-58 helicopter crews trained with airborne troops and conducted large-scale airlift exercises to refine combat tactics. Helicopter crews were also taught special techniques to evade enemy interceptors. IAF helicopter pilot training was conducted using Bell 47 and Alouette light helicopters and was as intense as that experienced by fighter-pilot trainees.[8]

During the 1960s the IAF's fleet of basic trainer and liaison aircraft was modernized. Older light planes were taken out of service and replaced by new Piper Super Cub and Cessna 185 Skywagon aircraft. A small number of specialized aircraft like the Dornier DO 27 and Pilatus Turbo-porter short-take-off-and-landing liaison planes were also put into service.

The years following the 1956 conflict were relatively peaceful for Israel. Although no formal peace treaties had been signed to end Arab/Israeli conflict, UN forces located in the Sinai helped guarantee safe passage for Israeli shipping and also helped keep the peace. During the next several years, internal unrest in Lebanon, Jordan, Iraq, and Syria forced these nations to focus their attention on domestic problems. Still, sporadic terrorist attacks did not cease with the Israel/Syria border area being the most embattled area.

Air confrontations continued between Israel and its neighbors as planes crossed borders to test reaction times. On December 20, 1958, an Egyptian MiG-17 was shot down by an Israeli pilot flying a Mystere IVA. The Super Mystere B2 achieved its first combat victory on April 28, 1961, when a patrol of two Super Mystere fighters intercepted a pair of Egyptian MiG-17s. One of the MiGs escaped, but the pilot of the other lost control of his jet and bailed out.[9] In the fall of 1962 four IAF Super Mystere fighters clashed with four Syrian MiG-17 fighters over the Golan Heights. During the air battle one Israeli jet was heavily damaged and no MiGs were hit.

During the arms race between Israel and its Arab neighbors in the early 1960s, Egypt rapidly developed a powerful air force and gained considerable combat experience through participation in the civil war in North Yemen. Israeli defense planners were particularly worried about the threat of attack by the thirty TU-16 medium and forty IL-28 light bombers of the EAF, which could deliver over 350 tons of bombs against Israeli targets in a single raid. The Iraqi Air Force also operated both of these bombers, while the air arm of Syria had a small contingent of IL-28s. A coordinated Arab air strike, protected by fighter escort, was a possibility that Israel had to face. No less important was the threat of air attack by the hundreds of fighter-bombers in service with the air arms of Egypt, Syria, Jordan, Iraq, Lebanon, and other Arab countries. By the mid-1960s, this force outnumbered the IAF by more than three to one and included over 250 supersonic MiG-19/21 fighters and 350 MiG-15/17, SU-7, and Hawker Hunter fighter-bombers.[10]

To even the odds, Israel planned to strike the first blow in a future conflict. Titled the "operational plan," this offensive doctrine called for a simultaneous surprise attack of Arab airfields. The Israelis calculated the number of sorties that would be required to deliver enough bombs, rockets, and cannon shells to destroy a majority of the Arab aircraft on the ground. Even if all IAF aircraft reached their targets and performed successfully, the air arm was not large enough, nor could the IAF carry a large enough payload to complete the job in a single wave. Because most of the frontline IAF aircraft were designed to perform air-to-air combat rather than ground attack, the useful ordnance payload that most IAF fighters could carry per sortie against typical target airfields was limited (Vautour—4,000 pounds; Mirage IIIC—2,000 pounds; Super Mystere B2—2,000 pounds; Mystere IVA—1,000 pounds; and Ouragon—500 pounds). In figuring the chances for a successful preemptive attack, Israeli planners had to account for aircraft lost due to enemy fire, maintenance problems, and pilot error. A preemptive attack would only succeed if the exact location of enemy aircraft could be determined. To maximize the number of effective sorties, IAF ground crews would rapidly have to refuel, rearm, and return to service the aircraft that had completed their mission. A conveyor belt-like system would be necessary in order to destroy all the potential targets.[11]

The airfields targeted for initial attack housed Egyptian TU-16 and IL-28 bombers and MiG-19/21 fighters. To protect Israeli cities and minimize the risk to the heavily laden Israeli fighter-bombers, it was imperative that the first wave of Israeli planes either destroy or damage these Egyptian aircraft. Subsequent waves of attacking aircraft could eliminate crippled jets, blast lower priority targets, and hit the main base of other Arab air forces. To make this plan work, almost all IAF aircraft had to be committed to the attack, with less than one squadron of fighters to be held in reserve to provide air defense. This offensive plan also counted on surprise and confusion among the Egyptians and their Arab allies. A confused enemy would not be able to react quickly to the strikes, and the enemy's aircraft would be destroyed before an effective defense or counterattack could be organized.

The operational plan was tested often by the Israelis. Pilots constantly practiced ground attack techniques, navigation, and air-to-air tactics. Model target airfields, constructed in the Negev Desert, gave pilots a chance to practice and hone their skills. Large-scale mock attacks helped train pilots and give ground crews experience in dealing with rapid servicing, rearming, and refueling.

Any Arab aircraft that made it into the air during the planned offensive were to be engaged immediately and shot down. Israeli pilots flew mock dogfights and air-to-air exercises. The defection of two Arab pilots with their aircraft in 1965 and 1966 gave the IAF an opportunity to evaluate and fly simulated combat against their principal adversaries' frontline fighters—the MiG-17 and MiG-21. These tactical insights, plus rigorous training, tempered the IAF into a force that had air combat skills unmatched anywhere in the world.

Tension between Israel and Syria increased in the early 1960s as terrorist raids and shellings intensified along Israel's northern borders. In 1964, Syria began efforts to divert the Jordan River to deprive Israel of its primary source of irrigation water. Fighting erupted on the Golan Heights in November 1964 with artillery, tanks, and aircraft trading fire.

A high state of unrest continued into the summer of 1966, when Syrian and Israeli fighters engaged in several dogfights. The Israelis scored the first Mirage air combat victory on July 14, 1966. A strike force of Mystere IVA fighter-bombers, attacking Syrian artillery batteries in response to heavy shelling, was threatened by a flight of Syrian MiG-21 fighters. A top-cover flight of Mirages tangled with the MiGs.

Capt. Yoram Agmon was the first to spot the Syrian MiG-21s:

I suddenly noticed something shining on my left, at very
low altitude. It was moving in a southeasterly direction
towards the confluence of the Jordan and the Yarmuk. I
radioed to the lead that I had made eye contact with the
plane. I did everything without taking my eyes off that
shining spot. I was flying low, about 500 feet off the
ground, at high speed, and, at about 2,000 meters, I
identified a pair of MiG-21s. I was getting closer when
they were warned of my presence and turned sharply to
the left. Although I knew that the MiG-21 maneuvered
well, I was surprised at the extraordinary angle of the
turn. I lost sight of the right-hand MiG, but pulled
sharply upwards to try to slow down and close in on the
left-hand one. At about 350 meters I got alongside him
and shot off a short round, though with no result. I
maneuvered again quickly, and reduced the distance
between us to 250 meters. I aimed the second round
carefully and was immediately rewarded with a powerful
explosion in his right wing, which was torn off at the
fuselage. The plane began to spin downward; I passed
alongside and saw the pilot bail out. I took my way
westward and joined the formation near the Sea of
Galilee.[12]

A month later a second Mirage pilot claimed another Syrian
MiG-21 that was strafing an Israeli patrol boat in the Sea of
Galilee.

In response to increasing terrorist attacks along the
Jordanian/Israeli border, on November 13, 1966, Israeli armored columns moved into Jordanian territory to attack guerrilla bases. Jordanian troops counterattacked this Israeli force
and two Royal Jordanian Air Force Hunters took part in the
engagement. These aircraft made several successful strafing
passes, but were subsequently intercepted by a flight of Israeli
Mirage fighters. After a prolonged dogfight, one of the Hunters
was shot down. Israeli raids against targets in both Jordan and
Syria experienced heavy opposition from antiaircraft fire, and
several IAF aircraft were damaged or lost.

Two weeks after the air battle over Jordan, Israeli aircraft fought with Egyptian MiGs over the Negev Desert and scored additional victories. An Israeli Piper Cub, which was flying a reconnaissance mission along the Israeli/Egyptian border, was suddenly attacked by two EAF MiG-19 fighters. Diving to the deck, the Cub pilot turned and twisted low over the desert to escape and radioed for help. The two MiGs were toying with the Piper Cub and did not notice the two delta-wing Mirage fighters that lined up on them. One of the Israeli Mirage pilots tracked a MiG on his radar and locked onto it. When a light on the Mirage pilot's instrument panel came on, indicating that his Matra 530 air-to-air missile was seeking its target, the Israeli pilot fired the weapon. The missile quickly covered the mile and a half to the MiG and its 60-pound warhead ignited the MiG-19's fuel tanks, causing a massive explosion. The second Mirage pilot swept in and raked the other MiG with cannon fire, quickly shooting it down. This dogfight, which took place on November 28, 1966, saw the first successful use of air-to-air guided missiles in Middle East combat.[13]

During 1966 Gen. Mordechai Hod replaced Ezer Weizman as the commander of the IAF. A fighter pilot in the 1948 war, Hod led the IAF's only Ouragon squadron in the 1956 conflict and served as the assistant to General Weizman during the early 1960s.

In the decade between the end of the 1956 conflict and the 1967 war, the IAF had enlarged its inventory, introduced Mach 2 fighters, and substantially improved its pilot cadre, tactical doctrine, and operational effectiveness. By 1967, the IAF operated almost 100 supersonic fighters, nearly 150 subsonic fighter-bombers, 60 combat-capable jet trainers, and a sizable complement of transports, helicopters, and light aircraft.[14]

The spring of 1967 saw an increasing number of clashes along the northern border between Syria and Israel. The largest air battle fought in the Middle East since the 1956 conflict occurred on April 7, 1967, when a heavy Syrian artillery barrage led to a sizable Israeli air strike. Syrian MiG-21s intercepted the attack and a large air battle ensued, resulting in the loss of six Syrian aircraft.[15]

Tensions increased as Egyptian President Nasser, in support of Syria, mobilized additional troops and strengthened Egyptian positions in the Sinai. On May 18, President Nasser ordered UN forces to withdraw from Sharm el Sheikh and positions in the Sinai along the Egyptian/Israeli border. Two days later, Israel responded by mobilizing a number of reserve units and putting the IAF on a state of full alert. Egyptian forces subsequently blockaded the Straits of Tiran, halting shipping to the Israeli port of Eilat. Although neither Egypt nor Israel appeared to want war, events were out of control.

# 5

# *The Six-Day War*

*A*t about 8:45 A.M. on June 5, 1967, Israeli fighter-bombers simultaneously attacked the major EAF bases at El Arish, Jebel Libni, Bir Thamada, Bir Gifgafa, Kabrit, Inchas, Cairo West, Abu Suweir, and Fayid. They blasted the runways of these bases with bombs and then swept back and forth to strafe parked aircraft, control towers, hangars, and antiaircraft positions.

The attacks came as a complete surprise, and the Israeli fighter-bombers left dozens of flaming Egyptian aircraft and damaged facilities in their wake. Within minutes, additional groups of attackers appeared and the cycle of destruction continued. Despite the surprise, about a dozen EAF fighters made it into the air and fought back. Egyptian MiGs shot down Israeli aircraft near Abu Suweir and Cairo West air bases, while antiaircraft fire claimed victims at several other airfields. A total of eight IAF aircraft were lost during the first series of strikes. Four Israeli planes were shot down by Egyptian fighters and four were lost to antiaircraft fire. However, the EAF lost more than one hundred planes during the first in a series of Israeli air strikes, which lasted about forty-five minutes. Most of these aircraft were destroyed on the ground, but ten were shot down by IAF fighters, a few others were destroyed while trying to land on damaged runways, and some ran out of fuel.

By 9:30 A.M., the IAF launched a second series of strikes against Egyptian airfields. Israeli fighter bombers that had returned from the initial attacks were refueled, rearmed, and sent back into the air in ten minutes or less. Repair crews worked furiously on battle-damaged fighters, quickly returning them to operational status. The 115 sorties of the second wave reattacked some airfields hit earlier and also struck new targets, including Mansura, Helwan, El Minya, Almaza, Luxor, Deversoir, Hurghada, and Bilbeis air bases. This series of raids destroyed about one hundred EAF aircraft, with the loss of only a single Israeli aircraft.

By 1:00 P.M., the repeated Israeli air strikes had eliminated half of the EAF. Nearly three hundred Egyptian aircraft had been destroyed, including most of the TU-16 and IL-28 bombers that posed a threat to Israel, and many of the advanced MiG-21 and MiG-19 fighter aircraft. The EAF also suffered significant personnel losses and damage to air base facilities.[1]

During the late morning and early afternoon, Jordanian and Syrian aircraft struck back at Israel. Jordanian Hawker Hunters attacked Kfar Surkin and Netania airfields, destroying a transport. Syrian MiGs bombed an oil refinery at Haifa and strafed Megiddo airfield. IAF fighters were in action against Egypt and did not intercept these raids.

When artillery shells began to hit near Ramat David airfield and Jordanian ground troops attacked Israeli forces near Jerusalem, IAF fighter-bombers went into action against Jordan. The Royal Jordanian Air Force bases at Mafraq and Amman were hit beginning at about 12:45 P.M. Eighteen Hawker Hunters, most on the ground, were destroyed in the attacks, but one was shot down in air combat. Several Jordanian transports and helicopters were also hit, and airfield facilities were damaged. The Jordanian radar site at Ajlun was bombed and destroyed. A single IAF Mystere was lost in air combat with the Jordanian Hunters.

Israeli fighter-bombers struck Syrian airfields at Damascus, Marj Riyal, Damyr, and Seiqal at about 1:00 P.M. A more remote airfield, T-4, was hit just after 4:00 P.M. During these air strikes, a total of sixty-one Syrian aircraft were damaged or destroyed on the ground, while seven MiG-21s and three MiG-17s were shot down in air combat. Since the element of surprise had been lost, the attacking IAF fighter-bombers had to brave fierce antiaircraft fire and numerous MiGs, which were airborne over their bases. Two Mysteres were lost to antiaircraft fire over Damascus. Another Mystere pilot was surprised by a flight of four MiG-17s while strafing ground targets and was shot down. A total of four IAF aircraft were lost to the Syrian defenses.[2]

In retaliation for a 2:00 P.M. Iraqi air strike that hit a factory at Netania, three Vautour fighter-bombers were dispatched to attack an airfield in Iraq. The aircraft flew across Jordan and struck the Iraqi airfield at H-3. While the air base sustained damage, defending Iraqi MiG-21 and Hawker Hunter fighters forced the Israeli pilots to withdraw.

Throughout the afternoon and early evening, IAF fighter-bombers continued to strike at Arab airfields. Delayed-action bombs were employed in order to disrupt runway repair efforts. Egyptian radar sites also were hit; all sixteen in the Sinai were put out of action and many west of the Suez Canal were also destroyed.

Yallo Shavit discussed his role in the Israeli air attacks on June 5:

In 1967 I was commander of the one Super Mystere squadron. It was like two squadrons as we had almost forty aircraft. French aircraft were at Bedek IAI for depot overhaul and we used them during the war. . . . They didn't like it but it was war.

We had excellent pilots because this was the channel of supply for pilots for the Mirage squadrons. We were caught in 1967 with a bunch of good pilots who were about to graduate.

The armament which won the 1967 war was the cannon, no doubt about it. We just went down to low level, got in close, and shot one target after the other. We spent hours at the ranges. If you didn't hit the target of 4 by 4 by 4 [feet] in the middle, it didn't count. It was the same with the air-to-air gunnery, so the tough rules of the training paid for themselves later in war.

The first day was a tough one. . . . We got up at about 3:00 A.M. The briefing started at 5:00 A.M. We went to the aircraft at about 6:15 A.M. and took off around 7:00 A.M. It took us some forty minutes to reach Inchas. I was there at 7:55 A.M., ten minutes after the first raid of four Mirages. We bombed and hit the runways and strafed the aircraft on the ground. My number three was hit or made a mistake and crashed into the ground. We did five passes and on the last one, I was hit by 12.7-mm antiaircraft fire. It was a mistake to make so many passes, but there were so many MiGs. They hit my auxiliary hydraulic system and the air brakes were caught out, and I got a warning that one of the undercarriage doors might be open. So I kept my speed below 250 knots. Can you imagine flying back at 250 knots and seeing all the war around you? I saw a MiG taking off from Inchas after I was hit. I asked my number two and three—they were youngsters—to fly next to me to protect me in case the MiGs attacked. Out of the blue came one of the MiGs and I pulled up and fired at him. He pulled down and disappeared at low level.

When I came back for a landing, it was tough because many aircraft were hit on the first mission. We had a lot of casualities on the first mission because of our inexperience and their heavy defenses.

A lot of other aircraft were also damaged, so there was a problem where to land. Bene Peled, my wing commander at Hatzor, told me to bail out as he was afraid that I would block the runway. I told him, "Not me, I will circle around and then get in." I crossed the intersection so I would not block the runway, and landed. I finished the runway on the overrun. The aircraft survived with minimum damage. The ground crew took the aircraft and prepared it for flight the next day.

I went to the brief, changed aircraft, and flew to Mansura, again with bombs and cannon. I came back and then attacked Mafraq, Jordan. The antiaircraft fire there was tough, but no big thing—you get hit, this is war. Three missions by 2:00 P.M.

In the afternoon I flew to Seiqal, a base in Syria on the edge of the Iraqi desert. . . . MiG-21s were flying top cover over the air base. We had four aircraft. My number three got hit by a bullet as we flew over the West Bank. He was hit in the external fuel tank and was low on gas. I ordered him to follow me, drop his bombs, and then climb up to look for MiGs. So we went into bombing, the four of us.

After the attack, I turned left and saw a long train—two of them (MiG-21s) were sitting on us. I asked

number two to follow me, number three to go up, and
number four to turn the other way. I saw number four
and the two MiGs coming out of the turn, and I told
number four to take a left so that we can sandwich
them. But their number two saw me and he pulled up. I
asked my number two to take him, and I continued with
their number one. I had experience fighting with the
MiG-21 because I was one of those who did the dogfights
with the MiG-21 brought by the defecting pilot from Iraq
that arrived in 1966. We flew the Super Mystere against
the MiG-21, and I knew exactly the position where he
sees me and does not see me. What their number one did
when he saw me was level off, gain speed, and climb. I
knew that I couldn't follow his tactic because I would be
on my back and he would come down and shoot me. So
what I did was drop my fuel tanks, and played a little
trick on him. When he pulled out, I went to a position
where he could see me and I showed him my belly. He
saw me and said, "Ah, ha!" and put his nose down to 60
or 70 degrees, diving toward me. I knew from training
that if a MiG-21 and Super Mystere crossed the horizon
going down at the same time, it would take the MiG
more time to recover from the dive because the Super
Mystere was more agile.

I came into a barrel roll and I got him with his nose
down. It was at low altitude, about 2,000 feet. He went
into a tight turn, and I almost lost him because he had a
lot of energy, but he made a mistake by changing
direction. When he did this, I got into firing position.
Then my number three said over the radio, "Number
one, with all due respect, you are doing OK."

I said, "Shut up, I'm in the middle of a dogfight." I
got the MiG at very low speed—150 knots—300 feet over
the hangars. He did a turn and I fired. He exploded and
fell right into the hangars in the middle of the base. I
went down to minimum altitude, below 100 feet and
gained some speed. One of my guys shot the other MiG,
and I saw the wing of the MiG-21 separate above me at
about 4,000 feet, and the pilot bailed out. We met and
flew back to Hatzor and landed in the dark.

At 8:30 P.M. we were back in the air with bombs. My number one had flares and we were attacking Jordanian artillery, which was shelling Jerusalem. We reloaded and went back around 10:00 P.M. and came back at 11:00 P.M. It was a full day of six missions.

Early the next morning on the first mission, we lost a Super Mystere shot air-to-air by rockets or missiles from a MiG. He was flying over the Sinai like he was over Tel Aviv on Independence Day, and they got him.[3]

Operation Focus, the preemptive attack of Arab air forces that had been practiced for years, succeeded beyond all expectations. By the evening of June 5, twenty-five Arab airfields had been attacked with some 350 Arab aircraft damaged or destroyed. Most were hit on the ground but over two dozen had been shot down in air combat.

Surprise was the key to this victory. For years the IAF had made a habit of scrambling a large number of training sorties at dawn, which flew west over the Mediterranean, as if toward Egypt. The EAF responded by flying patrols over the northern Sinai, which usually took off just after sunrise. So the actual Israeli air strikes were timed to arrive over Egyptian airfields when the Egyptian morning patrols had landed and at a time when senior officers would be in transit from their home to work. Israeli aircraft took off according to a precise schedule that enabled them to arrive simultaneously over their respective targets at 8:45 A.M. Cairo time. The aircraft flew at low level, below radar coverage, and maintained complete radio silence.

Israel used various means to deceive and confuse enemy radars. Prior to and during the attacks, C-47 transports flew back and forth along the Israeli/Egyptian frontier, dispensing chaff. Other electronic countermeasures also were employed to disrupt Egyptian radar and radio communications and to deny electronic intelligence to the many other forces monitoring the Middle East.[4]

The Israeli attacks had been so successful that Arab leaders speculated that the IAF must have received assistance from the USAF and RAF. Other analysts suggested that the precise nature of the attacks and destruction of hundreds of parked aircraft must have been the result of the use of a new air-to-ground guided missile. The real secret of the success was the years of planning and training and the willingness of Israel to risk an all-or-nothing surprise assault with nearly all of its available aircraft. The IAF committed all but a dozen aircraft to the initial series of raids, and sequenced the sorties so that the targeted airfields were under almost constant attack. Rapid turnaround ensured that this cycle of attacks was maintained for several hours.

During the initial air strikes the IAF introduced a new weapon designed to maximize damage to enemy runways known as the "dibber" bomb. Low-level attacks against runways with conventional bombs did not prove to be a very effective tactic because the weapons frequently would bounce back into the air, causing only limited runway damage and creating a hazard to the attacking aircraft. High-angle dive-bombing tactics would have solved this problem, but attacking fighter-bombers would have been exposed to enemy defenses. Instead, Israeli fighter-bombers used runway destruction bombs—the product of the state-owned ordnance firm Israel Military Industries. These bombs could be released safely from low altitude and at high speed, and still cause considerable damage to runways. When released, a parachute opened to ensure separation from the aircraft and orient the weapon perpendicular to the ground. After two or three seconds, a booster rocket fired that drove the hard-nosed bomb deep into the runway, where its explosion would cause a much larger crater than would conventional bombs.[5]

On the initial series of airfield strikes, Mirage III and Mystere IVA aircraft carried two special antirunway bombs plus fuel tanks. Vautours were armed with four 1,000-pound bombs, while Super Mysteres carried two 500-pound bombs and external fuel tanks. Even the aging Ouragon was used on the first strike. The Ouragons were armed with four 200-pound bombs or rockets. Once pilots had delivered their bombs or rockets, they made several low-level strafing passes with their cannons.

The primary targets of the initial strike were the EAF TU-16 and IL-28 bombers, which could threaten Israeli cities and airfields. Located at Cairo West and Beni Sueif airfields, the TU-16 bombers were parked in concrete revetments. Accurate cannon fire destroyed these aircraft in their revetments.[6] Abu Suweir, home of an IL-28 light-bomber regiment, was repeatedly attacked and most of those aircraft destroyed. Also targeted and destroyed in the initial raids were MiG fighters, Sukhoi fighter-bombers, transports, and helicopters.[7]

The vital element of surprise was nearly lost on the morning of June 5. At about 8:05 A.M., an IL-14 transport carrying General Amer, the Egyptian chief of staff, General Sidki, the EAF commander, and a Soviet air force general took off and headed into the Sinai Peninsula. After several minutes, the IL-14 headed south toward Sharm el Sheikh. If the aircraft had turned north toward Gaza, the crew might have been able to spot the large number of Israeli aircraft that were heading east to attack Egyptian airfields. In the end, however, the flight of this transport also aided Israel. Egyptian antiaircraft gunners were warned not to fire on any planes at that hour lest they hit these senior officers. Once the attack began, the chief of staff and air force commander were out of the action since they could not find a safe place to land.[8]

Also that morning, Jordanian radar operators at the mountain top station at Ajlun noticed considerable activity over Israeli air bases. At 8:38 A.M. they sent a message to Egyptian War Minister Shams al Din Badran regarding this activity. But a recent directive had forbidden direct communication between Jordanian and Egyptian forces, so the message was not relayed from the war minister's office to frontline commanders in time.[9]

While the bulk of the IAF was striking Egyptian airfields, Israeli armor was pouring over the border at several different points into the Sinai. An *ugda* (roughly a division) led by Brig. Gen. Israel Tal crossed the border into the Gaza strip and attacked Egyptian forces at Khan Yunis on the Mediterranean, while a supporting brigade moved into Gaza. This force fought a tough battle at Rafah and then moved west along the northern coast to the outskirts of El Arish. The Suez Canal was Tal's *ugda*'s ultimate goal. A similar-size force under the command of Brig. Gen. Avraham Yoffe moved across the desert and engaged Egyptian forces on the route toward the important Giddi and Mitla Passes in the central Sinai. Brig. Gen. Ariel Sharon's division was charged with the destruction of the strong Egyptian defenses in the central Sinai near Abu Aweigila. The Israeli attack force included two armored divisions, one mechanized division, and several supporting brigades with more than 70,000 men and 750 tanks.

Egyptian forces in the Sinai totaled about 90,000 men and over 900 tanks organized into five infantry and two armored divisions.[10] Most of these forces were located in the central and northern Sinai behind a strong network of fortifications.

While most IAF sorties flown on June 5 were directed against Arab airfields, fighter-bombers and armed trainers also flew numerous interdiction and attack missions in support of advancing Israeli troops. Beginning at about 8:00 A.M., IAF Fouga Magister armed trainers flew close support sorties.

IAF transports delivered supplies and ammunition to mobile columns in the Sinai from the outset of hostilities. Helicopters were used to rescue downed pilots, evacuate wounded from the battlefield, and ferry troops and supplies. After nightfall on June 5, IAF S-58 and Super Frelon helicopters transported paratroopers behind the positions at Abu Aweigila for a surprise assault. The paratroopers defeated Egyptian artillery units that had been holding up the Israeli advance.

Eliezer Cohen led the helicopter squadron used in this operation:

There is a saying that comes from the Bible that says you have to use some tricks and fight with your brain to win a war. The story was that we were to be involved to achieve air superiority. When we entered the war, I was standing by to take paratroopers to attack airfields in the Sinai. But the results of the fighter attacks in the first two or three hours—you know how good it was. At 10:00 o'clock the head of operations of the Israel Air Force called me on the phone and said, "Listen, you are out of a job because we destroyed all the airfields and the airplanes." Now General Sharon is in trouble trying to penetrate with his division in the Sinai because the Egyptians installed twenty-five batteries of 122-mm and 130-mm cannon and they were hitting our troops badly. . . . General Sharon was already planning this helicopter movement behind enemy lines the day before. . . . At 2:00 P.M. I went to a briefing with General Sharon and he told me and Danny Matt, the paratroop commander, to take the paratroopers behind enemy lines and to attack the three or four batteries in the center with grenades and Uzis.

I saw that I had no time to prepare. Darkness came at 5:30 P.M. and I had to start flying before then to drop the pathfinders who will set up lights and radio devices. When we left the general, it was 2:30 P.M. and we had to take off at 4:30 P.M. . . . At the time all the helicopters were out searching for pilots who had ejected during the attacks against enemy airfields. . . . When I went to meet Sharon, I had only seven helicopters. At the time we had thirty S-58s. Now in a very short time, I had to prepare the paratroops into groups and ready the aircraft. We didn't have enough time, so everything was made highly simple. Danny Matt said, "Your group, go with these helicopters." He was just pointing with his fingers. . . . The pathfinders took off and got into position. I climbed to 5,000 feet and got on the radio and told all my pilots to switch to squadron channel. I told them in plain language, "Listen, we are going to start a big operation. Stop whatever you are doing. Everyone come to me." We started the operation with seven helicopters but the second round was with fifteen. By the third round, we had twenty, and the fourth we did with twenty-four helicopters.

We dropped five hundred paratroopers behind the artillery, returned, and waited for their attack. When a big cannon is firing, it is like daylight. Dozens of them were shooting in the distance, and it was daylight. The paratroopers came with Uzis and hand grenades, and they hit four batteries in the center, and all the others stopped. They started that attack at ten before midnight and at 12:15 it was total darkness, and we knew that we did it.[11]

The Israelis had hoped that they would not have to go to war with Jordan or Syria, since Egypt was the primary threat and Israeli military planners did not want to fight a multifront war. The Jordanians had concentrated nine brigades of troops, mostly infantry units but with sizable armor and artillery support, on the West Bank after the initiation of the Jordanian, Egyptian, and Syrian pact of May 30. Brig. Gen. Uzi Narkiss, commander of the six brigades of Israel's central command, was promised two additional brigades plus support from troops of the northern command (whose troops were to defend the Israeli/Syrian border) in the event of war with Jordan.

Israeli troops expected limited action, but when shells started hitting near Ramat David airfield and falling on the suburbs of Tel Aviv and serious fighting began in and around Jerusalem, offensive plans were put into action. The urban terrain of Jerusalem and its historic nature forced the Israelis to rely on infantry, with support from armor, artillery, and limited air power. Early in the afternoon of June 5, Israeli troops began to assault Jordanian positions in Jerusalem. IAF fighter-bombers went into action against Jordanian artillery and Jordanian army units, which were moving forward toward the front line. The air strikes made a significant contribution by silencing Jordanian artillery and hampering the movement of support forces.

On the first day of the 1967 war, the IAF paid a high price for its success. The air force suffered the loss of nineteen aircraft: two Mirage IIIC, four Super Mystere B2, four Mystere IVA, four Ouragon, one Vautour, and four Fouga Magister planes. Aircrew losses on June 5 were eight killed and eleven missing.[12]

During the night of June 5, Egyptian, Syrian, and Iraqi military commanders dispersed their surviving aircraft to remote bases and began repairing damaged runways and facilities. While badly hurt, Arab air forces were not completely out of action. At dawn on June 6, the Arab air arms began to strike back at the Israelis. Two Egyptian SU-7 fighter-bombers swept and attacked an element of Tal's *ugda* in the northern Sinai. However these fighter-bombers were intercepted by a flight of Mirages and sent rapidly crashing to earth. A number of Egyptian air strikes successfully hit their targets later in the day, causing some Israeli casualties.

Early on June 6, an Iraqi TU-16 Badger bomber penetrated Israeli airspace and dropped three bombs that caused several casualties in the town of Netania. The aircraft then tried to bomb Ramat David air base but was intercepted by an Israeli Mirage III that damaged the TU-16 with a missile. The damaged bomber overflew an Israeli convoy as it headed east toward Iraq and was shot down by antiaircraft fire. At about 9:00 A.M. two Hawker Hunter fighters of the Lebanese Air Force flew into Israeli airspace. Israeli Mirages intercepted the intruders, shooting down one of the Hunters and driving the other off.

During the first twenty-four hours of fighting, Israeli forces in the Sinai had taken El Arish and had overcome strong defensive positions in the northern Sinai at Abu Ameigila. Egyptian defenders had fought with courage and caused considerable Israeli casualties, but the defenses had been penetrated. Heavy air support could now be brought into play to restrict the mobility of the Egyptian army and assist Israeli ground forces. Israeli aircraft went into action against Egyptian columns in the Sinai at dawn on the morning of June 6. Mirage IIIJ, Super Mystere, Mystere IVA, Ouragon, Vautour, and Fouga Magister fighter-bombers attacked Egyptian convoys on the roads from Egypt to the Sinai.

On the second day of fighting, Gen. Hakin Amer, Egyptian commander-in-chief, ordered the commanders of units in the Sinai to pull back to the Suez Canal. However, Israeli fighter-bombers disrupted the flow of Egyptian forces from the Sinai toward Egypt proper. With the northern coast road blocked at El Arish, Egyptian forces had only three paths to take west toward their homeland: the Ismailiya road, the road through Giddi Pass, and the highway through Mitla Pass. Aircraft pounded retreating convoys from the west while Israeli armor harassed them from the east. The forces under the command of Generals Tal, Yoffe, and Sharon fought several battles against counterattacking Egyptian units as they continued their advance across the Sinai. During the day, Israeli infantry and paratroops assaulted Gaza with support from tanks and IAF aircraft and artillery. Heavy fighting continued throughout the day, but by evening the town had fallen into Israeli hands.

IAF aircraft continued to attack Arab airfields sporadically throughout the day. In retaliation for the TU-16 attack against Israel, the IAF staged an air strike against the Iraqi airfield at H-3. The IAF sent a flight of four Vautours with an escort of two Mirages to strike the airfield. Like the attack flown on the previous day against H-3, the strike force ran into intense Iraqi fighter opposition. The Iraqi fighters aggressively defended their base but the Israelis shot down two Hunters and a MiG-21, destroyed ten aircraft on the ground, and damaged the runways. Ben-Zion Zohar, a Vautour pilot, downed one of the Hunters while a Mirage pilot claimed two victories.[13]

On the Jordanian front, heavy fighting continued in Jerusalem and on the West Bank, with Israeli paratroopers and infantry bearing the brunt of the fighting. The troops of the Jordanian army fought tenaciously and ground was given at considerable cost to both sides. Brig. Gen. David Elazar, the officer in charge of the northern command, sent a reinforced armored brigade into action to assist in the capture of Jordanian territory on the West Bank. Jordanian forces fought back aggressively and several counterattacks hit Israeli armor by surprise, causing heavy casualties. Israeli commanders called for close air support, and these air strikes damaged and destroyed many Jordanian vehicles. Iraqi units also suffered from Israeli air strikes. A brigade of Iraqi armor moving up to support Jordanian troops on the West Bank was repeatedly hit by IAF fighter-bombers and suffered many casualties.

On the second day of the 1967 war, the IAF had concentrated on supporting advancing ground troops on the Egyptian and Jordanian fronts. However, a sizable number of attack sorties were flown against Arab airfields. The IAF admitted that seven aircraft had been lost in action on June 6, the second day of the conflict. Israeli losses in two days of fighting thus totaled twenty-six aircraft.[14]

Heavy fighting continued in the Sinai on June 7, the third day of the conflict, as advancing Israeli forces met retreating Egyptian forces on the few available roads. Using flares, IAF fighter-bombers attacked several Egyptian convoys at night, but with the dawn, concentrated air strikes began. An Israeli column of paratroopers and armor advancing on the northern coast road was attacked several times by Egyptian fighter-bombers, causing numerous casualties. The EAF continued to fly attack sorties against the Israelis in the Sinai with the small number of aircraft that had survived the initial air strikes.

An Israeli armored brigade moved forward against heavy opposition in order to seal off Mitla Pass, while another force headed for the Giddi Pass. Late on June 7, a small group of Israeli tanks blocked Mitla Pass. This force ambushed several Egyptian convoys and was nearly overrun itself by the Egyptians. Air strikes against Egyptian vehicles helped save this small Israeli force. Continued air and ground attacks turned Mitla Pass into a graveyard of burned-out tanks and armored vehicles.

Elements of the Tal *ugda* fought a major battle with rearguard Egyptian armor near Bir Gifgafa on June 7. After six hours of heavy fighting, Israeli tanks, with heavy support from IAF fighter-bombers, succeeded in routing an element of the defending Egyptian 4th Armored Division. The Israelis also captured the large air base near Bir Gifgafa that was the EAF's headquarters in the Sinai. Later that night, Egyptian T-55 tanks, using night vision systems, attacked and drove back an Israeli armored unit in the central Sinai. The Egyptian counterattack was stopped when an Israeli relief force of Centurion tanks supported by flare-dropping Vautour fighter-bombers came to the rescue.

Israeli torpedo boats fired on the Egyptian positions at Sharm el Sheikh on June 7. When the boats did not receive return fire, a force of paratroopers was dispatched by helicopter to find out why. These troops took control of the airfield and found the Sharm el Sheikh defenses to be deserted. Additional paratroops were subsequently flown in by transport aircraft.

June 7 was also a day of heavy fighting on the Jordanian front. Israeli paratroopers attacked Jordanian positions around Jerusalem just after dawn and pushed into the old city. The IAF's aircraft attacked and scattered a Jordanian column that was moving up to reinforce units in Jerusalem. By late in the day, Jerusalem was totally in the hands of Israeli forces.

Israeli armor repeatedly attacked the Jordanian 40th Armored Brigade on the West Bank near the town of Qabatiya. After a four-hour battle, Jordanian troops began to withdraw. Israeli armored units overran Bethlehem, Hebron, Jericho, and other towns, completing the capture of Samaria, Judea, and the West Bank. Israel and Jordan agreed to a UN-sponsored cease-fire in the afternoon and the fighting ended at 8:00 P.M. on June 7. Jordanian forces had fought hard, but the Israelis had nevertheless seized control of the West Bank territory. In three days of heavy fighting, Jordan suffered some 3,000 casualties and lost 187 tanks, hundreds of other vehicles, and over 20 aircraft. Israeli losses on the Jordanian front were 550 killed and 2,400

wounded, while 112 tanks, dozens of vehicles, and several aircraft were destroyed.[15]

During the third day of fighting, the IAF flew hundreds of
close air support, interdiction, and fighter patrol sorties against
Jordanian, Egyptian, and Iraqi forces. For the first time SA-2
surface-to-air missile (SAM) sites in Egypt near the Suez Canal
were attacked. Mirage fighters fought several air battles and
shot down seven Arab aircraft. By the end of the day, the IAF
had claimed that more than four hundred Arab aircraft had
been destroyed—most on the ground, but nearly fifty had been
shot down in dogfights.[16] Israeli aircraft raided a number of
airfields in Egypt, Syria, and Iraq during the day. However, an
attack on the H-3 air base in Iraq did not go according to plan.

Colonel S, an IAF wing commander during the 1967 war,
recalled this tough mission against the Iraqi H-3 airfield:

> In the 1967 war, most of my sorties were with the
> Mirage, but then one sortie I remember I did with the
> Vautour. It was an attack on H-3, the Iraqi airfield, the
> third attack with Vautours on the third day of the war.
> On the second day, there was an attack with Vautours
> on H-3 with no casualties. Now on this sortie, I was
> number two because I didn't have enough knowledge on
> the Vautour then. There was a formation leader: I was
> his number two, and then there were numbers three and
> four. We were escorted by four Mirage fighters. These
> planes carried bombs, and they intended to use them in
> case there was no opposition, or to drop them and
> protect us in case we met enemy fighters. The first plan
> was to go alone, only Vautours, but I knew that we
> might meet Hunters so I demanded an escort of Mirages.
> OK, low-level flight, we reached the target, and then
> about two or three kilometers before the airfield, we saw
> that there were Hunters in the air. We didn't know how
> many, but more than four, six, or eight. The Mirage
> flight started to get speed, dropped their bombs, and we
> had to do our job.
>      At that time, the leader lost communication.
> Everything continued as planned. We bombed the
> runway. The Vautour is very tricky—you had bombs in

the bomb bay and when you have the bombs outside of the bomb bay, you cannot do more than one-and-a-half *g*s with the aircraft. After you drop the bombs, until you get the bomb rack inside, you cannot do more than one-and-a-half *g*s. So you have got to fly very smoothly and it takes about twenty seconds until the bomb bay closes. So you drop the bombs and then continue more or less smoothly. During the attack, I got shot at by ground cannon. When the bomb bay had closed—at the same second—I got a warning that a Hunter was very near behind me. So I started to turn in order to save my life. At that time, I couldn't see my number one because we split during the attack. Until now I don't know who warned me. I was in a very difficult position because I lost all my speed, all my height, and the Hunter was closing. When he was very near, I changed the direction of the maneuver and I saw him going out. During those maneuvers, I saw that two aircraft were shot down, just flames in the sky, and I didn't know at the time whose planes they were. Now I know it was one Hunter and one Mirage that were shot down over the airfield. So I started to gather speed because I was very slow and had the flaps down. By that time the attack was over, and I heard the remaining aircraft reorganize for the return. I gathered speed headed home.

What happened was, number one was lost at the beginning. Nobody knows when and why he went down. At the end, he was found some kilometers away from the airfield, crashed. The pilot and navigator were dead. He was flying a glazed-nose Vautour and the rest of us had single seaters. Now number three finished his first attack and went back for another strafing run. On this second attack, they got him and he bailed out. Number four did the mission, was left alone, and he came back home. The Mirage flight did their best; they shot down two Hunters. One of them was shot down himself and he bailed out. So we had two prisoners in Iraq—number three of the Vautours and one of the Mirages. . . . It was a very tough mission because of the Hunters. Nobody anticipated that we would meet so many aircraft in the air. . . . Some say they were Iraqis; some say they were Jordanians. We don't know for sure. They were flying from Baghdad to H-3 and, by surprise, they found us. I tend to think it was an accident, because they were not flying in a way to cover the airfield. They were coming toward final from the other side, so we just collided. They found themselves in the air with Vautours, a big aircraft, as their target. So this attack, it was not a very big success, but, as a matter of fact, from then on we didn't have any more attacks from the Iraqis or Jordanians.[17]

June 8, the fourth day of the 1967 conflict, saw Israeli forces consolidate their hold on the Sinai Peninsula. An element of the Tal *ugda* on the northern coast road overcame Egyptian defenses and reached the Suez Canal at Qantara, while other Israeli forces drew near the canal. Advancing Israeli units continued to suffer losses to Egyptian ambushes and attacks by EAF aircraft. Patrolling Mirages intercepted some of the attacking fighter-bombers and downed three in air combat.

On the afternoon of June 8, Israeli aircraft detected a ship off the Sinai coast, and military commanders decided to send the IAF into action against the vessel. Mirage III and Mystere IV fighter-bombers made multiple attacks and hit the ship with rockets, napalm, and cannon fire. A motor torpedo boat of the Israeli navy then intercepted the damaged ship and attacked it with torpedoes and gunfire. Despite the heavy damage caused by these attacks, the USS *Liberty*, a U.S. Navy intelligence-gathering vessel, was able to limp away and eventually reach Malta. Thirty-four of the crew of the USS *Liberty* were killed and 164 wounded by the Israeli assault. The reason for the attack has never been fully explained but probably had to do with the ship's ability to gather intelligence about Israeli military activities.

The fighting in the Sinai ended on the early morning of June 9, when both sides agreed to the United Nations' call for a cease-fire. After the cease-fire, Egyptian troops continued to move west in an attempt to cross the canal to safety. They left behind about 700 tanks, 500 artillery pieces, and 10,000 trucks and other vehicles. Egyptian forces suffered over 10,000 killed and wounded and another 5,500 were captured. Israeli losses on the Sinai front totaled about 300 killed and more than 1,000 wounded.[18]

During the first four days of the 1967 war, Syrian forces participated in the conflict in only a limited way: Syrian aircraft struck targets in Israel on June 5, several limited ground attacks were made against four Israeli border settlements, and Syrian artillery sporadically shelled Israeli targets. On the first day of the conflict, the IAF attacked several Syrian airfields, destroying over sixty aircraft. Subsequently, numerous air strikes were flown against Syrian artillery positions on the Golan Heights in an attempt to end the shelling. Israeli military leaders refrained from large-scale attacks on the Golan Heights because ground troops and air support were committed in the Sinai and on the Jordanian front. However, once the fighting on these fronts was successfully concluded, Israel turned its attention to Syria. While the United Nations was pushing for a total cease-fire, Israel elected to settle an old score with its northern neighbor.

The Israel/Syrian border in 1967 ran from the Sea of Galilee to the Lebanon border near Mount Hermon and had a length of some 50 miles. The border included the Sea of Galilee and the steep hills of the Golan Heights, ideal defensive positions for the Syrians. Since the War of Independence in 1948, the Syrians had fortified the border area with mine fields, barbed-wire fences, and concrete bunkers. These fortifications were manned by over thirty thousand Syrian troops, who were supported by several hundred tanks and artillery pieces.

On June 8, the IAF initiated a blistering series of raids against Syrian positions on the Golan Heights. During the next two days, the IAF flew hundreds of ground support sorties over the Golan Heights, more than were flown on any other front. Syrian antiaircraft fire was intense and several Israeli aircraft were lost during these attacks. While these air attacks and artillery fire disrupted efforts to reinforce Syrian frontline defenses during daylight hours, they had little impact on the concrete-reinforced fortifications.

An Israeli force, composed of two armored brigades, a mechanized brigade, the Golani Infantry Brigade, and supporting units, was given the task of seizing the Golan Heights. This force of about 20,000 men and 250 tanks, under the command of Brig. Gen. David Elazar, assaulted the Syrians beginning at about 7:00 A.M. on June 9, the fifth day of the conflict.[19] The main thrust was made by the Golani Brigade and the two armored brigades. These units assaulted the tough terrain of the Golan Heights with the objective of seizing the town of Quneitra, the site of the headquarters of Syrian forces on the Golan Heights.

Additional Israeli units struck into Syrian territory in the central and southern parts of the Golan Heights to support the main effort in the north. The steep terrain, mines, and heavy Syrian fire slowed the assault and Israeli forces suffered dozens of casualties despite support from artillery and air strikes. Syrian defensive positions were only overrun after costly hand-to-hand fighting which resulted in heavy casualties on both sides. Syrian counterattacks slowed the Israeli advance but the timely arrival of IAF fighter-bombers and additional troops stopped the Syrian assault. During the night a renewed Israeli attack breached the Syrian line in a number of positions and penetrated onto the Golan Heights.

Israeli units continued the offensive on June 10 despite heavy Syrian resistance and the United Nations' call for an immediate cease-fire. Syrian resolve slackened late in the morning and troops began to pull back from defensive positions around Quneitra. Taking advantage of this withdrawl, IAF helicopters ferried paratroopers into positions behind Syrian lines to capture important road junctions and speed the advance of Israeli armored forces. The IAF's fighter-bombers continued to hit retreating Syrian columns with bombs and cannon fire. By late afternoon, Israeli units had advanced to within 40 miles of Damascus. At 6:30 P.M., Israel finally agreed to end the fighting and a UN-sponsored cease-fire came into effect. During the fighting with Syria, Israel suffered the loss of 127 killed and 625 wounded, plus 160 tanks, dozens of vehicles, and several aircraft destroyed. However, Israel had captured the Golan Heights. Syrian forces suffered about 600 killed, 700 wounded, and were forced to give up valuable terrain to Israel.

In the 1967 war, the Israel Defense Forces won a significant victory. In six days of heavy fighting, the armed forces of its principal adversaries—Egypt, Jordan, and Syria—were battered. Israel had captured the Sinai Peninsula, the West Bank territory, and the Golan Heights. While the war was won on the ground, Israeli aircraft made a significant contribution to the victory.

The IAF quickly achieved air superiority over its Arab opponents through a surprise first assault and air-to-air combat. The air force then assisted the army in winning the ground battle by flying thousands of ground attack sorties, by moving supplies to advancing troops, and by using helicopters to transport paratroopers into enemy rear area positions, evacuate wounded, rescue downed pilots, and conduct reconnaissance sorties.

What were the ingredients of the successful IAF air campaign? The first ingredient was the successful achievement of a surprise attack. For years the IAF had prepared for this one mission. The force was developed, trained, armed, and equipped to perform the surprise assault. Accurate intelligence efforts enabled aircraft to be dispatched to the right targets. For the second ingredient, nearly all IAF fighter-bombers were committed to the surprise attack. This almost total concentration of force on the primary objective was a big risk but it payed off. And for the third ingredient, Arab aircraft were not housed in protective shelters and most airfields were not heavily defended. This made the task of destroying the Arab air forces on the ground much easier.

The successful preemptive assault had both real and perceived effects on the outcome of the conflict. The destruction of Egyptian, Jordanian, and Syrian air power disrupted battle plans, damaged Arab morale, and almost totally eliminated the air threat to Israel and its advancing armies. Without defending fighter cover, Arab armies could only rely on antiaircraft fire for defense against Israeli air strikes. Once it achieved air superiority, the IAF was able to reduce the number of air combat patrol sorties to a minimum and concentrate on flying ground attack missions. Air superiority also meant that IAF transports, helicopters, reconnaissance, and liaison aircraft were able to perform their important missions with minimal interference from Arab fighters.

The IAF flew 3,279 fighter-bomber sorties during the conflict. Reportedly 469 Arab aircraft were destroyed during the War: 391 on the ground, 60 in air-to-air combat, 3 shot down by

Israeli antiaircraft fire, and 15 lost due to fuel exhaustion or flying into the ground.[21]

The IAF admitted the loss of forty-six aircraft, with twenty-three more heavily damaged. Aircrew casualties included twenty-four pilots killed, eighteen wounded, and seven taken prisoner. In six days of fighting, more than 20 percent of the IAF's frontline tactical aircraft had been destroyed and 8.4 percent of its pilots killed.[22]

Mirage IIIC, Super Mystere B2, Vautour, Mystere IVA, and even aging Ouragon fighter-bombers were used on the initial assault against Arab airfields. After the first pass to deliver special antirunway weapons, conventional high-explosive bombs, or rockets, these fighter-bombers made several strafing passes against aircraft or airport facilities. Later these aircraft joined Fouga Magister trainers in the ground support and road interdiction roles. High-explosive and napalm bombs, rockets, and cannon fire were used with telling effect against Arab vehicles, defensive positions, and troop concentrations. Hundreds of Arab vehicles were destroyed in the Sinai, on the Jordanian front, and on the Golan heights. Attacking aircraft regularly faced heavy antiaircraft fire, which destroyed most of the Israeli aircraft lost during the war.

The Six-Day War saw IAF aircraft in dozens of air combat engagements with Arab aircraft. Many battles were fought over Arab airfields during the initial air strikes, and dogfights occurred on each day of the conflict as Israeli fighters met Egyptian, Syrian, Jordanian, or Iraqi aircraft that flew in support of their forces. Despite Israeli air cover, numerous successful Arab air strikes were flown. However, many Arab attacks were intercepted by IAF fighters and sixty Arab aircraft were shot down in air combat. Mirage pilots achieved over 80 percent of the air-to-air victories, but flyers of older IAF jets also shot down Arab aircraft: Supere Mystere pilots downed five planes, Mystere IV pilots three, while Vautour and Ouragon aviators each hit a single Arab jet. Aircraft cannon were used to achieve all of these victories.[23]

According to official releases, only three or four IAF aircraft were lost to Arab fighters. However, a high-ranking IAF officer later disclosed that in fact ten aircraft had been "bounced" by enemy fighters and shot down.[24]

The IAF transport force of C-47 and Nordatlas aircraft moved thousands of tons of supplies to the front and air-dropped food, fuel, and ammunition to advancing columns. Captured Arab airfields and desert strips were used by the transports to deliver troops and supplies and to evacuate wounded.

Helicopters were used extensively in the 1967 conflict to carry troops, rescue downed pilots, and move casualties rapidly to forward field hospitals. Super Frelon and S-58 transport helicopters delivered paratroops into position on numerous occasions to assault Arab defenses from behind or capture important road junctions.

During the 1967 war, the IAF proved that it could have a dramatic impact on the course of battle in the Middle East. Israeli airpower had reigned supreme. However, Arab forces had learned a bitter lesson and immediately began to take steps to change the status quo.

# 6

# War
# of
# Attrition

*L*ess than a month after the cease-fire that ended the
Six-Day War, Egyptian and Israeli troops fought a two-
week series of bitter battles around Port Fuad at the northern
end of the Suez Canal. Both sides committed aircraft to the
fighting: Egyptian forces lost a MiG-17 to antiaircraft fire on
July 4, 1967, while an SU-7 EAF fighter-bomber was shot down
by an Israeli Mirage on July 8. Another major battle erupted
along the Suez Canal on July 15, during which five Egyptian jets
and a single Israeli aircraft were shot down.

Israel, flush with victory, had hoped that Egypt, Jordan, and
Syria would enter into negotiations for a peace treaty that
would bring an end to the hostilities that had continued since
the birth of Israel in 1948. General Dayan stated that he was
expecting a call from Cairo or Amman at any time. However,
instead of a phone call, the Arabs responded with military and
political action.

An Arab summit conference held in Khartoum in August and
September 1967 dashed any Israeli hope for peace. Participants
in the conference stated that there would be no recognition of
Israel and agreed upon a strategy of confrontation that included
economic boycott, political efforts, terrorism, and military confrontation. Evidence of Arab resolve to fight back came on October 21, 1967, when the Israeli destroyer *Eilat* was hit and sunk
by several Styx antiship missiles. Forty-seven Israeli sailors
were killed and ninety-one wounded in the attack. In retaliation,
Israeli aircraft bombed Egyptian naval facilities at Alexandria
and Port Said and Israeli artillery batteries severely damaged
the Egyptian oil refinery near the city of Suez.

The United Nations, continuing its efforts to prevent renewed
conflict, passed Resolution 242 on November 22, 1967. It called
for Israel to pull back to its pre-1967 borders in exchange for
Arab recognition of the State of Israel, establishment of demili-

tarized zones between Israel and Arab countries, and discussions regarding the fate of Palestinian refugees. Neither side accepted this resolution. The territories acquired in the Six-Day War considerably strengthened Israel's strategic situation: Egyptian forces now had to cross the Suez Canal and Sinai Peninsula to threaten Israel, while in the east, capture of the Jordan River Valley and Golan Heights gave Israel much more defensible borders.

However, Israel now had to administer the nearly one million Arab civilians who lived in the captured territories of the West Bank and Gaza Strip. And immediately after the 1967 war, Egyptian and Syrian forces received hundreds of tactical aircraft, tanks, and other military systems from the Soviet Union, which also sent scores of "advisors," whose arrival forced Israel to increase its preparations for renewed conflict.

Israel needed new fighters to replace the forty-eight jets lost in action during the Six-Day War. The IAF inventory after the 1967 conflict included approximately three squadrons of Mirage IIIC fighters (about sixty-five aircraft), one Super Mystere squadron (twenty-five aircraft), one Vautour squadron (fifteen aircraft), two Mystere IVA (thirty-five planes), and two Ouragon squadrons (thirty aircraft). The subsonic Vautour, Mystere IVA, and Ouragon aircraft had been delivered in the late 1950s and were reaching the end of their service lives. In an emergency, the IAF could press into service two squadrons of Magister trainers (eighty aircraft), but this aircraft suffered heavy losses during operations in the 1967 war. Support services were provided by two squadrons of transports, one flying C-47s and the other Noratlas aircraft, and a composite wing of S-58, Super Frelon, Alouette, and Bell 47G helicopters.[1]

Prior to the 1967 conflict, the IAF had worked closely with the French aircraft manufacturer Dassault to develop an upgraded version of the Mirage IIIC fighter. An order for fifty of these improved aircraft, designated the Mirage V, had been placed in 1966 and the jets were already on the assembly line. The IAF planned to purchase at least one hundred Mirage Vs and intended to evaluate the then-new Mirage F1 fighter. These jets were never delivered to the IAF because President Charles de Gaulle of France imposed an arms embargo against Israel.

As a result of the embargo, Israel Aircraft Industries, with the assistance of numerous Israeli and foreign firms, set out to establish a production line for an aircraft essentially identical to the Mirage V. Israeli firms had gained experience by overhauling and modifying French combat aircraft, producing the Fouga Magister trainer, developing the Arava transport, and upgrading the Westwind Business Jet. The plans for the Mirage and its Altar 9C turbojet engine were provided by Alfred Frouenknech, a Swiss engineer who later served a two-year jail term for his part in the transfer of these documents. Israeli engineers worked around the clock to develop and produce the new Nesher (Eagle) fighter.[2]

In the early 1960s, Israeli officials tried to purchase U.S. combat aircraft in an attempt to find another source of supply for the IAF. While the initial answer was negative, the U.S. government agreed to supply Israel with defensive weapons such as the Hawk surface-to-air missile system. A delegation headed by the IAF commander, Gen. Ezer Weizman, visited Washington, D.C., in late 1965 to ask the United States to sell Israel fighter aircraft. The delegation was successful and a contract for the sale of the first U.S.-built jets, forty-eight A-4 Skyhawk fighter-bombers, was signed in late 1966. However, Israeli requests for F-4 Phantom or A-6 Intruder aircraft were turned down. Senior U.S. leaders felt that these advanced jets would upset the balance of power in the Middle East, and the aircraft were needed by U.S. forces to support air operations in Viet Nam.

The IAF wanted to buy a high-performance fighter, like the Mirage V or F-4 Phantom, that could perform both air combat and attack missions. However, the U.S. agreement to sell combat aircraft to Israel was a major breakthrough, and the Skyhawk fighter-bomber had good range, could carry a sizable weapons load, and cost only about two-thirds as much as a new Mirage. The IAF eventually received more than three hundred Skyhawks of eight variants, making it the most widely used combat aircraft in the history of Israel's air force.

The A-4 Skyhawk is a small attack jet capable of operating from an aircraft carrier. The Israeli version of the Skyhawk, the A-4H, differed from U.S. Navy versions in having 30-mm cannon armament, a rear-mounted brake parachute, a larger square-tipped tail, and minor avionic changes.[3] With the Skyhawk came American training, maintenance concepts, and weaponry. The first Skyhawk was delivered in the fall of 1967 and all forty-eight aircraft were in service by late 1968.

Terrorist activities intensified along the Syrian and Jordanian borders in late 1967 and early 1968. These confrontations were the prelude to a prolonged struggle. Large training camps located in Jordan and Lebanon generated a steady supply of Palestinians who were ready and willing to fight to the death to hit back at Israel. Jordanian troops and Iraqi forces that were stationed in Jordan collaborated with these guerrilla groups and often supported their efforts with artillery fire and logistical assistance. Terrorists directed their attacks against civilian targets like settlements, schools, and public places in an attempt to undermine personal security and erode public confidence. Israeli efforts against these attacks were constrained by political restrictions that limited action in the occupied West Bank and prevented the launching of full-scale assaults against guerrilla bases in Jordan, Syria, and Lebanon. Israeli forces heavily patrolled the border and terrorists who crossed the border were pursued or ambushed. However, the Israelis used air attacks, surprise commando assaults, and artillery fire to hit terrorist base camps and staging areas to disrupt their operations. The IAF's tactical aircraft flew hundreds of fighter-bomber sorties against terrorist positions in Jordan in 1968 and 1969. Helicopters such as the S-58 and the new UH-ID Huey were used to assist Israeli troops in their battle against terrorists in the Jordan River Valley.

Russian resupply and training efforts quickly rebuilt the Egyptian and Syrian armed forces. By mid-1968, the Egyptian army had regained most of its pre-1967 war strength and thousands of Russian advisors assisted in training efforts. Nearly 150,000 Egyptian troops were well entrenched in positions along the Suez Canal. These men were supported by almost one thousand artillery pieces, plus more than five hundred tanks. The EAF was strengthened and Russian advisors drilled it in their training concepts. The EAF in late 1968 included 110 MiG-21 and 80 MiG-19 fighters, 120 MiG-15/17 and 40 SU-7 fighter-bombers, and 40 IL-28 and 10 TU-16 bombers. New airfields were built to accommodate the additional air force units and concrete shelters were constructed to protect aircraft

and vital support equipment. In 1968 an independent Egyptian
Air Defense Force was established to protect Egypt and its forces
from air attack. A network of radars, SA-2 surface-to-air missile
batteries, and antiaircraft guns was set up to protect Cairo and
important military and industrial positions.[4]

The Syrian Air Force also benefited from Russian resupply
and intensified training efforts. By late 1968 the force had a
strength of sixty MIG-21 fighters and seventy MIG-15/17 and
twenty SU-7 fighter-bombers. The Royal Jordanian Air Force
had received a dozen Hawker Hunter fighter-bombers and was
in the process of acquiring a squadron of supersonic F-104A
fighters from the United States.[5]

The IAF had taken over several former Egyptian air bases in
the Sinai and deployed a sizable number of aircraft to these new
airfields. Major air bases, headquarters, and logistics centers
were hardened against attack and were protected by antiaircraft guns. Several Hawk surface-to-air missile batteries
were also positioned to defend Sinai positions.

Israeli ground forces manned a limited number of observation
posts located along the Suez Canal in order to monitor Egyptian
activities. Held back, out of range of artillery fire, was a force of
about ten thousand men organized into two armored brigades
and supporting units. These Israeli troops in the Sinai had many
tanks and armored vehicles, but only a limited amount of artillery. In the event of an Egyptian attack, these units were to move
forward and destroy any bridgehead across the canal.

On September 8, 1968, a massive artillery barrage was
launched by Egyptian forces all along the Suez Canal. During
the six-hour-long barrage, over ten thousand shells landed; ten
Israeli troops were killed and eighteen were wounded. Israel
retaliated by shelling the cities of Suez and Ismailiya and the oil
refinery near Suez. To demonstrate its determination, Egypt
staged another intensified artillery attack on October 26, which
killed thirteen Israeli soldiers. In addition, civilians living in
Suez, Ismailiya, and other towns near the Suez Canal were
evacuated by Egyptian authorities.

As a deterrent to future artillery attacks, on October 31 Israeli
paratroops, carried deep into Egypt by IAF helicopters, sabo-
taged a dam, destroyed two bridges spanning the Nile, and

damaged a power transformer substation near the town of Naj Hammadi.

Eliezer (Cheetah) Cohen, then chief of operations for the IAF, discussed these operations:

> We started to do special helicopter operations and they
> didn't have an answer for it. We did it as a deterrent.
> When you put a small bomb on a dam on the Nile you
> are giving a message: Next time we will come with a
> bigger bomb. We released the bombs from the
> helicopters. Using the cargo sling, the helicopter hovered
> over the dam and we put the bomb—a special-shaped
> charge, one like those used to attack tanks—next to the
> wall and destroyed the dam. There are many dams on
> the Nile. Once we came and destroyed a small dam, we
> demonstrated that we had the ability to hit targets well
> behind the front lines. This sent a message. They thought
> about it and stopped fighting along the Suez Canal for a
> few weeks because they knew that we could do terrible
> things to them . . . We showed that we could cut their
> electricity, break the dams, and flood their fields.[6]

These raids startled the Egyptians and their Soviet advisors, resulting in the strengthening of air and ground defenses around vital rear-area Egyptian assets. Except for small-scale artillery attacks and reconnaissance sorties, the Suez Canal front remained quiet into 1969.

Israeli forces used this quiet period to their advantage and constructed a series of concrete-and-steel-reinforced fortifications along the Suez Canal. Each of these positions included two or three tanks and several squads of troops. The positions were to serve only as lookout posts to deter the Egyptians from crossing the Suez Canal. Concrete, sand, and steel protected the troops of the so-called Bar Lev line from artillery fire, but defense of the Sinai still rested with Israeli armored forces. Aside from an air battle near the Suez Canal on December 12, 1968, which resulted in the destruction of a single EAF MiG-17, air action on the Sinai front was limited during this period.

Throughout 1968 the IAF flew attack missions against guerrilla camps in Lebanon, Syria, and Jordan, as well as Jordanian

and Syrian army artillery batteries that continued to shell Israeli settlements. Hundreds of helicopter missions supported
border patrols and antiterrorist commando raids. Pilots of the
new A-4 Skyhawk squadrons flew most of their missions in
support of these antiterrorist operations.

A successful attack carried out against an EL AL airliner at
Athens Airport on December 25, 1968, prompted the Israeli
government to take action. Guerrilla groups based in Beirut
were identified as being responsible for this and earlier assaults
against EL AL aircraft.

At 9:30 P.M. on the night of December 28, four IAF Super
Frelon helicopters landed on the main runway of Beirut International Airport and a large number of heavily armed paratroopers disembarked. Moving swiftly, the paratroopers seized
control of the main terminal. Passengers on aircraft belonging
to Arab airlines were escorted off the planes and into the terminal. Once the aircraft were emptied, demolition charges were
placed aboard and, one by one, fourteen airliners were blown
up. A fifth helicopter landed next to the main highway that
linked the airport to Beirut. Paratroopers from this helicopter
blocked the highway, preventing police or the Lebanese army
from interfering with the operation. Within an hour the paratroopers had left, leaving behind fourteen destroyed airliners
but no civilian or military casualties.[7] This raid was staged to
serve notice that Israel could and would strike out against those
who supported terrorism. The political repercussions from this
raid were high, though, as it prompted the French to impose a
total arms embargo against Israel and generated widespread
criticism.

Tensions along the Israeli/Syrian border intensified early in
1969 and on February 12 the first air battle between Israel and
Syria in nearly two years occurred. Syrian fighters contested
IAF aircraft again on February 24, during an Israeli raid against
a terrorist camp near Damascus. Israel claimed to have downed
three Syrian MiGs and to have suffered no losses in these air
battles.

A new, more dangerous phase of the confrontation on the Suez
front began on March 8, 1969. Just before noon, a flight of
Egyptian MiG-21 fighters penetrated into the Sinai near Great
Bitter Lake. Israeli Mirages intercepted this patrol and one

Egyptian jet was shot down. Six hours later, Egyptian forces initiated a massive artillery barrage against Israeli fortifications all along the Suez Canal. The same day President Nasser announced the start of a "War of Attrition" against Israel. Using artillery and commando raids, Egyptian forces hoped to destroy Israeli fortifications near the Suez Canal and inflict heavy casualties. Israeli artillery responded in kind to these attacks. On March 9, the Egyptian chief of staff, Gen. Abdul Moneim Riadh, and some of his staff who were observing the action from forward positions near Ismailiya were killed by Israeli artillery fire.

Heavy shelling continued for days, and in early April, Egyptian forces staged a number of successful commando raids against Israeli patrols, supply convoys, and fortifications. Egypt took advantage of its superiority in artillery firepower, numerical strength, and willingness to accept a moderate level of casualties.

Israel regularly struck back in response to attacks along its borders, but increasing tension and rising casualties created a serious concern. At an April 17, 1969, news conference, Defense Minister Moshe Dayan stated that Israel had suffered sixteen hundred casualties in the nearly continuous border clashes that had taken place in the twenty-two months since the end of the 1967 war. By way of contrast, he pointed out that there had been thirty-six hundred Israeli casualties in the Six-Day War. Dayan said that Arab claims of success were greatly exaggerated. Commenting on Israeli and Arab aircraft losses, he stated, "We have lost seven jets and one Piper Cub since the [1967] War, all downed by ground fire. The Egyptians have lost fifteen jets and the Syrians three."[8]

While military action along the Suez Canal continued at a high level in the spring of 1969, there was no reduction in counterterrorist operations along the Jordanian, Syrian, and Lebanese borders. Terrorist bases and several radar stations in Jordan were bombed on April 22, and one of the attacking Israeli aircraft was lost to antiaircraft fire. Arab confrontations, including terrorist attacks and shelling, continued and Israeli forces responded with commando raids and air attacks.

In May, heavy fighting broke out along the Israeli/Syrian border, and on May 29, a Syrian MiG-21 was shot down by a missile fired from an IAF Mirage. Syria moved additional troops, tanks, and artillery up to the border and shelling continued. A major air battle erupted over the Golan Heights on July 8, and Israeli Mirage fighters downed seven MiG-21 aircraft. This was the biggest Israeli/Syrian aerial confrontation since the 1967 war.

Throughout the spring of 1969 the United Nations attempted to mediate a total cease-fire in the Middle East. While many meetings were held and many proposals put forward, none of the warring factions were willing to end the fighting.

Almost daily shelling and commando activity occurred along the Suez Canal and air activity intensified. Egyptian fighter-bombers flew a heavy series of raids against Israeli targets in the Sinai on May 21. However, Israeli defenses were ready—three EAF MiG-21s were shot down by Israeli Mirages and a single MiG fell to a Hawk surface-to-air missile. On June 17, two Israeli Mirages flew at supersonic speed over President Nasser's home at Heliopolis, producing a loud sonic boom that shattered windows and caused considerable unrest. This "attack" prompted Nasser to replace the EAF commander, Air Vice-Marshall Musstafa Shalaby el-Hennawy, and the chief of air defenses, Maj. Gen. Hassan Kemal. President Nasser also responded by ordering an increase in the number of commando raids, artillery barrages, and EAF air strikes against Israeli positions in the Sinai. Air battles, which occurred on several occasions in late June and early July 1969, resulted in the loss of nine Egyptian jets. However, Egyptian shelling, commando raids, and air strikes increased the Israeli casualty toll to 106 dead and wounded in July.

Israel responded to this worsening situation along the Suez Canal by changing its tactics. On July 19, a force of naval commandos stormed Green Island, an Egyptian fortress located at the southern end of the Suez Canal. The raiders captured the fortress and set demolition charges that destroyed the structure. The following day, the IAF flew a massive series of air strikes against Egyptian military positions all along the Suez Canal. This was the first time that the IAF had flown a large-scale air offensive against Egyptian forces since the end of the 1967 War.

The EAF contested these air strikes and flew raids into the

Sinai, resulting in several large air battles. Israeli authorities claimed their forces shot down five Egyptian jets, including two SU-7 and two MiG-17 fighter-bombers and a single MiG-21 fighter, on July 20. During the battles, two Israeli aircraft were lost, including a Mirage that was shot down in a dogfight with Egyptian MiG-21s. This was the first Israeli admissions of the loss of an aircraft in air combat since the 1967 war.[9]

The military objective of Israel's new air offensive was the suppression of Egyptian forces along the Suez Canal at a minimum cost to Israel. Israeli air strikes continued for several weeks. Egyptian fighters rose to challenge the Israeli attackers while EAF fighter-bombers frequently struck Israeli positions in the Sinai. During several large air battles on July 24, Israeli forces claimed six Egyptian MiGs and an SU-7. Israeli raids against Egyptian positions continued almost daily and on August 19, the IAF pounded numerous Egyptian artillery positions for several hours. However, during the day a Skyhawk fighter-bomber fell to Egyptian antiaircraft fire.

S. Gilboa, a former Mystere squadron commander, commented about his flying experience during this period:

> As a reserve officer in 1969, I continued to fly Mysteres. I remember bombing some cannon sites very near the Suez Canal. We were in formations one behind the other, a difference of three minutes. It was very simple. On some days we used to make four sorties. We used to pick one or two targets and hit them and hit them like a hammer until they would go down. It was a way of delivering a message. At that time, the missiles were not in the area and the antiaircraft fire was not very accurate. We came in at 8,000 feet, roll in, drop, and out—no strafing, just one or two bombing runs and then back home. Formation after formation, we hit the targets. For a time we didn't think it had an impact but later on we found out it affected them very strongly. We knew this due to two facts: an Egyptian soldier who swam to our side told us about the situation, and one day our aircraft took a photograph of a graveyard. We started to take pictures every two or three days and to count. We saw that they were digging graves at a higher

rate, and we understood that they were suffering heavy casualties.[10]

During September 1969, conflict along the Suez Canal intensified to the highest level since the 1967 war. During the night of September 7, Israeli naval commandos blew up several Egyptian patrol boats at their anchorage at Ras el Sadat in the Gulf of Suez. This opened the way for Israeli landing craft to cross the gulf and bring ashore a sizable raiding party of armored vehicles. To achieve surprise in the assault, the Israelis used Russian-built tanks and armored vehicles captured in the 1967 war. Dozens of Egyptian vehicles and defensive positions were destroyed during the raid. Israeli aircraft bombed and strafed several Egyptian SA-2 batteries and other military positions in support of this attack. One Israeli aircraft was hit by antiaircraft fire during these air strikes and its pilot was lost after ejecting into the Gulf of Suez.

After the raid, the IAF continued to plaster the Egyptian positions with bombs. Israeli aircraft attacked a radar site near the Gulf of Suez on September 9 and an SA-2 battery near the Suez Canal on September 10. In the six weeks since the initiation of intensified air strikes against Egyptian forces along the Suez Canal, the IAF had flown over one thousand sorties and Israeli forces had shot down twenty-one Egyptian planes for the loss of only three aircraft.

On September 11, the EAF sought revenge for the Israeli assault across the Gulf of Suez. Three separate air raids totaling sixty to seventy sorties penetrated into the Sinai and struck at Israeli positions. Israeli officials stated that eight Egyptian aircraft had been brought down by IAF fighters, three by antiaircraft fire, and two by Hawk missiles.[11] This was the biggest one-day Israeli claim since the first day of the 1967 war. Late in the afternoon, Israeli aircraft flew a series of raids into Egypt and a Mirage fighter was lost to antiaircraft fire.

At a September 13 press conference, Defense Minister Moshe Dayan stated that the recent armored raid and air attacks were undertaken to force the Egyptians to "think twice" about their strategy along the Suez Canal. Dayan added that Nasser should know "that his front is wide open in the Gulf region." The defense minister said, "We have opted for selected response, and

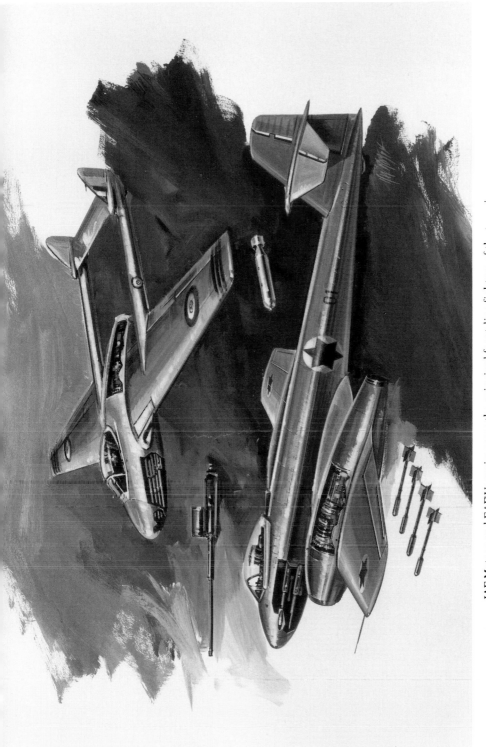

IAF Meteor and EAF Vampire were the principal front-line fighters of the two air arms during the mid-1950s.

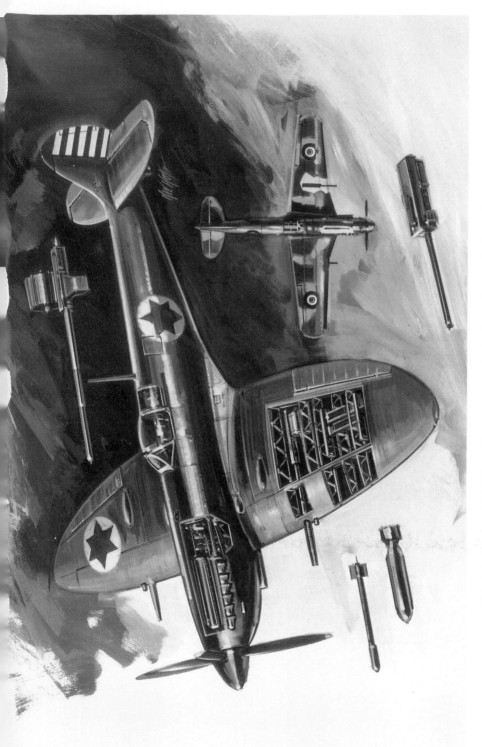

IAF Spitfire Mk 9 and EAF Fiat G55 were adversaries in the 1948 War of Independence.

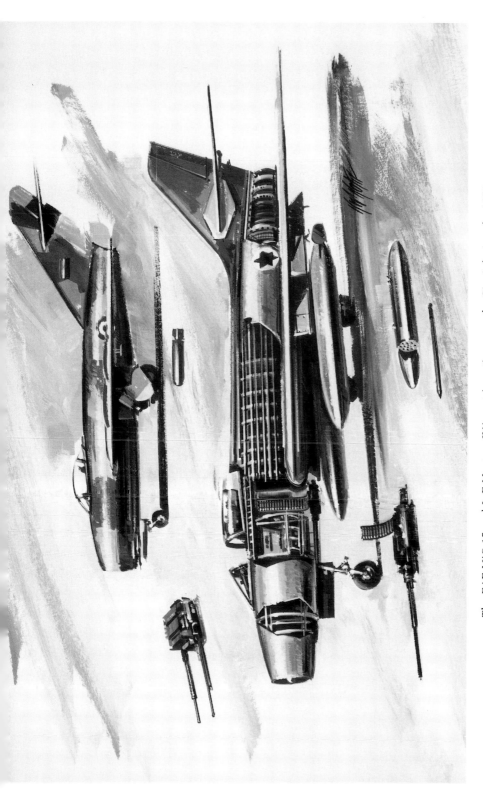

The EAF MiG-15 and IAF Mystere IVA met in action over the Sinai during the 1956 conflict.

Front-line fighters of the Middle East in the early 1960s included the Israeli Super Mystere, Jordanian Hawker Hunter and Egyptian MiG-19.

The A-4 and the SU-7 were the primary attack aircraft employed by the Israeli and Arab air forces during the War of Attrition.

Adversaries in the 1973 War included the Egyptian MiG-21 fighter and the Israeli F-4E Phantom.

The IAF F-15 Eagle fought the SAF MiG-25 Foxbat in the skies over Lebanon in 1982.

The IAF F-16A and SAF MiG-23 met in action over Lebanon during the 1982 conflict.

we maintain the right to choose the targets, the weapons, and the magnitude of the blow."[12]

It was not a hollow threat. In late 1968 the U.S. government had agreed to supply Israel with fifty F-4E Phantom aircraft as a result of the intensification of fighting in the Middle East and increased Soviet involvement in Egypt and Syria. The first of these supersonic fighter-bombers, which the IAF nicknamed the Kurnass (heavy hammer), arrived in Israel on September 5, 1969. A single F-4E Phantom could carry the same number of bombs as eight Mirage or Mystere fighters. With its speed, range, payload, and capability to perform both the fighter and attack missions, the Phantom was the perfect airplane for the IAF's offensive-oriented tactics. A second batch of forty-two A-4H Skyhawks, which had been ordered in early 1968, also began to arrive in Israel during the fall of 1969.

The Egyptians struck at Israeli targets in the Sinai on October 6 and the raid was intercepted by Israeli forces. Three MiG-21 fighters were shot down in air combat and a MiG-17 fighter-bomber fell to a Hawk missile. While many EAF aircraft were downed or damaged, Egyptian pilots continued to brave the Israeli defenses and many strikes hit home. This added to Israeli casualties caused by Egyptian artillery barrages, commando raids, and tank fire. In retaliation, the IAF continued to bomb Egyptian SAM sites and stepped up its attacks against positions further inland. On October 22, IAF F-4 Phantom crews flew their first combat missions against an SA 2 surface-to air missile site at Abu Suweir, Egypt. Each of the Phantoms in the two-plane raid carried eleven bombs. They "crossed the Canal north of Quneitra" and, according to one of the pilots, "We were doing 540 knots, turned south and pulled up to 20,000 (feet). We came in long and let go. We hit well, and could see lots of smoke coming from the target."[13] Early on November 4, Phantoms woke up Cairo with a sonic boom that broke windows, and on November 11, the first air combat victory was achieved by an F-4. An Egyptian MiG-21 was shot down over Jebel Ataka by a missile from a Phantom. Two other Egyptian MiGs were shot down on this day by Mirage fighters.

Most of the Egyptian SAM positions near the Suez Canal had been knocked out by November 1969, and the IAF had gained a high degree of air superiority over the Suez Canal area. The

Israeli chief of staff, Lt. Gen. Haim Bar Lev, commented about the Egyptian air raids into the Sinai during a November 1969 interview:

> Their planes attack, but they do not hit anything. They don't take time to get a proper angle of attack. They get rid of their bombs all at once, as soon as possible. They do everything to be over our territory as short a time as possible.
>
> Today, for instance, we were bombing on their side. And we have been hurting Nasser, so for the first time in two months the Egyptians sent up their MiGs—eight MiGs. We shot down two by cannon and one by an air-to-air missile. We prefer to use cannon because with a missile you have to have certain conditions. You have to be at a proper distance. And if the other pilot sees the missile, he can avoid it. With cannon, you go the way he goes and follow him. We use missiles when the conditions are right for them. But mostly, we use cannon.[14]

The IAF Mirage IIIC fighter could carry the French Matra 530, American AIM-9B/D Sidewinder, or the Israeli-developed Shafrir air-to-air missiles. These weapons all utilize infrared-homing guidance, which requires the attacking aircraft to approach a target from the rear, where the missile seeker can "see" the hot jet-engine exhaust. The Shafrir was developed by the Israeli RAFAEL Armament Development Agency. The IAF F-4 Phantoms carried both the infrared-homing Sidewinder and the longer-range, radar-guided AIM-7 Sparrow air-to-air missile. This weapon could be used at night and could hit a target head-on or from the side, but its complicated firing procedures reduced the likelihood of a successful attack in the swirling dogfights that were common in the Middle East. Cannons and missiles were complementary weapons: The range of the cannon was from zero to 4,000 feet, while missiles were effective from 2,500 feet to over 5 miles, depending upon target speed and altitude. Not all the Egyptian aircraft shot down fell to Israeli fighters. Between May and November 1969, fifty-one Egyptian aircraft were downed: thirty-four in air battles, nine by antiaircraft fire, and eight by Hawk surface-to-air missiles.[15]

During the fall of 1969, the IAF also flew hundreds of sorties in support of antiterrorist activities along the Lebanese, Syrian, and Jordanian borders. The IAF aircraft rocketed, bombed, and strafed terrorist training camps and Jordanian and Iraqi artillery batteries. Yallo Shavit, a retired IAF brigadier general, commented about the antiterrorist role of the air force during this period:

> During the War of Attrition I was deputy wing
> commander of Base One. We had Mirages, Skyhawks,
> and Phantoms. As the wing commander and deputy were
> allowed to fly with any squadron, I might fly a Skyhawk
> in the morning, then a Mirage, and then a Phantom late
> in the day. The Skyhawk was easy: You take the book,
> learn the emergency procedures, and fly the plane. We
> flew many missions against Jordanian targets. I believe
> that the first time the Israeli government used the air
> force to stop the shelling of Israel was in the Jordan
> Valley. Listen, we hit them below the belt so badly that
> up until today it is quiet there. The people there know
> what we can do. You know Irbid Heights, it is between
> Mafraq and the Jordan Valley, south of the Golan
> Heights. They were shelling targets in Israel from there.
> So we took off with eighteen Mk.81 [250-pound] bombs
> on a Skyhawk and eight aircraft—144 bombs—and we
> would drop them in the middle of the village next to the
> artillery battery firing at Israel. It went on like this for
> two or three weeks and then the firing stopped. It was a
> tough war, they were shelling our kibbutzim day and
> night. With each of our missions a Jordanian village
> would disappear. It hurt and they learned a lesson.[16]

On November 17, the IAF flew dozens of strike sorties against radar sites and artillery positions in Jordan. During an air strike against a radar site near Mazar, one of the attacking Israeli aircraft was downed by Jordanian antiaircraft fire. This was the seventh Israeli fighter-bomber to be lost over Jordan since the 1967 war. An IAF spokesman stated that "the Jordan figures were high because they occurred shortly after the war when pilots were going into their targets on a wartime basis, taking more risks. We had to tell the pilots to be more cautious and we rethought our tactics."[17] An IAF base commander also commented on IAF losses over Jordanian targets: "When we bombed artillery, antiaircraft sites, or El Fatah camps, the batteries were heavily defended. We made mistakes: we used the wrong weapons sometimes; we used the wrong tactics. But we learned a lot since July 20, 1969, when the current Suez War of Attrition began from the Israeli side."[18]

The morale of Egyptian forces had declined to a low point by mid-December 1969. Vice-President Sadat and Defense Minister General Fawzi made an urgent visit to Moscow to appeal for assistance. In fighting with Israel, more than sixty Egyptian aircraft and several dozen pilots had been lost and almost all of the air defense network near the Suez Canal had been put out of action. Although Egyptian forces struck back and inflicted casualties on the Israelis, each success caused an intensification of the Israeli air attacks.

With Soviet assistance, the Egyptians began to reconstruct their air defenses. Missile batteries, radar systems, and anti-aircraft guns were placed near the Suez Canal and fortified with sand and concrete. Israeli reconnaissance aircraft detected this buildup. On December 25, in an unprecedented eight-and-one-half-hour series of heavy air strikes, the IAF hit every major air defense position from Suez City to Qantara. The following day a second series of intense raids blasted the Egyptian defenses.

That night Israeli commandos staged a raid that snatched a whole Soviet-built radar warning system from Egyptian territory. Soviet advisors had installed an advanced P-12 Spoonrest surveillance radar near Ras Gharib to upgrade Egyptian radar coverage along the Gulf of Suez. A specially trained group of commandos was landed by helicopter near the radar site after sunset on December 26. Israeli fighter-bombers and artillery struck at positions surrounding the site to divert the attention of nearby Egyptian army units. The commandos quickly overpowered the guards and dismantled the radar van and antenna into two loads that could be lifted out by helicopter. Two Sikorsky CH-53D heavy-lift helicopters came in and carried out the equipment. This was the first major success of the American-built CH-53D helicopter, which had only been in service with the IAF for a short time. Israeli technicians were able to evaluate the performance of this advanced radar system and shared this information with the United States.

Since Israel had the upper hand in the ongoing conflict with Egypt, senior Israeli government officials had no incentive to make the compromises that would have been necessary to reach a negotiated settlement to end the fighting. The Israeli leadership decided to use the air force as a bludgeon in an attempt to force Egypt to seek peace. On January 7, 1970, IAF fighter-bombers initiated a strategic bombing campaign by attacking three military bases within thirty-five miles of Cairo.

On the following day, dozens of Egyptian aircraft penetrated into the Sinai to hit back in response to the new Israeli deep-strike raids. Egyptian fighter-bombers successfully hit several targets, causing casualties and moderate damage. However, two SU-7 aircraft were lost to Israeli ground fire.

Israeli interdiction missions were resumed on January 13, when a supply depot of El Khanka, fifteen miles northeast of Cairo, was hit. Three separate targets around Cairo were bombed on January 10. However, one of the Israeli jets was shot down by Egyptian antiaircraft fire. The goal of the new air offensive was to relieve pressure along the Suez Canal and Disrupt Egyptian military preparations. Golda Meir, Premier of Israel, stated, "Nasser is not happy. The war has been brought home to him. . . . He can't fool his people anymore. Maybe that is the most important thing that has happened. You can't lie anymore when people hear planes right over Cairo."[19]

Israeli deep-strike attacks and commando raids battered Egyptian forces to the point that President Nasser made an urgent trip to Moscow on January 22. During four days of meetings in the Soviet Union, the Egyptian president acknowledged that his forces were unable to deal with the Israeli attacks. Nasser requested that Egypt be supplied with advanced attack aircraft that would be used to strike back at Israel. Soviet leaders would not supply offensive weapons, but did agree to upgrade the Egyptian air defense capability rapidly.

Soviet Premier Kosygin sent a personal note to President Nixon on January 31, stating that Israel was attacking Egypt at will and that if the United States would not restrain Israel, the Soviet Union would be forced to come to the assistance of Egypt.[20] A massive Soviet airlift of war materiel to Egypt began almost immediately. While Soviet and Egyptian consultations continued, Israeli jets struck targets near Cairo on January 23 and 28. President Nixon replied to Premier Kosygin on February 4. His note denied responsibility for the current situation but Nixon agreed to work toward a cease-fire.

On February 6, President Nixon said he was seriously considering the sale to Israel of an additional twenty-five F-4 Phantom II and eighty A-4 Skyhawk aircraft along with other war materiel. This sale was discussed to let the Soviet Union know that the United States planned to support Israel to help maintain the balance of power in light of the Soviet assistance that was being provided to Egypt and Syria. These airplanes would come from the production lines and thus could not be delivered until 1971.

On February 8, Egyptian fighters clashed with Israeli jets flying a deep-strike raid and two MiG-21 aircraft were shot down by IAF fighters. This was the first time that Egyptian fighters challenged IAF aircraft during one of the air strikes over the Nile delta. Egyptian fighter-bombers struck back, flying several successful raids against Israeli positions in the Sinai on February 9. When Israeli fighters jumped the Egyptian fighter-bombers, they were engaged by top-cover MiG-21s and one Israeli Mirage was shot down. Israel acknowledged this loss as the second aircraft to be shot down in air combat, while eight others had been lost to antiaircraft fire on the Egyptian front since the 1967 war.

During a television interview aired in the United States on February 8, 1970, President Nasser stated, "The Israelis think they are strong—all right, they are strong. They know they have air superiority." He added, "The problem is not the airplanes really. The problem which we feel here in the Arab countries—not only here in Egypt—is the problem of pilots. We have more planes than pilots; the Israelis have two pilots for every airplane; so the Israelis have air security and air supremacy." President Nasser said that in its recent raids against targets near Cairo, Israel demonstrated "the arrogance of power."[21]

A deep-strike raid by Israeli aircraft near Cairo on February 12 mistakenly hit the Abu Zohal concrete factory, killing sixty-eight civilians and wounding ninety-eight. This strike intensified Egyptian and Soviet resolve. By late February, massive quantities of Soviet equipment were arriving in Egypt. Thousands of Soviet advisors were helping to reestablish an air-defense network to protect vital targets in Egypt.

On March 18, the United States disclosed that Soviet forces had deployed dozens of new SA-2 and SA-3 air-defense missile batteries around Cairo, Alexandria, the Aswan Dam, and other vital rear-area locations. A senior Israeli military officer said that these new air defenses were a threat and would be attacked, "because they represent a new obstacle to attacking aircraft." According to the officer, the SA-3 had never been used in combat, "not even in Vietnam." He added that the missile had a range of about twelve miles and was thought to be much more effective than the earlier SA-2.[22]

A massive series of Israeli raids were flown in late March 1970 to destroy new air defense sites being deployed along the Suez Canal. Egyptian fighters aggressively challenged these raids, and numerous air battles occurred, resulting in the loss of nine Egyptian aircraft in less than a week. An Israeli spokesman stated that the nine Egyptian jets shot down were all MiG-21 fighters and that fifty-four of this type of aircraft had been downed since the 1967 war.[23]

Israeli aircraft continued to bomb Egyptian positions in central Egypt. However, Israel refrained from striking locations known to be protected by Soviet troops. A flight of IAF fighter-bombers heading for a target in the Nile valley was called back on April 17, when Israeli ground controllers discovered that they were headed for an intercept with a formation of MiG-21 fighters flown by Soviet pilots. The Soviets controlled several airfields and had been flying fighter patrols over Egypt. Israel was not ready intentionally to engage in combat with Soviet pilots. Israel ended its deep-penetration attacks against rear-area targets in Egypt because of the threat of direct conflict with Soviet military personnel. Since January 1970, the IAF had flown 3,300 sorties over Egyptian territory and delivered more than 8,000 tons of bombs.

The northern borders of Israel were also the scene of considerable action during late 1969 and spring of 1970. Israeli commando raids and air strikes conducted against guerrilla positions in southern Lebanon led Israeli and Syrian forces along the Golan

Heights to trade artillery and tank fire. Both sides committed aircraft to the fighting, and on December 11, 1969, the Syrians lost three planes to Israeli Mirages. Another air battle took place over the Golan Heights on January 8, 1970, resulting in the destruction of three Syrian MiGs. These battles raised the total of Syrian aircraft losses since the 1967 war to seventeen. Ground action, including artillery and tank fire, did not let up along the Israeli/Syrian border and on January 23, a Syrian MiG-21 over-flew the city of Haifa at supersonic speed, smashing windows. Later in the day, IAF Phantoms reciprocated by "booming" Damascus and several other Syrian cities. Border fighting continued and on February 2, an Israeli Mirage on a reconnaissance mission was lost to Syrian antiaircraft fire over the Golan Heights.

While the Egyptian front was the focus of IAF activity during the spring of 1970, terrorist attacks were answered with air strikes along the Lebanese, Syrian, and Jordanian borders. Israeli forces initiated large-scale attacks against Syria on April 2, in response to repeated cease-fire violations. "If the Syrians are not impressed by one blow, then we shall deal them a second," said Lt. Gen. Haim Bar Lev. He added, "If the cease-fire line ceases to be quiet, our blows will grow harder." Israeli planes pounded Syrian positions all along the Golan Heights and shot down three MiG-21 fighters in air combat. However, Israel admitted the loss of one aircraft, thought to be an F-4 Phantom, to Syrian antiaircraft fire.[24]

During a strike flown by ten Skyhawks against terrorist camps near Mt. Hermon on May 12, a pair of IAF Skyhawk fighter-bombers was attacked by Syrian MiG-17s. Lt. Col. Ezra Dotan, a Skyhawk squadron commander, heard his number two shouting into the radio: "MiGs! MiGs!" "Are you sure?" he asked him, "I don't see any aircraft!" "Affirmative," came number two's reply. "Get them!" he commanded.

Dotan continues his story:

I still didn't see them, and I wasn't 100 percent sure that they were really MiGs. But the instant I broke, I saw them—MiG-17s. By then, my number two was inside their formation, threatening one of the MiGs. However, at that time, the IAF Skyhawks weren't equipped with air-to-air gunsights, and my number two had to estimate the range. As a result, he started firing from too far away.

I saw he didn't have a chance to succeed, and I decided to go in after him. Quickly, I climbed to high altitude and rolled left, into the Syrian formation. I acted so fast, they didn't have time to react. Right out of the roll, I went after their number two. While I was diving, he turned left, then straightened out. But it didn't help—I came out of my dive only 130 meters behind him!

I closed in on him as close as possible and thought fast. What could I fire at him? I decided to use . . . my AT rockets! I fired two clusters; they passed underneath his tail. The Syrian pilot didn't even notice he was being fired on. But I didn't give up—I still had plenty of rockets. I fired two more clusters, estimated range from my air-to-ground gunsight, pulled the Skyhawk's nose up—just like an air-to-ground attack—and fired two more clusters. The Syrian's craft was ripped to shreds; trailing black smoke, he fell at the foot of Mount Hermon.

"Break! MiGs after you!" my number two shouted into the radio. A glance at my mirror confirmed the warning: a MiG was firing on me at that very moment, his tracers slipping past my right wing, and another pair of MiGs was on my tail. Later it turned out that I'd been in the middle of eight MiGs.

I slowed down and let one of the pair pass me. I could have got him—but I realized that if I tried, his wingmen would wipe me out. So I decided to save my skin and my Skyhawk, broke left and down. It surprised the MiGs, and they were ahead of me before they realized what was happening. One of them used his afterburner and streaked away—I realized this meant he was using up valuable fuel, which put him at a disadvantage. So I jettisoned my heavy rocket clusters and streaked right after him.

The Syrian realized I was closing in and dipped close to the ground. That was when I thanked Heaven for my

Skyhawk—its fantastic maneuverability let me keep chasing after him, in and out of streambeds, between hills. At one point, there were so many trees and rocks streaming past my cockpit, I couldn't follow the MiG by line of sight! I climbed a bit higher, then spotted him below and ahead of me. I closed in on him as fast as I could—my Skyhawk was faster than his MiG, and I almost passed him. I slowed down, but couldn't get my nose down far enough to hit him with my guns.

If the Syrian had had the sense to keep flying straight, he might have got away. But he decided to break suddenly, which meant he had to climb a bit. That was when he got into my sights. I dropped down a bit—by then he was filling my entire windscreen—and fired at the base of his wing. The wing flew off, and the MiG plummeted to the ground.

Then I climbed to join my number two, who had been covering me from above, and we returned to base together. The whole base saw our victory roll![25]

On the Suez front, air action had increased because of Egyptian attacks. Since Soviet pilots were responsible for flying protective patrols over Egypt, the EAF was free to concentrate its operations against Israeli targets. During the period April 18–24, 1970, EAF aircraft flew several major air raids against Israeli positions in the Sinai, causing considerable casualties and damage. Israeli fighters and antiaircraft defenses downed several SU-7 and MiG-17 fighter-bombers and two IL-28 bombers that had penetrated 125 miles into the Sinai to attack targets near El Arish. In concert with these air attacks Egyptian forces intensified shelling, damaging Israeli positions along the Suez Canal. On May 2, President Nasser remarked, "A change has taken place. Our armed forces have regained the initiative with bold military operations in the air and on land."[26]

In early May, Egyptian and Soviet troops began to reconstruct the air defense network parallel to the Suez Canal. New SA-2 and SA-3 sites, protected by antiaircraft guns, were installed from Port Said on the Mediterranean Sea to as far south as the Aswan Dam. At the same time, heavy Egyptian air attacks hit Israeli positions almost every day. Israeli defenses claimed seven Egyptian aircraft during the May 14–16 period. On May 14, Egyptian commandos destroyed an Israeli patrol boat at the port of Eilat and the Egyptian navy sank an Israeli fishing boat in the Mediterranean. In retaliation for these assaults, Israeli Phantoms bombed an Egyptian destroyer and a missile boat in the Red Sea.

Beginning on May 30, an intensified series of Israeli air raids began. Within a week more than four thousand bombs fell on Egyptian fortifications. The strike capacity of the IAF had expanded considerably with the introduction of the Skyhawks and Phantoms. At times the pace of operations was so intense that the air force ran short of bombs.

In the summer of 1970, the IAF had in service two F-4 Phantom squadrons (about forty aircraft), three Mirage squadrons (about sixty aircraft), three A-4 Skyhawk squadrons (about eighty aircraft), one Super Mystere squadron (about twenty aircraft), one Vautour squadron (about ten aircraft), and one Mystere IV squadron (about twenty aircraft). Ouragon and Fouga Magister aircraft were used in the operational-training role. Support services were provided by about forty Noratlas, Stratocruiser, and Dakota transports. The vertical-lift component included about twelve Super Frelon, ten Sikorsky CH-53, twenty-five Bell 205, and twenty Alouette light helicopters.[27] To combat Soviet-built surface-to-air missiles, the United States supplied Israel with jamming pods. These advanced electronic countermeasure (ECM) systems had been used successfully by U.S. forces against the SA-2 radar in Vietnam. Several two-seat Vautour aircraft were also equipped with ECM equipment to jam or deceive Egyptian air defense systems.

In June, U.S. Secretary of State William Rogers announced a renewed effort to bring peace to the Middle East. Israel, Egypt, and Jordan indicated a willingness to consider a cease-fire, but each faction made final efforts to ensure it had a strong bargaining position. For Israel this meant concentrated attacks against the rapidly expanding network of Egyptian air defenses along the Suez Canal.

In June, Egyptian troops, with assistance from the Soviets, began moving their air defense network closer to the Suez Canal. Israeli fighter-bombers hammered the new defenses despite the knowledge that Soviet troops were operating some of the missile sites. Egyptian aircraft provided cover for their ground forces and frequently attacked Israeli positions. In the process, about ten planes were lost to Israeli defenses in June.

During the night of June 29, the Egyptians, with Soviet assistance, moved twelve SA-2 batteries, several SA-3 batteries, and protective antiaircraft guns forward to form a missile screen parallel to the Suez Canal. The following morning a patrol of Israeli Phantoms was ambushed by these new sites and two of the F-4s were shot down. Israeli fighter-bombers aggressively hammered at the air defense batteries, but the Egyptians rapidly repaired battle-damaged sites and fought back with heavy missile and antiaircraft fire. During the next week, seven of the missile batteries were destroyed or damaged by Israeli raids. However, another Phantom jet was lost. Maj. Gen. Haim Bar Lev, Israeli chief of staff, commented that the new Egyptian air defense screen was intended to "drive us from our freedom of air operation along the canal and to enable the Egyptians to concentrate and intensify their offensive ability along the Canal." He added, "In the whole system we feel the Russian hand—in planning, directing, and operating the whole system."[28]

According to Major General Bar Lev, the missiles were more effective because the sites were located close enough to protect each other. Also, ripple fire tactics were used—whereby all the missiles of a battery were fired at a target—making it difficult for the aircraft to escape. The SA-2 batteries used in the June 30 ambush were described as improved models having greater performance, better computers, and optical-tracking capability. A typical SA-2 battery had six ready-to-launch missiles, a central tracking and guidance radar, and a number of antiaircraft guns for close-in protection. The SA-2 was effective against aircraft flying at medium and high altitudes, to a range of 20 miles. Major General Bar Lev was most concerned with the SA-3s because they were effective against low-flying aircraft and were manned by Soviet crews. A typical SA-3 battery consisted of a detection and guidance radar (known by the NATO code name of Low Blow) and four two-round missile launchers. The SA-3 missile had a maximum range of 13 miles and could hit targets below 500 feet.

Israeli fighter-bombers flew hundreds of strike missions against the missile sites and Egyptian frontline positions along the canal. On July 10, IAF fighters shot down three Egyptian MiG-21s that interfered with one of these raids. However, on July 18, a Phantom was shot down by an SA-3 missile and another F-4 was damaged. Despite the intense bombing, the Israelis were not able to eliminate the Egyptian air defenses along the Suez Canal.

Israeli planners began talking of a ground offensive across the Suez Canal to destroy the new air defense network, and the possibility of a direct confrontation with Soviet troops appeared a distinct possibility. Brig. Gen. Mordechai Hod, commander of the IAF, stated that the new threat was a "Russian fist covered by an Egyptian glove."[29]

In concert with the new ground-based air defense network, Soviet fighters began patrolling closer to the Suez Canal. On July 25 a Soviet pilot flying a MiG-21 attacked an Israeli Skyhawk and damaged its wings and tail with an Atoll heat-seeking air-to-air missile. The identity of the MiG-21 pilots was determined by Israeli intelligence units that monitored radio communications between the aircraft and their ground controllers.[30] The next day Israeli fighters shot down two Egyptian MiG-17s that crossed into the Sinai. Senior Israeli government and military personnel debated the next move and decided that the Russians should be taught a lesson. On the afternoon of July 30, a flight of Israeli Mirages flew a reconnaissance patrol into Egyptian air space to bait the Soviet pilots into action. More than a squadron of Soviet MiG-21s scrambled after the decoy and they were met by flights of Mirage and Phantom fighters.

One of the Israeli pilots who participated in the air battle described the situation:

> I was number two of a pair of Phantoms; we and two Mirages were up against about ten MiGs. It was a little unsettling to see so many aircraft at once, so many fuel tanks being jettisoned all over the place. I didn't care about numerical superiority—I was just afraid someone might bump into my aircraft!
>
> One of the Mirages fired an air-to-air missile seconds after the battle began. The missile hit a MiG and set it on fire. The pilot bailed out; the aircraft went into a spin and dropped like a stone from 30,000 feet. The Russian

pilot's parachute opened right away—it's not supposed to: chutes are designed to open automatically at 10,000 feet, so their wearers don't freeze or suffocate at high altitudes. But this pilot used the manual apparatus and opened the chute himself! Maybe he didn't want to be taken alive . . . or maybe he just didn't know any better.

Now some more of our aircraft had joined the battle; the Russians no longer had numerical superiority. I started looking for a MiG to kill. Finally I found one—its pilot was making a right turn, trying to close in on my number one. I broke to the right—the MiG left my number one and started chasing me! We stuck together for a while, dropping to about 15,000 feet; at that point he was only about 150 meters from me. I could see the pilot's helmet clearly.

By this time I'd realized the Russian pilot was inexperienced; he didn't know how to handle his aircraft in a combat situation. At 15,000 feet he proved this fact by trying to escape in a steep dive to 7,000 feet. All we had to do was follow him and lock our radar onto him— and fire a missile. There was a tremendous explosion— but the MiG came out of the cloud of smoke apparently unharmed. That made me mad and I fired a second missile—which turned out to be unnecessary. The Russian aircraft had, in fact, been severely damaged by the first missile; suddenly it burst into flames and fell apart. By the time the second missile reached it, it wasn't there any more.[31]

Israeli Phantom and Mirage pilots shot down five Russian jets in the short dogfight with no loss to themselves.

Heavy fighting continued along the Suez Canal, but Israeli, Soviet, U.S., and Arab representatives began to make serious headway toward a cease-fire. On August 3, 1970, Israel admitted that another Phantom had been lost during attacks against air defense positions near the Suez Canal. This plane was acknowledged to be the sixteenth aircraft lost in action with Egyptian forces and the twenty-sixth plane lost in combat on all fronts since the 1967 war.

Israeli warplanes continued to strike at targets in Egypt, Jordan, and Lebanon right up until the cease-fire took effect on August 8. The cease-fire terms called for both sides to freeze the number of ground forces, air defense systems, and other weapons deployed near the Suez Canal.

During the 1,141 days that had elapsed since the end of the 1967 war, the IAF flew thousands of combat sorties. During these missions, hundreds of thousands of pounds of ordnance were delivered against targets in Egypt, Syria, Jordan, and Lebanon. A total of 113 Egyptian, Syrian, and Soviet aircraft were shot down in air combat during the period while another 25 fell to Israeli Hawk missile and antiaircraft fire.[32] During the War of Attrition, the IAF had modernized much of its force structure, replacing older French aircraft with new American systems. The IAF inventory of helicopters was expanded, and those vehicles played a vital role in defeating terrorist raids, evacuating wounded, and moving troops involved in commando raids. Transport, liaison, and training aircraft provided necessary support and assistance.

However, the IAF was stressed almost to the breaking point during the period that ran from mid-1969 to the cease-fire of 1970. The strain of sustained combat operations on multiple fronts, training and maintenance requirements, and the introduction of new sophisticated systems (such as the A-4 Skyhawk, F-4 Phantom, and electronic-warfare systems) took their toll. Toward the end of the War of Attrition, the IAF faced off against a Soviet-developed air defense network that was one of the most advanced in the world. The system in place along the Suez Canal surpassed even the defenses around Moscow in density and depth. Israeli air attacks damaged this air defense network but were unable to destroy it. The massive Soviet and Egyptian investment in weapons and troops plus the commitment to prevail, no matter what the cost, fundamentally changed the balance of power along the Suez Canal. Because of this new air defense network, the IAF could no longer provide large-scale close air support for Israeli ground troops with an acceptable loss rate, as it had in the 1967 war.

Immediately before the August 8 cease-fire, Egyptian and Soviet forces moved additional SAM batteries and antiaircraft guns to forward positions near the Suez Canal. During the fall of 1970, additional missile batteries were positioned along the waterway. These new systems extended missile coverage into the Israeli-held Sinai and strengthened the already formidable Egyptian air defense shield.

Israel vigorously protested these cease-fire violations and threatened to renew hostilities unless the new missile sites were pulled back. However, Egypt ignored these threats. The United States delivered advanced ECM pods, Shrike antiradar missiles, and other weapons to Israel and promised to supply additional F-4 Phantom and A-4 Skyhawk aircraft to strengthen Israel and maintain a balance of power between the two countries.

Meanwhile Israel Aircraft Industries and other Israeli firms were in the process of refurbishing and upgrading IAF aircraft. Mirage IIIC fighters were reworked to extend their service life, while Super Mystere B-2 aircraft were fitted with a new American engine—the Pratt & Whitney J52 turbojet—and new electronic systems. Even the relatively new Phantoms and Skyhawks were upgraded. IAF A-4E/H Skyhawks were fitted with a computerized weapons delivery system that considerably improved the air-to-ground weapons delivery capability of the Israeli Skyhawk. This new system allowed IAF pilots to bomb more accurately, thus reducing the number of sorties necessary to hit a given target.

IAF officials liked the Skyhawk so much that they bought a new version of the jet that was custom designed to meet their requirements. Known as the A-4N, this new airplane combined the sophisticated attack system installed on other IAF Skyhawks with the airframe that was developed for the U.S. Marine Corps. With its increased power, speed, payload capacity, and accuracy, the A-4N was, at the time of its delivery in 1972, one of the most effective attack aircraft in the world. Israel also improved its F-4 Phantoms by fitting them with leading-edge flaps to improve their maneuverability and by adding new systems and weapons.

One of the biggest IAF programs involved the production of the Nesher, a copy of the embargoed Mirage V, in Israel. The prototype Nesher first flew in late 1969, and by the early 1970s deliveries were underway. Even as the first versions of the Nesher were being assembled, IAF engineers were working to integrate a new engine into the airframe to improve performance. The General Electric J79 jet engine, used in the F-4 Phantom, had greater thrust, better fuel consumption, and was much more reliable than the French-designed Attar turbojet that propelled the Mirage III and the Nesher. After successful flight tests in a Mirage IIIB two-seat trainer, Israeli Aircraft Industries began the difficult task of producing a new aircraft that combined the J79 turbojet, a revised Nesher airframe, and an advanced weapon-delivery system. The prototype Kfir fighter reportedly flew for the first time in June 1973.[33]

Despite tension over the cease-fire violations, the Suez Canal front remained relatively quiet until September 11, 1971, when an EAF SU-7 was downed over the Sinai. A week later Egyptian missile batteries shot down an Israeli Stratocruiser transport that was flying over the Sinai, fourteen miles back from the Suez Canal. Israel and Egypt traded artillery fire along the waterway for more than a week after this incident. During late 1971 and early 1972, Soviet-piloted MiG-25 reconnaissance aircraft overflew the Sinai on numerous occasions. The MiG-25 flew at a speed of more than Mach 2 and an altitude of over 70,000 feet, which was above the reach of Israeli Mirage and Phantom interceptors. Israel responded to the MiG-25 overflights by sending Teledyne Ryan Firebee reconnaissance drones over Egyptian territory. On June 13, 1972, Israeli and Egyptian fighters fought over the Mediterranean Sea and two EAF MiG-21 aircraft were shot down.

In late 1970 and early 1971, Jordanian troops fought a bloody series of battles and expelled terrorist groups that had contested the throne of King Hussein. Once the terrorist groups were expelled, the border between the Israeli-held West Bank and Jordan became quiet. However, the guerrillas did not give up. They moved to Syria and Lebanon. During the next several years, hundreds of air strikes were flown over Lebanon to hit these guerrilla camps.

The Israeli/Syrian border remained relatively calm until the fall of 1972. Intensified terrorist activity and shelling was answered by Israeli air strikes. In August 1972, four Syrian aircraft were shot down over the Golan Heights. Eight more Syrian fighters were destroyed during several large air engagements in November 1972. In January and again in September 1973, the

IAF fought large-scale air battles with the Syrian air force, resulting in the destruction of twenty Syrian fighters for the loss of a single Israeli aircraft.

By 1973 the IAF had grown to a strength of 120 F-4E Phantom, 160 A-4E/H/N Skyhawk, 70 Mirage III/Nesher, and 16 Super Mystere combat aircraft. Support types included 6 RF-4E reconnaissance aircraft, 86 Magister trainers, and 10 Stratocruiser, 20 Noratlas, 10 C-47, and 2 C-130E transports. The helicopter component of the IAF included 12 Super Frelon, 12 CH-53, 45 AB-205, and 5 Alouette II helicopters. In 1971, antiaircraft defense weapons were officially transferred from the army artillery branch to the air force. The IAF thus gained functional control over 10 Hawk surface-to-air missile batteries and more than 300 20–40-mm antiaircraft guns.[34]

# 7

# *The Yom Kippur War*

*A*fter the War of Attrition, Israel continued to hold the Sinai Peninsula, Golan Heights, and Jordanian territory that had been captured during the 1967 war. Israel showed no willingness to negotiate a peace treaty and return the territory, so Arab leaders began planning for war. Egypt and Syria secretly prepared for a simultaneous attack against Israeli forces on the Golan Heights and an invasion across the Suez Canal into the Sinai Peninsula. Egyptian President Sadat (who became president after the death of Nasser in 1970) and Syrian Premier Assad hoped to overwhelm the Israeli defenses, capture terrain, and then call for a cease-fire before the Israeli reserves could counter attack.

Egyptian and Syrian efforts to disguise their preparations for war had been highly successful. Israeli leaders misjudged Arab intentions and discounted the possibility of war. However, evidence of a massive shift of Arab forces to forward positions late on October 6, 1973, prompted Israel to mobilize the army hurriedly and prepare the air force for action. Within hours the IAF was ready to fly a massive series of preemptive air strikes similar in concept to the operation staged in 1967. However, Prime Minister Golda Meir refused to authorize the air attacks so as not to appear to have started the conflict. As a result of both the political decision not to strike first and the late mobilization, regular army units on the Golan Heights and in the Sinai and the air force had to bear the brunt of the initial Arab assault. IAF pilots flew attack missions against the well-defended advancing Arab armies in an attempt to slow this advance and buy time for the Israeli reserve forces to move to the battlefield. Israeli air and ground forces fought with determination and the massive Arab invasion was halted, but at a great cost to Israel. At the end of the conflict, Syrian forces had been driven back from the

Golan Heights and the Egyptian army was held in check in the Sinai. However, it was a pyrrhic victory because of the shock caused by the surprise Arab attack, and the heavy casualties and loss of materiel suffered by Israel.

The fifth major Arab–Israeli conflict began on October 6, 1973, the Yom Kippur Jewish holiday. Since it was the major holiday of the year, Israeli forces were at a reduced level of readiness. The war, which lasted for almost three weeks, can be divided into three phases. The Arab assault took place from October 6 to 9. An Israeli offensive on the Golan Heights and holding actions in the Sinai were the major actions of the second phase, which lasted from October 10 to 14. An Israeli invasion into Egypt and continued fighting on the Golan Heights constituted the final stage, which ran from October 15 to 25. The IAF played a significant role in the war.

Egyptian, Syrian, and Iraqi fighter-bombers spearheaded Operation Badr, the Arab assault, and were active throughout the war. In mid-1973 EAF had a strength of over 400 Soviet-built combat aircraft, including 210 MiG-21 fighters, 100 MiG-17 and 80 SU-7 fighter-bombers, and IL-28 and 16 TU-16 bombers. Several hundred helicopters, and transport, training, and liaison aircraft were also in service.[1] Egyptian forces were augmented during the conflict by a squadron of Algerian SU-7 fighter-bombers, an Iraqi Hawker Hunter unit, and two squadrons of Libyan Mirage aircraft.[2]

The Syrian Arab Air Force in 1973 had a total inventory of more than 500 aircraft, including some 200 MiG-21 fighters, and 120 MiG-17 and 45 SU-7 fighter-bombers.[3] Syrian aviation units were supported by squadron-sized detachments of Iraqi Hawker Hunter and MiG-21 aircraft.

The Arab invasion began at about 2:00 P.M. on October 6, when Egyptian, Syrian, and Iraqi fighter-bombers conducted a coordinated attack on dozens of Israeli targets. Over two hundred Egyptian aircraft penetrated into the Sinai and bombed three Israeli airfields, several Hawk missile batteries, two artillery positions, a number of radar and ECM sites, plus several military headquarters. Kelt air-to-surface missiles fired from Egyptian TU-16 bombers also hit several Israeli targets.

Captain N was a pilot on alert at an air base in the southern

Sinai near Sharm el Sheikh on the afternoon of October 6:

I decided to take off—the controller was screaming that there were orders not to take off. However, I decided that the orders were from 400 kilometers away and they didn't know what was going on. I cranked the engines and told my number two to do the same and to scramble as quickly as possible. Standby is very close to the runway so we cranked the engines, went to the runway, and took off. I looked back to see that number two was airborne and that everything was okay, and I saw smoke plumes on the runway, like cotton balls. And I didn't understand. I told my navigator, "Look! What do you make of this?" He said, "They are bombing the runways, this must be war!"

Then we saw a glimpse of a MiG that was shining in the sun—it was far away, perhaps four miles. There were a lot of them. From then on I don't remember everything. It is just a collection of still pictures. I remember telling number two that there is an attack on the field and nearby facilities and that he should split from me and work on his own to cover the navy base to the south.

First he shot down a MiG-21 right over Sharm el Sheikh. I saw it go down.

My navigator was experienced, he had participated in the battle against the Syrians over the sea on the thirteenth of September 1973, when we shot down thirteen Syrian MiGs and lost only one Mirage. . . . This was my first battle. He said, "Hey, you didn't punch your external tanks!" So I jettisoned them. Then we rushed into what looked like a mass of hornets, there were so many MiGs together. Very quickly I found myself in some maneuvers with two MiG-17s. I was turning after one and the other was at my six o'clock. The one behind us was shooting rockets at me. I saw them missing and I thought, "Don't look back, look forward." Then I shouted to my navigator, "Lock the radar up, I want to shoot the MiG-17 with a radar missile." It didn't work because we were too low, my navigator shouted that it wouldn't lock on because there was too much clutter. So I selected a heat missile, an AIM-9D Sidewinder. I pushed the button and nothing happened. The one-second delay time seemed like eternity. I almost fired another missile. Then the Sidewinder went out and boom, a big explosion. And I thought, well, I shot down an aircraft! It was a black-and-red ball of fire and I kept staring at it. My navigator yelled, "Leave it, there are others."

There were two MiGs making a pop-up maneuver on my left so I turned after them. They saw me and broke very hard so we went into a sort of a scissors maneuver. One MiG-17 turned too sharp for a Phantom and I could not stay with him in the turn so I went into the vertical, looked, and came very close to gun range. The MiG was jinking very sharply and he tried to shake me away. The Phantom is very heavy and not very agile. . . . We went into a pass and I fired. I saw the bullets hitting his wings but he didn't explode, so I left him. He was smoking but there were so many MiGs and I saw another one coming.

I went into a scissors with another MiG who was jinking in an attempt to escape. I shot a missile from a very short range and boom! I saw the missile go in the jet pipe and there was a huge explosion.

Of course you get lost in such a battle and I saw that we were south over the coast. I saw two MiGs strafing the Hawk battery that was there. I came in to interfere with their attacks and they saw me. They split toward me and I made a hard turn down toward one. I passed him head on and went after the other and started shooting the gun at him. My bullets hit him but he didn't explode. That MiG-17 is a tough aircraft. Then I started sinking. The MiG-17 was flying straight and level and opening from me—I couldn't understand what was happening. I looked at the instruments and saw that one engine was out. I got stall stagnation when I shot the gun. Here we are at 1,000 feet. I told my navigator that we have a slight problem and that we have to restart the

engine. I shut it down, lit it, and it started. By that time
the MiG was at about one mile. He was running very
low along the coast. We opened both burners and within
15 seconds we were within range and we shot a
Sidewinder missile at him. It hit and he exploded over
the water.

All this time I had heard my number two shouting
about his fight. After my battle I turned around and saw
a Phantom chasing a MiG-21. They were flying so low
that you could see shock waves behind both aircraft on
the water. I yelled to number two to be careful because
he was too close to the water. He said, "I know, I know,"
but kept chasing the bouncing MiG.

I took off north and came upon a couple of MiGs
which were attacking our airfield. I flew straight into
them. They saw me and started turning, but I was
experienced now! I took the rear one and nailed him
with my last Sidewinder. He exploded over the ground.
The other one I engaged with the gun and hit him. I
fired again, then silence—I was out of ammunition and
too low for a radar missile so he got away.

It was quiet. I circled around and saw several smoke
plumes from the ground. I called my number two. He
said that he was okay and that he had shot down two
MiG-17s and one MiG-21. I told him that I had shot at
six MiGs and was sure that four had exploded. We went
in to land because we were out of weapons and low on
fuel. We saw a hole in the middle of the runway and
another in the middle of the taxiway. Then four Neshers
came from up north and they shouted, "What's going on,
where are the MiGs?" They caped [flew a protective
patrol over the airfield] and we called the tower, but
there was no answer. We picked 04 runway and landed
hard, right on the end like on a carrier, and stood on the
brakes. We stopped just short of a hole which was more
like a hill. When I looked at it I was amazed because it
was such a big pile of debris.[4]

The Israeli airfield at Refidim in the central Sinai was taken
by surprise and put out of action by several flights of Egyptian

SU-7 fighter-bombers; many other positions suffered damage from these Egyptian air strikes. On the Golan Heights, over one hundred Syrian aircraft conducted similar attacks that caused damage to many Israeli positions. Because of the element of surprise and the use of low-altitude tactics, only one Syrian aircraft was lost to Israeli defenses during these attacks. Syrian Mi-8 helicopters lifted commandos to the top of Mount Hermon and the Israeli outpost on top of the mountain was captured following a brief battle. This was a serious loss for Israel because the position was an important observation post.

While the Syrian air strikes were underway, the ground assault began. Five Syrian divisions with more than 75,000 men and 1,200 tanks attacked two Israeli armored brigades with a combined strength of only 8,000 men and 170 tanks. The Syrian force received heavy fire support from 1,000 guns and mortars while Israel had only 60 self-propelled cannons on the whole northern front.

In the Sinai, the Egyptian fighter-bombers continued to pound Israeli positions. Israeli fighters, Hawk surface-to-air missile batteries, and antiaircraft fire downed ten of the attackers. In concert with the air strikes, Egyptian artillery blasted Israeli fortifications with over 2,000 guns. More than 10,500 shells hit Israeli targets in the first minute of firing. As this barrage continued, thousands of Egyptian infantry crossed the Suez Canal in small boats and engineers established pontoon bridges across the waterway to allow armored vehicles and artillery to cross.

Israeli defenses in the Sinai relied upon sixteen fortified outposts of the so-called Bar Lev line that ran the length of the canal from near Port Said to the town of Suez. Manned by a total of only 450 reservists, many of these positions fell to the Egyptians on the first day of fighting. Held back from the Suez Canal were three Israeli armored brigades with a total strength of about 10,000 men and 280 tanks. These units initiated immediate counterattacks against the Egyptian bridgeheads and attempted to link up with the battered Bar Lev strong points. While some Israeli tanks made it to the Suez Canal, dozens were knocked out by tank, rocket, and cannon fire from attacking Egyptian forces.

In the late afternoon on October 6, some thirty Mi-8 transport helicopters flew into the Sinai to deliver Egyptian commandos. However, Israeli fighters and antiaircraft guns downed over a dozen of the Egyptian troop-carrying helicopters. The troops that made it into the Sinai assaulted Israeli command posts and struck at Israeli convoys that were moving to the front.

On both the Sinai and Golan fronts, the hard-pressed defenders called for reinforcements, artillery, and air support to stem the relentless Arab assault. However, the Egyptian and Syrian invasion planners took into account Israeli superiority in the air. The simultaneous attack on two fronts prevented the Israelis from concentrating their efforts. The IAF was forced simultaneously to fly air defense missions over the Sinai and northern Israel, to defend against Arab air strikes, and to strike advancing Egyptian and Syrian units. Cries from battered Israeli ground forces for close air support often could not be fulfilled. The IAF aircraft that flew over the battlefield ran into a barrage of missiles and gunfire. The Egyptian air defense shield, which proved to be such a difficult adversary during the electronic summer of 1970, had been considerably strengthened. The Egyptian Air Defense Force concentrated more than 60 of its 150 SAM batteries along the Suez Canal.[5] These missile batteries were positioned in an overlapping manner so that they could protect each another, and thousands of antiaircraft guns were situated near the missile sites for close-in protection. The effectiveness of the Egyptian air defense screen was further enhanced by a comprehensive command-and-control network that tied together visual spotters, dozens of search radars, and the weapons themselves. Many dummy missile sites were set up and both real and camouflage batteries were protected by sand-and-concrete fortifications.

Since the War of Attrition, large numbers of new, Soviet-supplied weapons were introduced into the Egyptian Air Defense Force. The SA-6 surface-to-air missile system consisted of a radar/fire control vehicle and four transporter/launcher units, each of which held three missiles. The SA-6 system was highly mobile since it was mounted on a tank chassis. After firing, the battery could immediately move to a new position to minimize the chance of a successful counterattack. The SA-6 system was effective against low-flying aircraft, had a high rate of fire, and was immune to Israeli ECM equipment. Capable of hitting targets at a range of over 17 miles, the missile was hard to evade because it was very fast.[6]

Another new Soviet-supplied weapon was the ZSU-23-4 radar-guided antiaircraft cannon, which used the same tank chassis as the SA-6 system. The ZSU-23-4 had a fire control radar and optical-tracking system that enabled the gunner to detect and fire at aircraft flying at low altitudes and high speeds. Because of its high firepower and effective range of over 2 miles, the ZSU-23-4 was a dangerous foe.[7] A third new system to see service with Arab forces was the SA-7 Grail antiaircraft missile. This infrared-homing weapon was first used by the North Vietnamese in 1972 and proved surprisingly effective against helicopters and slow-flying aircraft. Similar in appearance to a bazooka antitank weapon, the shoulder-fired missile traveled at a speed of Mach 1.5 and had an effective range of about 2 miles.[8]

A similar lethal network of air defense systems was established by the Syrian forces on the Golan Heights. Most of the thirty-four Syrian SA-2, SA-3, and SA-6 missile batteries were concentrated in the area between the Golan Heights and Damascus, but others protected important positions in central Syria. As on the Sinai front, hundreds of antiaircraft guns and SA-7 missiles accompanied advancing armored units to defend against Israeli fighter-bombers.

Following the air assault that initiated the 1973 war, the Arab air forces continued to fly attack strikes against Israeli targets on the Golan Heights and in the Sinai. However, a large percentage of the Arab fighter force was held back to protect rear-area positions. Defense against Israeli air strikes near the front lines rested primarily with the Arab air defense forces.

Israeli fighter-bombers began to fly close support missions and strike Arab targets within an hour of the attack, but the results of these initial air strikes were limited. On October 6, the first day of the Yom Kippur War, six Israeli aircraft were lost—four on the Egyptian front and two on the Golan Heights, with four of the aircrew being killed.[9] Egyptian authorities admitted that fifteen aircraft had been shot down, while the Syrians suffered only five losses to Israeli fighters and antiaircraft weapons. During the first day of fighting, Arab forces had made considerable gains on the ground and were moving up their air defense screen to check Israeli air strikes.

The second day of the conflict saw intense IAF activity as Israeli jets attempted to assist the ground forces in holding the line against the Arab assault. Just after dawn on October 7, dozens of IAF aircraft penetrated into Egypt and bombed seven airfields. These attacks caused damage, but the lasting impact was limited because Egyptian aircraft were protected by shelters and runway damage was rapidly repaired. During the attacks, Israeli fighters fought with defending fighters and many Egyptian planes were shot down. However, about five Israeli jets were lost to Egyptian defenses. Israeli jets also struck at the Egyptian bridges that spanned the Suez Canal and advancing armor, but they suffered heavy losses to missile and antiaircraft fire. Egyptian fighter-bombers flew a number of successful attack missions against targets in the Sinai on the second day of the war, but several EAF planes were shot down by Israeli fighters and antiaircraft fire.

For Israel, the situation on the Golan Heights was desperate. Syrian units had continued their assault throughout the hours of darkness using Soviet-supplied night vision equipment. While Israeli defenses in the northern part of the Golan Heights held, Syrian tanks in the south overran the Israeli 188th Armored Brigade. By morning this unit had been almost completely destroyed. Reserve tanks and infantry were shoved into the breach to stem the Syrian assault. The IAF was forced to ignore the enemy air defenses and fly attack missions against advancing Syrian columns. Later in the morning, Phantom fighter-bombers flew dozens of strikes against Syrian missile batteries. However, limited intelligence information, poor weather, and heavy opposition resulted in the loss of five F-4 Phantoms for the destruction of only a small number of air defense sites.

Col. Yallo Shavit, who was an air base commander during the 1973 war, discussed the problem that the IAF faced:

> The entire situation was very vague during the beginning. On Sunday, the second day of the war, they started in the north to clean the missile sites. It takes

time, this operation—six, seven, eight hours—you start with the decoys and the AAA [antiaircraft guns] and then the missiles. In the midst of the operation we were told, "Disaster on the Egyptian front, attack there." So in order to start there you had to take on the missiles. We had to start the same operation again. Meanwhile we paid the casualties on the Golan without results. We went to Egypt and paid the price with limited results. And then Sunday afternoon we went back to Syria because they almost took the Golan Heights. The air force was moved like a platoon—you cannot do that—the air force suffered casualties without getting their rewards. When you go to clean SAMs, the price was about one aircraft per battery—these were the statistics. But we paid more than that because we kept switching back and forth from the Syrian to the Egyptian to the Syrian front. But we were the only element which could help on the Golan Heights at that time so we did it.[10]

Syrian and Iraqi jets were also active on the second day of the war. IAF fighters and air defense units engaged these attackers and over a dozen Arab fighters and helicopters were shot down during the day on the northern front. However, the IAF suffered its highest losses of any single day of the war on Sunday, October 7, when twenty-two Israeli planes were shot down by the Syrian and Egyptian defenses.[11]

On the third day of the war, Israeli reinforcements halted the Syrian assault on the Golan Heights. At great cost to themselves, defending Israeli tanks, troops, and jets had destroyed hundreds of Syrian tanks and other armored vehicles. IAF fighter-bombers blasted convoys that were moving reinforcements, fuel, and ammunition to sustain the Syrian advance. As a result of heavy losses, the Syrians ceased their advance and began to dig in. Syrian units fought hard to hold the ground they had captured and struck back against the advancing Israelis with tank fire, air attacks, and artillery. The IAF flew dozens of fighter patrol missions on the northern front and shot down more than twenty Arab aircraft. Dozens of IAF attack sorties hit Syrian targets, including a series of raids against airfields. However, the Syrian defenses were ready and losses on the attacks against the Syrian airfields were heavy, totaling four F-4 Phantoms.

In the Sinai, Egyptian fighter-bombers struck at Israeli positions but Israeli jets intervened, resulting in several major air battles. Israeli armored columns rolled forward to hit the Egyptian bridgehead into the Sinai but the attacks achieved little, and heavy losses were suffered. Egypt had moved over seventy thousand men, five hundred tanks, and thousands of antiaircraft weapons into the Sinai. Expecting Israeli counterattacks, the defenders had dug in and protected their positions with mines, cannons, and missiles. In the afternoon the IAF flew nearly one hundred sorties against four SAM batteries that defended Port Said and was successful in putting these units out of action.

IAF air defense, helicopter, and transport elements were deeply involved in Israeli battle plans. Hawk batteries and antiaircraft units in the Sinai and on the Golan Heights were the target of dozens of Arab air strikes. Reserve antiaircraft units moved up to the battlefield and provided protective firepower with their 20- and 40-mm cannons. Noratlas, C-47 and C-130 transports flew around the clock in order to move men and material into the Sinai or to northern Israel to support combat operations. On many return flights these aircraft evacuated casualties for treatment at Israeli hospitals. Helicopters of the IAF were heavily involved in supporting the mobilization and rescuing aircrew shot down by Arab antiaircraft fire. These helicopters played a vital role in saving lives by moving the wounded rapidly to medical trauma centers. Maintenance and support personnel worked to exhaustion in order to ensure that combat and transport aircraft were ready for action.

By the fourth day of the war, a sizable number of reserve units had reached the northern front and Israeli forces began to push back the Syrians. However, the Syrians fell back in good order and frequently ambushed advancing Israeli units. Syrian forces began firing FROG-7 surface-to-surface missiles into Israeli territory with the hope of hitting Ramat David air base and the headquarters of the northern command. About a dozen of the Soviet-supplied missiles hit near civilian settlements that surrounded the air base and headquarters. In retaliation for these missile attacks, the IAF heavily bombed a number of strategic targets in Syria, including the air force headquarters near Damascus and the Homs oil storage facility. Israeli jets also bombed an Iraqi convoy moving through central Syria toward the front, a radar site in Lebanon, and several Syrian positions near the battlefield. Israeli fighters and air defenses claimed the destruction of ten Arab aircraft on the Golan Heights during the fourth day of the war.

On October 9, Egyptian tanks raced out from their defensive positions along the Suez Canal and struck south toward Ras el Sudr. This advance was stopped by Israeli armor and air attacks. Israeli units continued to arrive in the Sinai but, except for local attacks, these forces refrained from battle. Israeli army commanders were still moving troops into the Sinai and examining battle plans. The IAF flew over four hundred fighter patrol and strike sorties on the Egyptian front on October 9. Israeli jets struck at Egyptian bridges crossing the Suez Canal and military concentrations on both sides of the waterway. Egyptian airfields at Katamia and Mansura were hit, and air defense positions near Port Said were again blasted. Six Egyptian aircraft were said to have been downed during the day, although Egyptian fighters and antiaircraft fire probably claimed a similar number of the attacking Israeli aircraft.

By the end of the fourth day of fighting, the Israelis had halted the Syrian invasion of the Golan Heights and stabilized the situation in the Sinai. The desperate defense that halted the Arab advance cost Israel more than one thousand casualties and the loss of three hundred tanks and other armored vehicles. The strong Arab air defenses also took a heavy toll of Israeli aircraft; more than fifty were shot down during the first four days of fighting and dozens more were damaged. More than 20 percent of the IAF's frontline combat aircraft had been shot down or put out of action during these four days of intense fighting, and pilot losses were also heavy. Most of the aircraft downed during this period were hit while flying ground support or interdiction missions.

N. Merchavi, a pilot who flew both A-4 Skyhawk and F-4 Phantom aircraft during the conflict, commented on the situation:

We played the game by our rules and suddenly we didn't know the new rules or how to play. Until 1970 we had total air superiority. We were good at air-to-air missions and could attack any point in the Middle East without any chance to be interrupted. But then came the SAMs, the SA-2, improved SA-2, the SA-3, and then in 1973 the SA-6. When you look at the statistics you see that we didn't lose all that many aircraft to the missile threat. . . . What the missile threat did was to take away the capability of the pilot to search and find targets. During the Yom Kippur War the systems that were supposed to support the pilot and help him do his job didn't exist. These were the ECM and intelligence systems. We came in to fight like we did in 1967 but the conditions were different. So it took us about seven days to overcome the uncertainness and understand how to do the job properly.[12]

Pilots on ground support missions had to find and identify their targets while flying at high speeds and low altitudes. At the same time they had to watch out for missiles, gunfire, and enemy fighters while accurately delivering their bombs and rockets. Targeting and intelligence data were generally many hours old, and it was not always possible to talk with ground controllers because of the changing tactical situation and communications jamming. As a result of this situation, many pilots were forced to make multiple passes and were hit or shot down in the process of searching for and attacking their targets.

The Israelis tried different tactics and used a variety of countermeasures in an attempt to reduce their losses. Missions were flown against preplanned targets or battlefield positions that could be marked by smoke from artillery. High-speed, low-level flight profiles were flown and strike aircraft made a single pass, popping up only to deliver their weapons. Several aircraft hit a single target from different directions, while helicopters, low-flying aircraft, or ground observers provided warning of SAMs, antiaircraft fire, or the approach of enemy fighters. To hit targets behind the front lines, flights of aircraft would penetrate at medium altitude, which placed them above the effective altitude of most antiaircraft fire. Shrike radar-homing missiles were fired to force Arab air defense radars to shut down or face destruction. Stand-off jammers were employed to disrupt Arab radars. Strike aircraft carried their own jamming pods and dispensed decoy flares and chaff during the attack in order to confuse the defenses. Aircraft fired upon by missiles made violent maneuvers in order to escape.[13]

The Israelis also used remotely piloted vehicles (RPVs) to perform dangerous reconnaissance missions over the battlefield and as decoys to distract and confuse the Arab air defenses. Drones built in the United States and supplied to Israel in the early 1970s flew these dangerous missions.[14]

Pilots flying interdiction missions against rear-area targets such as airfields, bridges, or oil storage facilities, used indirect flight paths in order to skirt battlefield defenses and achieve surprise. These new tactics and techniques, plus improved intelligence and targeting selection, considerably reduced the Israeli loss rate during strike operations.

During the second phase of the conflict, which lasted from October 10 to 14, the Israelis cleared the Syrians from the Golan Heights and reached a stalemate in the Sinai. At an October 10 news conference, Maj. Gen. Aaron Yariv, advisor to the chief of staff, stated, "It is not going to be a short war. The people of Israel can expect no early and elegant victories. We will have to do a lot of fighting." He added, "I don't want to say that the Syrians have been broken but we have dealt them a severe blow." On the Sinai front the general said that Israel had done no more than "redress the situation" caused by Egyptian numerical superiority. General Yariv acknowledged that "quite a number of our aircraft have been lost" due to the Arab air defenses. But he added that in air power, "the balance is very heavy in our favor."[15]

During the next several days (October 10–12) the IAF staged an intense series of interdiction raids against Syrian targets including airfields, military headquarters, power plants, and the oil storage facility at Homs. These attacks were hotly contested. The following interview with an Israeli Phantom pilot tells the story of one of these missions:

Four attacking Damascus International Airport. Early morning. All is calm. As we drop from the mountains toward Damascus, we notice a cloud of black smoke from burning fuel tanks. Flying low we pass underneath

the cloud. Poor visibility. Terrible AA smoke rising
toward us.

One minute to climb. The first pair climbs and so do
we. The airfield is beneath us. Two long runways.
Impossible to miss. I aim and press the bomb button.
Bombs released, the aircraft shudders—almost sighs with
relief. Beneath us Damascus Valley seems to be boiling
and steaming; missiles are flying through the air and AA
shells are everywhere. Two minutes later the first pair
breaks away. They're on to us. Jettison tanks. Full
afterburner. Break left as hard as I can. Everything is
happening so fast! To the west I see a Phantom breaking
left, with a MiG on its tail. I get behind them. If the MiG
straightens its wings, I tell myself, I'll launch a missile
at it. The MiGs wings straighten, I launch.

My earphones crackle with S's voice: "Break you son-
of-a-bitch! Break!" Another MiG, some 600 meters behind
S and me, is firing its gun like a madman. "He won't hit
us," I assured S. "We're out of range." The MiG I fired
on explodes—and in that instant, we're hit in the right
wing. The Syrian has crept up behind us into range.
Formation leader says to break contact. "Number four
aircraft stuck with MiGs," I reply. Number three flies
over us and begins to fire his gun. Amazingly, it helps:
the MiGs scatter.

We limp back to the rendezvous point. I report to the
formation leader: the aircraft is skidding out of control,
right engine temperature is shaky and we're low on fuel.
Nevertheless I manage to land. Ground crews swarm all
over the aircraft. A hole as big as a bucket in the right
wingtip.

Mission score: four good hits on the target, one MiG
killed, landed safely home.[16]


While a number of IAF jets were lost during this series of
interdiction missions, many Syrian and Iraqi fighters were shot
down in dogfights. The Syrians also pulled a number of their
missile batteries back from the front lines in order to defend
against these attacks. In addition to these deep attack missions,

IAF aircraft continued to fly a large number of ground support and fighter patrol missions over the Golan Heights each day.

As Israeli forces advanced across the Golan Heights, the Syrian leadership began to call for help from Arab allies and the Soviet Union. The Syrian Air Force stepped up its ground attack efforts, while Iraq committed additional forces and aircraft to the northern front. Sizable air battles occurred over the Golan Heights; IAF fighters and air defense systems claimed thirty-six victories on the northern front during the period October 10–12.

In response to Arab requests for assistance, the Soviet Union began flying replacement aircraft and military equipment to Syria and Egypt. Dozens of Soviet transport planes arrived daily and additional materiel was dispatched via cargo ships. An Iraqi armored division arrived in Syria, and Jordan sent an armored brigade into battle. During the night of October 12, Israel staged a dramatic commando raid against an Iraqi column that was moving toward the front on the Baghdad–Damascus Highway. A squad of troops was lifted into position above the highway by a CH-53 transport helicopter. The paratroopers destroyed a bridge, planted mines, and waited for the arrival of the Iraqi convoy. The paratroopers destroyed the lead vehicles of the convoy and then withdrew to the helicopter pickup point. Israeli Phantoms then swept in and blasted the stalled convoy, with bombs destroying many additional vehicles.[17]

The war on the Golan Heights was still being fought with considerable intensity. N. Merchavi commented:

Israeli ground forces came and took the territory
occupied by the Syrians back and moved into Syria to
Tel Sharms, which is about five miles east of the green
border [1967 cease-fire line]. But the missile sites were
further back so the Syrian air defense system, at about a
week after the war started, was still very good. On the
twelfth of October I got a mission from the headquarters
to attack with four Skyhawks fully loaded with weapons
and fuel and go to the Damascus area at 6:00 o'clock in
the morning to hit SAM sites. The mission plan from
headquarters said that we should go in at about 14,000

feet, which makes the aircraft in our loaded condition able to fly at about 280 knots at maximum power. . . .

We had the E model with the fixed gunsight, without RWR [radar warning receiver], and the old [8,600-pound-thrust Pratt & Whitney J52 turbojet] engine. So I decided not to go to the Damascus area directly from our border at 14,000 feet. I preferred to go to the north because there I leaned on Mount Hermon, and then I at least had one side clear from the missile sites. To make a long story short, we tried to attack several times. On our initial attack I entered first and put numbers three and four three miles behind to warm me about missile launches. I got close to a fixed SA-2 site, rolled in to bomb it, then I saw about twenty launches of SA-6s! At the time we knew all about missiles and how to identify them because we saw many. I was very surprised to see the simultaneous launching of so many missiles. None of us were shot down during the ambush because we all maneuvered like crazy. But I saw my number two release his bombs, start to recover, and then I saw a missile pass by me and I warned him to break. He turned and I saw an explosion and the aircraft come out of the orange smoke of the SA-6. He got out of it without serious damage and we got back to Mount Hermon. We tried to come back two more times but had to leave because the defenses were alerted.[18]

On the Golan Heights, Syrian and Iraqi armor, supported by aircraft, made several serious counterattacks, but Israeli units held the line and continued their slow advance. By October 15, fighting on the Golan Heights had reached a stalemate. During the previous three days the IAF had flown almost two hundred strike sorties against Syrian airfields, fuel dumps, and battlefield targets. Many Arab aircraft were engaged during Israeli fighter patrol and strike sorties, and over two dozen were shot down during October 13–15. Israeli aircraft losses were relatively light, but heavy Syrian tank and artillery fire and air strikes caused dozens of casualties among the ground forces.

There was a lull in ground action on the Sinai front during October 10–13 as both sides built up their forces for renewed

offensive action. However, Israeli and Egyptian units continued
to make frequent small-scale probes and trade artillery fire. The
Egyptians held a narrow strip of territory, running the entire
102-mile length of the Suez Canal, that varied in width from two
to nine miles. Opposing them was an Israeli force of about five
divisions, which included more than sixty thousand men and six
hundred tanks.

Despite the relative lull on the ground, heavy air action continued. The IAF struck at battlefield targets, including bridges
across the Suez Canal, armored formations, and air defense
sites. Many counter-air missions were flown against Egyptian
airfields, but since aircraft were protected by shelters and runway damage was rapidly repaired, most airstrips were back in
operation within several hours. Egyptian radars and observers
detected most of the approaching Israeli strikes so the defenses
were ready for the attackers. As a result, Israeli fighter-bombers
suffered losses to the strong missile and gun defenses that protected Egyptian air bases. Attacking Israeli jets also had to
contend with formations of MiG fighters that hovered over their
home airfields. The following account describes the outcome of
one of these deep strike missions:

> There were four of us. We felt really good; we kept
> singing into the radio. The attack was successful and we
> knew it. We could see the explosions, right on the
> target—a good feeling.
> We formed up again and headed for home. We kept
> looking around for MiGs, but there was nothing there.
> Total silence—and suddenly, total uproar. The aircraft
> next to us had climbed slightly—and there were two
> MiGs after him. Then I felt a blow to the aircraft. I
> thought H—my pilot—had jettisoned the fuel tanks. But
> it was a MiG firing behind us. I shouted for H to break
> left. Meanwhile, I saw another MiG firing on a Phantom
> from our formation. The Phantom was seriously
> damaged: flames streamed out its left-hand engine. The
> first MiG was still on our tail, closing to 400 meters and
> firing. I told H to break away; the burst missed us. But
> the MiG kept closing on us and firing; we were losing
> speed and the aircraft was sluggish. I had a feeling that

the next burst would run right through the cockpit and it would be all over.

The MiG got within 150 meters of us—and we were hit. The whole aircraft shook with the blow; the rear fuselage and wings burst into flames. I don't remember hearing anything over the radio from that point on— maybe because I was shouting myself. The entire aircraft was now in flames. I shouted to H to jump and pulled my ejection handle. I watched the fight continue on my way down; MiGs were firing all over the place, and another Phantom's crew bailed out. I saw H land safely—and then I was too busy with my own landing to see anything else.[19]

IAF Phantoms engaged and downed many MiGs in dogfights that broke out during the deep-strike raids, but they also suffered their share of losses to Egyptian fighters and ground defenses.

At dawn on October 14, the Egyptians made their long-awaited breakout from their defensive positions along the Suez Canal. Columns of Egyptian tanks attacked toward the Mitla and Giddi Passes, moved west along the Tasa road, and north into central Sinai. The attack was preceded by a massive artillery barrage and air strikes flown by dozens of Arab fighter-bombers. Algerian SU-7s and Libyan Mirages flown by Egyptian and Pakistani pilots participated in these strikes. North Korean pilots were also supporting the Arab effort by flying MiG-21 patrol missions over central Egypt.[20]

Israeli tanks engaged the advancing Egyptian columns from prepared, hull-down positions that gave them a considerable tactical advantage. The ensuing tank battle was the largest to be fought since World War II. Israeli tank fire, artillery, and dozens of air strikes repulsed the Egyptian attack. Over 220 Egyptian tanks and other armored vehicles were knocked out and 10 Arab aircraft shot down, while Israeli forces suffered only limited losses.

The IAF flew many sorties in support of Isareli ground forces and also staged dozens of attacks against Egyptian missile batteries and airfields. Captain N, the pilot who fought with Egyp-

tian MiGs over Sharm el Sheikh at the start of the war, participated in one of these missions:

> On October fourteenth I took part in an attack against
> Tanta [an Egyptian airfield], which was where the
> Mirages were operating from. My squadron leader led
> the attack and I brought up the rear. On our way in to
> bomb the air base we flew at low level and high speed.
> Over the Nile Delta a MiG-21 made a quarter pass at my
> aircraft with his cannon, but he didn't lead me enough
> and missed. I looked out and saw a MiG lined up with
> my wingman at 400 yards and firing—a great flame was
> jumping out from his cannon. I yelled for him to break
> right and he did. I cleaned up my plane by dumping my
> bombs and fuel tanks and broke with the MiG. I yelled
> to my wingman to turn so that I could fire my missile
> out at the MiG and he did. The Sidewinder guided to the
> right, I thought it was going for my wingman, but it
> came back and hit the MiG, blowing him up.
>
> After this I called my leader and he said that we
> should head for home. Now, I had no bombs or missiles
> left. Separate from my wingman, we headed northeast at
> high speed flying very low and passing out of Egypt over
> the Mediterranean.
>
> I was very low on fuel and I started to climb to save
> gas for the flight back. All of a sudden a missile flashed
> by! I looked back and saw a MiG-21. I went up and the
> MiG climbed with me and he came within 100 meters. I
> could see him clearly—he was wearing a leather flight
> helmet. We were so close I could see the instruments in
> his cockpit. I thought to myself, so this is how it will
> end—no missiles, almost no fuel, over the cold water and
> this guy seems to be good. Up we went. But I had one
> trick left. At 250 knots I engaged the afterburners and
> nosed over. He tried to follow me down but evidently
> lost control because he started spinning and flew right
> into the water with a big splash!
>
> I had made it but was now in real fuel trouble. I
> climbed to 35,000 feet, put one engine in idle, and got on
> the radio. I finally made it to El Arish, where I landed.

Just after I turned off the runway onto the taxiway the engines flamed out. What a mission![21]

On October 15, the United States publicly disclosed that it was supplying Israel with military assistance. Heavy losses and much greater than anticipated ammunition consumption prompted Israel to ask for support from the United States beginning on the second day of the conflict. The United States provided some vital supplies right away and these were transported to Israel on EL AL aircraft. Once the extent of the Soviet air-and-sea resupply effort and Israeli losses were learned, the United States initiated a massive operation. Some of the American aid was carried to Israel on U.S. Air Force C-141 and C-5 cargo aircraft, but additional material was organized for transport by ship. In addition to munitions, dozens of F-4 Phantom and A-4 Skyhawk fighter-bombers were flown directly to Israel. These aircraft were taken directly from U.S. Air Force, Navy, and Marine Corps squadrons and training units. A variety of advanced equipment was also provided to Israel including ECM systems and specialized laser, electro-optical guided weapons, Shrike antiradar missiles, and other high-technology munitions.[22]

On October 15, Egyptian forces again made a series of probing attacks into the Sinai, but the assault failed. The defeat of the Sinai offensive and the serious losses suffered by armored units forced Egypt to reconsider its tactics. This defeat reduced the Egyptian numerical superiority on the southern front and prompted Israel to begin its long-planned counteroffensive against Egyptian forces.

On October 15, the IAF flew hundreds of attack sorties against Egyptian battlefield and rear-area targets, while Israeli ground forces redeployed for a surprise attack. During the night, Israeli armor and infantry units forced their way to the Suez Canal at a point just north of Great Bitter Lake, which was the junction of the Egyptian 2nd and 3rd Armies. Tanks and other Israeli vehicles moved across the canal during the night and the troops established a bridgehead in Egyptian territory. Once across, Israeli forces fanned out and destroyed a number of SAM sites and defensive positions. These ground attacks opened a hole in the Egyptian air defense shield and allowed the IAF to operate with greater safety and effectiveness in the area. Egyptian commanders were initially unaware of the Israeli assault across the Suez Canal. They thought that the attacks on their positions in the central Sinai were an attempt to roll back their bridgehead. Egyptian units fought a fierce battle to push back the Israelis. On several occasions, strong Egyptian attacks closed the road to the Israeli crossing site. Israeli troops at the Suez Canal crossing site and on the west bank of the canal were surrounded. A determined assault by Israeli tanks and paratroopers reopened the road to the Israeli bridgehead.

Frantic calls for help from air defense sites and supply depots located in Egyptian territory alerted the Egyptian high command that Israeli forces had crossed the Suez Canal. Late on October 16, Egyptian forces began blasting the Israeli crossing site with artillery and air strikes. Israeli fighters hovered over the bridgehead and intercepted the Egyptian jets that came in to bomb the crossing site. The IAF downed ten Egyptian aircraft with its fighters and antiaircraft fire during one big battle on the afternoon of October 16. Egyptian tank attacks against the Israeli crossing site were also defeated. A pontoon bridge was established across the Suez Canal on the afternoon of October 17, and dozens of Israeli tanks poured into Egypt. While the bridgehead was still the focus of ground action, the IAF flew dozens of strike missions against missile batteries near Port Said, Qantara, Suez City, and several airfields.

Israeli forces pushed into Egypt; General Sharon's tanks moved north toward Ismailiya; General Adan's armor struck south toward the town of Suez. Taking advantage of the ever-expanding hole in the air defense screen, the Israeli jets pounded Egyptian forces near the Suez Canal, on the west bank of the canal, and flew nonstop fighter patrols to protect the advancing armor from Egyptian air strikes.

Optimism was high that this new offensive would turn the tide in favor of Israel and end the war. Defense Minister Moshe Dayan said, "I don't think this war is going to drag on." General Shlomo Gazit told reporters on October 18, that more than ten SAM batteries had been destroyed in the day's fighting and that Israeli planes were now, "completely free" to operate behind Egyptian lines in this sector. The general added that some missile batteries were captured intact and, "We have some things to bring back." He said, "Egyptian planes made repeated forays in the area and 25 were shot down."[23] Because of the destruction of its air defense shield, Egypt was forced to send in the air force to plug the gap and strike at Israeli ground forces. Egyptian MiG-21s engaged IAF Mirages in swirling dogfights over the Suez Canal while MiG-17, SU-7, and Mirage fighter-bombers flew in at low altitude to bomb, rocket, and strafe the bridges and advancing Israeli armor. Egypt sent in L-29 Delfin jet trainers and even Mi-8 helicopters to blast the Israelis. Barrels of napalm, rolled from the door of an Mi-8 transport helicopter, almost hit Defense Minister Moshe Dayan, who was visiting the Suez Canal crossing site. Israeli fighters and heavy ground fire took a heavy toll of the attacking Arab aircraft.

Thousands of additional Israeli troops and hundreds of tanks and other armored vehicles crossed the Suez Canal into Egypt on October 19 and 20 to support the invasion of Egypt. On October 20, there were in excess of ten thousand men and over three hundred tanks operating in Egyptian territory. This force was moving on a north–south axis, with the objective of cutting off the Egyptian 3rd Army. The ground offensive received considerable assistance from the IAF now that the Egyptian air defenses in the area had been neutralized. In addition, the IAF continued to hit rear-area targets and blast missile sites near the battle zone.

Egypt moved forces back from the Sinai to cut off any Israeli thrust toward Cairo and fought back with fierce determination. Scores of Arab aircraft struck at the crossing site and Israeli armor in the expanding bridgehead. Air action was intense and Israel authorities estimated that by October 20, over 110 Egyptian aircraft had been shot down.

Israeli forces had found a weakness, crossed the Suez Canal, and destroyed the air defenses and resupply units that supported the Egyptian invasion force in the Sinai. Airpower and armor, the most powerful Israeli military assets, could now be fully utilized in the battle against Egypt. Lt. Gen. David Elazar, Israeli chief of staff, commented to reporters, "The objective is to win the war and destroy the Egyptian armed forces."[24] Fearful that the gains of the early part of the war would be lost to the Israeli counteroffensive, Egypt began pressing for a cease-fire.

The Israeli offensive on the northern front had pushed the

Syrians off the Golan Heights and penetrated into Syria on the northern sector of the front. However, the Israeli assault into Syria had stalled just outside Sassa. The massive Soviet resupply effort strengthened the Arab armies, and counterattacks by Syrian, Iraqi, and Jordanian units halted the Israeli drive. Syrian artillery was especially active but Israeli forces returned the favor by using long-range 175-mm cannon to shell military targets in the suburbs of Damascus. On October 16 and 17, most of the IAF's sorties were flown on the southern front, but Israeli jets struck bridges in northern Syria, the Mount Hermon position, the Syrian Latakia naval base, and several battlefield targets. Syrian fighters contested these raids and conducted their own strikes against Israeli positions. Israeli fighters and anti-aircraft weapons claimed fifteen Arab aircraft on the northern front during the two days of heavy fighting.

On October 18, the IAF was fully committed to support the drive against Egyptian forces in the Sinai and did not see action on the Golan Heights. Several Israeli army units were withdrawn from the Syrian front and sent to the Sinai to support the invasion into Egypt. Syrian, Iraqi, and Jordanian forces staged a series of counterattacks on October 19 and 20, but Israeli units were well entrenched and the Arab attacks failed to gain any ground. Arab aircraft supported these attacks and four were reportedly shot down by Israeli fighters.

Realizing that a cease-fire was near, on October 21, the Israeli army made an all-out effort to recapture Mount Hermon. While IAF fighter-bombers made diversionary raids against targets near Damascus, CH-53 transport helicopters swept in and dropped Israeli paratroops near the summit. A column of Golani infantry and armor assaulted the hill from below, using the road that led up to the position. Both attacks stalled because of heavy Syrian fire, and Israeli units suffered many casualties. The Syrians flew in reinforcements but three of the Mi-8 transport helicopters were shot down by Israeli jets. Syrian fighters swept in to protect the helicopters and a big dogfight occurred, with both sides suffering losses. The Israeli ground assault continued throughout the night, and, by the morning of October 22, the outpost on the summit of Mount Hermon was in Israeli hands. On October 22, the IAF blasted Syrian armor that was attempting to move up to Mount Hermon, hit other battlefield targets, and fought several air battles with Syrian aircraft. Early on October 23, a major Israeli air strike hit a fuel storage depot northeast of Damascus. Two formations of fighters challenged the attackers, and nine Syrian jets were shot down by Israeli Mirages and Phantoms. A UN cease-fire came into effect on the evening of October 23, and the Yom Kippur War ended on the northern front.

In the Sinai, air and ground action continued with considerable intensity, and on October 20 and 21, Israeli forces captured hundreds of square miles of Egyptian territory. Air action was also heavy as IAF fighter-bombers blasted targets in the battle area. Israeli fighters achieved air superiority in the area of the Israeli invasion into Egypt, which enabled IAF transports to operate out of the captured air base at Fayid.

Early on October 22, the United Nations announced that a cease-fire would come into effect that evening. Prior to the cease-fire, Israeli forces made fierce attacks north toward Ismailiya and south near the town of Suez in an attempt to complete the encirclement of the Egyptian 3rd Army, which held positions in the Sinai running from the Gulf of Suez to Great Bitter Lake. During the day, over five hundred ground attack and patrol sorties were flown by the IAF in support of these Israeli attacks.

On October 18, the IAF initiated a five-day series of defense suppression raids that hit Egyptian missile sites all along the Suez Canal, from Port Said to the Gulf of Suez. Working in conjunction with ground forces, these efforts severely damaged the Egyptian air defense network. While Israeli army units hit SAM sites with artillery and tank fire, and captured many intact, the IAF plastered others with bombs and guided missiles. Shrike antiradar missiles were used with good effect, and the IAF also used recently introduced ECM systems to suppress surviving radar sites.

N. Merachavi, cited earlier in this chapter, participated in these raids:

On October twenty-second our squadron of F-4s had the mission to destroy six SA-2 and SA-3 missile sites near the town of Suez. It was a very smooth mission. We came in at close to 0.95 Mach with a full load of Mk 117

[750-pound] bombs with very good cover of ECM. We flew in at about 14,000 feet and after three or four minutes, all the sites were destroyed and none of us were hurt. . . . By the end of the war we had many calm and comfortable missions, the way you thought they should go. I think that we learned what to do and how to do it. If you look, you can get the impression that the air-to-air mission was the glory of this war, but I don't think so. Most of the real dirty work was done by the attackers, who mostly did a good job.[25]

The October 22 cease-fire broke down almost immediately as both Israeli and Egyptian forces continued to trade artillery fire. At dawn, Israeli units continued their attacks and by late on October 23, the Egyptian 3rd Army's supply line had been cut. Early on October 24, Israeli armored columns moved into the town of Suez in an attempt to capture it before a second cease-fire took effect. Egyptian commandos ambushed the Israeli columns and heavy fighting continued until well after sundown. Israeli forces were forced to pull out of Suez after suffering serious losses.

The IAF maintained a heavy pace of operations on the Sinai front during the last two days of fighting: Over six hundred sorties were flown, more than twenty Egyptian aircraft were shot down, and tons of supplies were moved to the west bank of the canal to support the ground offensive. Late on October 24, a second cease-fire ended the fighting between Israel and Egypt, and the Yom Kippur War came to an end.

After suffering heavy casualties due to the surprise Arab attack on two fronts, Israeli ground, naval, and air forces pushed back the Syrians and outflanked the Egyptians. In the course of nineteen days of fighting, Israel suffered 2,812 killed, and over 7,500 wounded, and lost 103 aircraft, 6 helicopters, 1 naval vessel, and more than 400 tanks and 500 other armored vehicles. Arab casualties totaled more than 8,000 killed and 19,000 wounded, and equipment losses included some 2,000 tanks, 1,000 other armored vehicles, 500 artillery pieces, 392 aircraft, 55 helicopters, and 15 naval vessels.[26]

The cease-fire of October 24 ended the fighting, but for some time Egypt, Syria, and Israel continued to maintain the positions they had captured during the conflict. Israeli troops held the Golan Heights and a sizable segment of Syrian and Egyptian territory. Egyptian forces were in possession of a large segment of the Sinai along the Suez Canal.

Skirmishes and air attacks continued on the southern front for some time after the cease-fire agreement. On December 6, an air battle occurred near the Suez Canal that resulted in the loss of an Egyptian MiG-21. It was not until January 18, 1974, that Israel and Egypt agreed upon terms to pull their respective armies back to prewar positions.

Disengagement on the northern front took even longer. Artillery fire and sniping continued along the cease-fire line, but on January 26, Syria intensified its shelling. Syrian authorities admitted that it was conducting a war of attrition to force Israel to continue its costly mobilization. United States Secretary of State Henry Kissinger established a dialogue between Israel and Syria in February 1974 in order to bring about a lasting peace. His efforts began to make progress but on April 13, 1974, Syrian forces attempted to capture the Israeli outpost on Mount Hermon. Heavy fighting continued daily into May and the air forces of both sides became involved. Kissinger's diplomatic efforts finally bore fruit on May 31, when a peace treaty was signed. Both Syria and Israel had suffered heavy casualties and lost many tanks, aircraft, and other weapons during eighty-one days of continuous fighting in the spring of 1974.

In order to review the activities of the IAF during the 1973 war, it is important to first identify the missions of the force: (1) to protect Israeli airspace, (2) to achieve air superiority over the battle zone, (3) to support ground and sea operations, (4) to fulfill IDF transportation, reconnaissance, communications, and intelligence needs.

The IAF clearly achieved its first mission, the defense of Israeli airspace. However, it can be added that the Arab air forces made only a few attempts to strike targets in Israel. Egyptian fighter-bombers hit targets in the eastern Sinai, while several Syrian strikes attempted to hit the oil refinery near Haifa. Israeli fighters intercepted and turned back most of these raids. The IAF was unable to intercept or interfere with the Syrian surface-to-surface missile attacks using FROG-7s, which caused minor damage to Ramat David air base and several surrounding civil-

ian settlements. IAF fighter-bombers blasted oil storage tanks at
the Homs refinery, hit electrical power plants, and struck other
targets in Syria in response to these missile attacks.

In the 1967 war, Israel had achieved air superiority by destroying enemy aircraft on the ground. During the War of Attrition, the IAF shot down or drove off many of the Arab jets that
penetrated into the Sinai or Golan Heights to interfere with
Israeli operations. The IAF used fighters, strike aircraft, and air
defense weapons to fight the air superiority battle during the
1973 war. The IAF aircraft capable of performing this air superiority role included about 75 Mirage/Nesher and 120 F-4E Phantom II fighters. Israeli air defense systems included ten Hawk
missile batteries and several hundred 20- and 40-mm antiaircraft guns.[27] Toward the end of the war, Israel received several Chapparal air defense systems from the United States. Hawk
batteries were positioned in hardened sites in the Sinai, on the
Golan Heights, and in Israeli territory in order to defend Israeli
positions. Antiaircraft guns were used to protect airfields, Hawk
sites, and ground forces. Israeli jets and antiaircraft weapons
fought hundreds of engagements and shot down more than three
hundred Arab aircraft. Since Arab fighter-bombers generally
employed high-speed, low-level attack profiles, many penetrated into the battle area and were able to hit Israeli frontline
units and defensive positions. IAF fighters were able to achieve a
high degree of air superiority over Israeli airspace and the areas
near the front lines. But the Arab air defense screen prevented
Israel from securing air superiority over the entire battle zone,
as had been achieved during the latter part of the 1967 war.

Israeli aircraft flew 3,961 top-cover, escort, air defense, and
reconnaissance missions during the 1973 conflict. Fighter aircraft were involved in 117 air engagements (65 on the Syrian
front and 52 on the southern front), which included over 450
aircraft. The IAF has stated that its pilots downed 334 Arab
aircraft for the loss of only 3 Israeli planes.[28] Other sources list
277 Israeli air combat victories during the 1973 conflict.[29] Air
combat usually took place over Arab territory following strike
operations, or else over the battle area. The most common sce-
nario involved groups of two or four Israeli fighters in engagements with four or more Arab aircraft near the battlefield. The
Mirage/Nesher fighters, which carried two Shafrir infrared-

homing air-to-air missiles and their 30-mm cannons, accounted for about two-thirds of the Israeli air combat victories. F-4 Phantom aircraft were used mostly in the ground attack role, but they also performed hundreds of patrol and intercept missions. Phantoms struck many rear-area targets such as airfields, oil storage facilities, and other strategic positions that were protected by Arab fighters. After delivering their bombs, Phantom crews frequently took on Arab fighters, attacking them with Sidewinder and Sparrow missiles or 20-mm cannons. One-third of the Israeli air combat victories were claimed by Phantom crews. About two-thirds of the Israeli air combat victories were achieved with air-to-air missiles, most of which were infrared-guided air-to-air missiles, but ten planes were shot down with Sparrow radar-homing missiles. The remaining one-third of the kills were made with cannon fire.[30]

While the IAF claims that only three of its aircraft were lost in air combat, some officers admitted that many of the Israeli aircraft losses placed in the unknown category probably were downed by Arab fighters. Some sources list twenty-one IAF air combat losses while the USAF estimated Israeli air-to-air casualties at 10 percent of the total. If the USAF estimate of eleven air combat losses is accurate, Israeli pilots achieved a kill/loss ratio of about 25 to 1. Even if the IAF had lost twenty-one jets to Arab fighters, the Israeli exchange ratio would be 13 to 1. By way of contrast, during the Korean War, U.S. F-86 Sabre jet pilots achieved a 6-to-1 kill ratio against the MiG-15. In Vietnam combat, the overall U.S. kill/loss ratio was less than 3 to 1 in favor of U.S. pilots. In the heat of battle Israeli forces accidently shot down two of their own aircraft. Since Arab air forces were flying Mirage aircraft, it is easy to understand how this could occur.

The IAF's antiaircraft weapons played an important part in the 1973 war. Even after mobilization, the Israeli inventory of air defense weapons totaled less than 10 percent of those in service with Egyptian and Syrian forces. These systems destroyed, damaged, or degraded the effectiveness of Arab aircraft that had evaded IAF fighters or penetrated below-radar surveillance coverage. During the 1973 war, Israeli Hawk and Chapparal missiles shot down thirteen Arab planes, while antiaircraft guns and small-arms fire downed thirty aircraft.[31]

Israeli fighters and air defense weapons engaged many of the attackers and took a heavy toll of Arab aircraft. However, Egyptian, Syrian, Iraqi, and Libyan aircraft did penetrate the defenses on many occasions, causing casualties and damage to Israeli forces.

During the conflict, IAF fixed-wing aircraft flew a total of 11,233 sorties, some 60 percent of which (7,272) were ground attack missions. The IAF flew 1,830 attack missions on the Syrian front and 5,442 strike sorties against the Egyptians.[32] For the first few days of the war, IAF fighter-bombers had to ignore enemy air defenses and concentrate on pounding the advancing Arab columns in order to assist the hard-pressed Israeli ground forces. During the October 6–9 period, more than fifty IAF aircraft were shot down by the Arab air defenses. Pilots of A-4

## Israeli Air Force
## October 1973 War
## Daily Loss Summary

| | | | Daily Sorties | | |
|---|---|---|---|---|---|
| Day | Date | A/C Lost | Egypt | Syria | Remarks |
| 1 | Oct 6 | 6 | 197 | 25 | Yom Kippur |
| 2 | 7 | 22 | 241 | 247 | |
| 3 | 8 | 9 | 434 | 188 | |
| 4 | 9 | 17 | 442 | 168 | |
| 5 | 10 | 3 | 296 | 230 | |
| 6 | 11 | 10 | 69 | 353 | |
| 7 | 12 | 5 | 172 | 197 | |
| 8 | 13 | 6 | 96 | 133 | |
| 9 | 14 | 2 | 229 | 48 | Second Egyptian offensive |
| 10 | 15 | 3 | 246 | 62 | |
| 11 | 16 | 2 | 283 | 30 | Sharon's counterattack |
| 12 | 17 | 5 | 213 | 18 | |
| 13 | 18 | 6 | 263 | 0 | |
| 14 | 19 | 0 | 375 | 2 | Fayid air base falls |
| 15 | 20 | 3 | 376 | 4 | |
| 16 | 21 | 3 | 327 | 55 | |
| 17 | 22 | 0 | 532 | 24 | |
| 18 | 23 | 0 | 354 | 42 | |
| 19 | 24 | 0 | 315 | 4 | Cease-fire |

Used with permission from John F. Kreis, *Air Warfare and Air Base Defense 1914–1973* (Washington, DC:, Special Studies, Office of Air Force History, USAF, 1988) 338.

Skyhawk and Super Mystere aircraft performed most of these dangerous missions. During the war, sixty aircraft were downed while flying ground support missions—thirty-three of these were lost on the Egyptian front and twenty-seven over the Golan Heights. IAF casualties were heavy—thirty-one aircrew were killed, fourteen were captured, and many other Israeli pilots and navigators suffered injuries.[33]

The IAF fighter-bombers delivered the full range of conventional air-to-ground munitions: high-explosive bombs, cluster bombs, and rockets. These weapons were delivered using low-level-attack, loft, or dive techniques. The U.S. resupply effort enabled the IAF to use large numbers of guided weapons, including guided bombs plus Shrike and Maverick missiles.

In attacks near the battlefield, IAF strike aircraft damaged or destroyed hundreds of Arab vehicles, positions, and fortifications. While hundreds of sorties were flown against Egyptian and Syrian airfields, these raids only destroyed twenty-two aircraft, because most planes were housed in protective shelters, but many bases suffered heavy damage to runways and facilities. The IAF also conducted a successful series of strategic attacks against Syrian command centers, fuel and oil storage sites, electrical power plants, and harbor facilities.

Arab SA-2, SA-3, and SA-6 batteries fired several thousand missiles at Israeli planes and shot down forty-one of them. Antiaircraft fire was responsible for the destruction of thirty-one Israeli planes while three were lost to both SAM and antiaircraft fire. Shoulder-launched SA-7 missiles hit and damaged many aircraft, but only three fell to this weapon; a further three were lost to a combination of SA-7 and antiaircraft fire.[34] The Arab air defenses reportedly shot down fifty-eight of their own aircraft, because many Arab jets did not have an IFF system, a system to identify friend from foe. Missile and gun crews also tended to shoot first and ask questions later. Israeli losses during the 1973 war included thirty-three F-4 Phantoms, fifty-three A-4 Skyhawks, eleven Mirage/Nesher aircraft, six Super Mysteres, and six helicopters.[35] Several other aircraft were lost in action during the fighting that continued on the Syrian front well into 1974.

A total of 236 IAF aircraft suffered damage during the war, and 215 of these were repaired and placed back into service

within one week.[36] These statistics call attention to the maintenance personnel of the IAF who, with the assistance of workers
from Israeli companies, were able to repair hundreds of battle-
damaged aircraft rapidly. Munitions handlers and personnel
who conducted routine maintenance and resupply also deserve
credit for their tireless efforts.

The helicopter and transport aircraft of the IAF flew thousands of sorties in support of Israeli operations. Helicopters
conducted rescue, medical-evacuation, scout, assault, reconnaissance, and liaison missions near and beyond the front lines.
Transport aircraft moved men and vital supplies to the front
and even operated from captured airfields on the west bank of
the Suez Canal.

Although the Arab air forces (Egyptian, Syrian, Iraqi, Algerian, and Libyan) had a numerical advantage at the start of the
war, they flew fewer sorties than the IAF. Together, the Arab air
units flew about 10,000 sorties during the conflict: about 7,000
were flown on the Egyptian front and 3,000 from Syrian bases.
Over 60 percent of this total were fighter patrol and air defense
missions, with the remainder attack and reconnaissance sorties.
Total Arab losses were estimated to be: EAF, 225 aircraft and 42
helicopters; Syrian Air Force, 121 aircraft and 13 helicopters;
Iraqi Air Force, 21 aircraft; while Algeria and Libya lost about
30 aircraft.[37]

Following the 1973 war many theorists declared that the Arab
air defenses had caused such heavy losses that the fighter-
bomber was obsolete. The IAF did suffer heavy losses during the
first few days of the conflict, when pilots braved enemy fire to
blunt the Arab attacks in the Sinai and on the Golan Heights.
However, the total Israeli loss rate dropped significantly as the
war progressed, because of the use of better tactics, widespread
use of ECM, and effects of the ground offensive. During the
conflict more than 550 Arab and Israeli aircraft were lost to all
causes. Ground-based air defense weapons were responsible for
the destruction of about 200 aircraft and helicopters. However,
nearly 350 were shot down by other aircraft in air combat—the
IAF was the victor in the vast majority of these engagements.
After the conflict, the IAF set its sights on overcoming the challenge of surface-to-air missile and gun systems.

# 8

# *Unending Conflict*

$\mathcal{F}$ollowing the 1973 conflict, there was no sense of celebration in Israel even though the country's army, navy, and air force had halted the Arab assault and defeated their combined adversaries on the battlefield. The surprise attack, bitter fighting, and heavy losses had shattered public confidence. After the war the Israeli government and military forces went through a period of recrimination and self-examination. The Israeli government appointed a committee, headed by Shimon Agronat, president of the Supreme Court, to examine the events leading up to the war and the political and military decisions made during the conflict.

The Agronat Report's conclusions and recommendations were classified as secret. However, the little information released revealed that the committee identified a number of errors and incorrect assumptions made by the intelligence branch and senior military and civilian leadership. Overconfidence concerning the ability of the regular army and air force to blunt a massive Arab assault delayed the call for mobilization and contributed to the early Israeli setbacks. The Arab armies staged a coordinated surprise attack, took advantage of their numerical superiority, and employed oil embargos and other political and economic leverage against countries that provided assistance to Israel.

After the Yom Kippur War, Israelis were forced to accept the facts that their military forces were not invincible and that many changes had to be made to ensure future security. These security investments included the expansion and reorganization of Israel's armed forces and negotiation, which led to a peace treaty with Egypt. Despite these changes, Israeli forces were soon involved in continuing conflict with terrorists along the Israel/Lebanon border.

The Israeli military leadership examined the lessons of the

1973 war and debated the future role of the army, air force, and navy. Military systems, such as aircraft, tanks, and ships, had proved to be very vulnerable to missiles, rockets, artillery, and other modern weapons. The high loss rate experienced in the 1973 war forced the Israelis to increase the number of weapons and combat units and to maintain larger stockpiles of hardware and ammunition. To rearm rapidly, Israel bought many new aircraft, tanks, missiles, and advanced systems from the United States. However, Israel also instituted a long-term program to encourage domestic industries to produce equipment, supplies, and ammunition, and thereby reduce the country's dependence on foreign sources. Israel's intelligence organization was reorganized and surveillance capabilities upgraded to prevent military surprises.

During the 1970s, the army and air force were expanded and new tactical doctrines tested. The new Israeli blitzkrieg tactics called for combat forces to operate as an integrated team: fighter aircraft, helicopters, tanks, armored personnel carriers, mobile artillery, and airborne forces would work together to overcome the enemy and achieve victory with reduced losses.

Maj. Gen. Benjamin Peled commanded the IAF during the 1973 war and continued to serve in this capacity for several years after the conflict. He strengthened the air arm and revised its missions and tactics to reflect the new Israeli combat doctrine. Following the war, General Peled acknowledged that aircraft losses in 1973 were two and one-half times the number suffered in the 1967 conflict. Peled pointed out that the Yom Kippur War lasted three times as long as the earlier conflict. He added that, even though enemy defenses were more formidable in 1973, Israeli pilots flew more missions per aircraft lost than in 1967. At the International Symposium on Military Aspects of the Arab–Israeli Conflict, which was held in Jerusalem in 1975, General Peled identified a number of lessons learned from the Yom Kippur War. He cited the need for rapid intelligence collection and dissemination, improved communications, better army and air force command and control, and better weapons. But people, he said, remain the dominant component of air warfare. "Psychological factors, skill, motivation, and pilot training are more important than any material consideration," he added. He listed air force mission priorities as (1) air superiority, (2) strategic, (3) deep interdiction, and (4) close support. Peled stated, "World War II–type close air support is not possible in a modern real war," and added that it is a waste of airpower to assist ground forces in accomplishing what they should be able to achieve on their own.[1]

In the years following the 1973 war, the Israeli army purchased hundreds of additional self-propelled guns, surface-to-surface rockets, and other advanced artillery systems. To increase army firepower, Israel deployed large numbers of multiple-rocket launchers. Although not as accurate or long-ranging as cannon, a barrage from only one multiple-rocket launcher equals the firepower of a battery of guns or of an air strike.

The Israeli army also purchased dozens of U.S.-built Lance surface-to-surface missiles. This 50-mile-range missile is armed with a warhead that contains 836 grenade-like bomblets. It can blast an area more than a quarter of a mile in diameter and is ideal for suppressing enemy surface-to-air missile sites.

The shock of combat had produced a tough, experienced air force. By the end of 1973, U.S. resupply efforts had nearly restored the air force's numerical strength to its prewar level. However, the Phantoms, Skyhawks, transports, helicopters, and other aircraft delivered to Israel were quite different from those in service. Air force and Israeli industry personnel worked at a feverish pace to repair battle-damaged aircraft and reconfigure newly supplied planes with common systems, radios, and other equipment. Major modification programs upgraded the navigation, attack, and ECM systems of Israeli combat aircraft. Israeli Skyhawk jets were fitted with a tail cone extension to minimize their infrared signature and reduce their vulnerability to the SA-7 shoulder-fired antiaircraft missile.

The IAF purchased large numbers of guided missiles, smart bombs, and advanced weapons in order to increase the ability of Israeli pilots to destroy point targets. Aircraft, weapon, and ECM upgrades and the use of modified tactics enabled IAF aircrews to reduce their exposure to enemy defenses and still perform their missions effectively. It took several years for the IAF to make up for the aircrew losses suffered during the Yom Kippur conflict. Intensified training programs replaced aircrew losses and created a larger pool of pilots, navigators, and aircrews. Performance standards were raised to ensure that IAF aircrews maintained combat capability.

The air force ordered additional A-4N Skyhawk and F-4E Phantom aircraft from the United States and increased the production rate of jets made in Israel. On April 14, 1975, the IAF received its first Israeli-built Kfir fighter. Produced by Israel Aircraft Industries, the new fighter-bomber integrated the General Electric J79 engine that powers the Phantom, an upgraded Mirage/Nesher airframe, and electronics and systems developed in Israel. This program demonstrated the Israeli resolve to produce high-technology weapons domestically in order to ensure a source of supply in times of tension. The supersonic Kfir fighter, which could perform both fighter and attack missions, first entered service with the IAF's premier fighter squadron in 1975 and subsequently replaced Skyhawks in other units.[2]

The air superiority capability of the IAF was significantly improved by the introduction of F-15 Eagles, the first of which arrived in Israel on October 10, 1976. Israel was the first foreign country to receive this new fighter. The premier air superiority fighter of the USAF, the supersonic F-15 featured a pulse Doppler radar capable of detecting low-flying aircraft and an armament of eight air-to-air missiles and a 20-mm cannon. In late 1977, Israel announced it had ordered seventy-five F-16 Fighting Falcon jets to replace aging Skyhawks. The F-16 could perform both fighter and ground attack missions.

While the IAF reduced its responsibility in the close support role following the Yom Kippur War, the air arm's commitment to assist the Israeli ground forces remained a high priority. New tactics called for Phantom, Skyhawk, and Kfir fighter-bombers to concentrate on the interdiction mission. These attacks hit targets behind the front lines with the goal of slowing the advance of enemy reinforcements. If enemy air defenses could be suppressed, Israeli fighter-bombers could blast targets near the front lines.

In 1974, the IAF purchased six AH-1 Cobra missile-armed attack helicopters to test new concepts for their use as a reaction force to support army units in repelling an unexpected attack. Following successful trials, the IAF ordered thirty more AH-1 Cobras and thirty 500M Defender helicopters armed with TOW antitank missiles.

Calls from the army for vertical-lift support during the Yom Kippur War underscored the need for an enlarged helicopter force. Following the 1973 conflict, Israel upgraded its fleet of Super Frelon transport helicopters through the addition of more powerful and reliable U.S.-built turbine engines and other improvements. In addition, older Bell 205 helicopters were sold and replaced by more capable Bell 212 utility transports. The IAF also bought additional Bell 206 scout helicopters and heavy-lift Sikorsky CH-53s.

During the 1973 war, the USAF gave Israel twelve C-130E Hercules transport planes. Following the conflict, the lift capacity of the IAF was expanded considerably by the Israeli purchase of an additional ten C-130H Hercules aircraft. Two of these aircraft were fitted with aerial refueling systems to extend the strike range of Israeli Phantoms and Skyhawks.

The IAF air defense force was also strengthened following the 1973 war. The Hawk surface-to-air missile was replaced by the much more advanced Improved Hawk Systems. Air defense units received mobile Chapparal missiles, Vulcan 20-mm guns, and Russian-built 23-mm cannons that had been captured from Arab forces. Modern air defense radars, command and control systems, and shoulder-fired Redeye missiles also improved the capability of Israeli forces to protect themselves against air attack.

Coordination between the air force and army was increased during the 1970s. Through closer communications, the leaders of Israeli air and ground forces developed a better appreciation of each others' strengths and weaknesses and a better awareness of how best to conduct combined operations. Organizational changes and streamlined command and control procedures improved the flow of intelligence information between the air and ground services. Tactical air control parties were assigned to army division headquarters and forward air control groups were located at brigade headquarters to coordinate fighter, helicopter, transport, and air defense activities.

Israel learned in 1973 that wars are won or lost on the basis of available information. During the late 1970s, the intelligence collection and dissemination capabilities of Israeli ground and air forces were improved. New intelligence collection platforms such as the E-2C Hawkeye radar early warning aircraft, OV-ID

Mohawk reconnaissance plane, and a variety of unmanned, remotely-piloted vehicles entered service. These new systems were used to monitor Arab military activities. Israeli military leaders vowed that they would not be surprised again.

Once Israel's defense against Syria and Egypt had been strengthened, combating terrorism became the prime security focus of the Israel Defense Forces. After Syria, Jordan, and Egypt had suppressed the PLO and other Palestinian groups, members of these organizations began to operate primarily from Lebanon. Well-funded terrorist organizations attracted a considerable following and expanded their power and influence in Lebanon at the expense of the central government and the Maronite Christian community. During 1974, terrorist groups stepped up their activities. Terrorists massacred several families in Galilee in April, killed dozens of children at a school in Maalot in May, and exploded bombs at theaters and public places throughout the year. In 1975, guerrillas began regularly to fire rockets at Israeli communities along the Lebanese border. In March 1975, the seaside Savoy Hotel in Tel Aviv was captured by PLO terrorists who came ashore in rubber boats. In retaliation for these raids and international terrorist attacks, Israeli forces strengthened their patrols along the border and began striking back. Israeli jets blasted known guerrilla bases in southern Lebanon and many terrorist camps were assaulted by helicopter-borne commandos.

The Lebanese civil war, which broke out in early 1975, pitted the Muslims and the various guerrilla groups against the ruling Christian community. This conflict disrupted the central government, destroying much of Beirut and killing more than sixty thousand people. While the attention of the PLO and other groups was focused internally on Lebanon, terrorism against Israel was reduced. In June 1976, Syrian forces moved into Lebanon, changing the balance of power there. In response to the civil war and Syrian intervention, Israel began to supply Christian armies in southern Lebanon with weapons, training, and support.

A dramatic hijacking triggered the first Israeli anti-terrorist operation to be conducted outside the Middle East. IAF C-130 Hercules and a Boeing 707 transport aircraft played a major role in this mission. On June 27, 1976, four gunmen, two from the German Baader-Meinhof gang and two from the Popular Front for the Liberation of Palestine, hijacked Air France flight 139, which was flying from Tel Aviv to Paris via Athens. After the takeover, the crew of 12 and the 246 passengers flew to Benghazi, Libya, for refueling and then on to Entebbe airport in Uganda. The hijackers took the passengers and crew off the plane and held them in the airport terminal with the blessing of Ugandan leader Idi Amin Dada. Non-Jewish hostages were released, but the 105 Israeli and Jewish passengers were threatened with death unless 53 prisoners held by Israel, Switzerland, France, Kenya, and West Germany were released.

The Israeli government refused to give in, but agreed to negotiate to buy time and gather information on the unfolding events. At the same time, Israeli military leaders began planning a rescue operation. Maj. Gen. Benjamin Peled, air force commander, directed logistics and Brig. Gen. Dan Shamron, chief paratroop and infantry officer, conceived the rescue plans in concert with many other senior Israeli officers.

Operation Thunderball, a daring rescue operation, involved an elite group of Israeli paratroops and commandos. Led by Lt. Col. Yonni Netanyahu, these troops repeatedly rehearsed the actual rescue operation.

Brig. Gen. (Ret.) Joshua Shani was the commander of the IAF's C-130 squadron in 1976. He was involved in planning logistics for the operation and flew the lead aircraft on the rescue mission. Shani recalled:

We started to do some planning on the first day, without anyone even approaching us, because, looking at the map, we knew that the only aircraft that could fly to Uganda and do the mission was the C-130. Although no one dreamed that we would conduct a military operation, my deputies and I studied the maps to see the distance, guess at payload, fuel requirements, navigation problems, and other needs. We did this to save time in case we were approached—then we would already have some answers.

The hijacking took place on Sunday, June 27, 1976, and we started our planning on Monday. On Tuesday evening, we were officially asked by air force

headquarters to come and give some answers about our
capabilities. I was at a wedding in Haifa, and it was
very unusual to get a telephone call like that. I went to
the headquarters from the wedding and we started to
work on our plan. First we talked among ourselves, air
force guys, then we met and coordinated with the army
and we came up with a plan which we never executed—
it was a bad plan. This plan was to drop paratroopers
from two C-130s into Lake Victoria in the middle of the
night. These troops would get into rubber boats and
sneak in very quietly up to the airport and storm the
terminal and free the hostages in Uganda, then tell Idi
Amin, "Everyone is free, no terrorists, now let us go."

We didn't trust Idi Amin. We also knew that we might
have to fight his troops, plus the drop into Lake Victoria
was dangerous enough, and then we found out it was
filled with crocodiles. Technically it was difficult to fly
the C-130 round-trip. We went through two full
rehearsals of this first mission. One was successful and
the other not very good.

Eventually we came to our senses and just made it
simple. To land was the only way to do the mission. We
and the army people came to the same conclusion at the
same time. After the second failed rehearsal, we met and
agreed to take three airplanes, to land on the main
runway, and do the job. Later we decided we needed
four planes. Of course, what we wanted to do was land
only one aircraft in the first ten minutes—maximum
surprise, minimum noise. Only after we got rid of the
terrorists would the other three C-130s come in.

We made one-and-a-half rehearsals for the actual
operation. One was a demonstration that I made for the
chief of staff of the army, General Gur, the chief of staff
of the air force, General Peled, and chief of operations of
the air force, Colonel Ben-Nun, now air force chief of
staff, on how I could land on a runway without lights.
They wanted to see it with their own eyes. We came in
at night and landed at Sharm el Sheikh. It wasn't
perfect but good enough. We knew that at Entebbe it

would be easier because there was more contrast between the water and the runway than at Sharm el Sheikh. That same night we did a full rehearsal with four airplanes, the special forces, the black Mercedes, Landrover jeeps, and even a building like the terminal. The minister of defense and lots of officials watched the rehearsal and it was very successful.

Early the next morning, Saturday [July 3, 1976], we held a big briefing at my squadron with all the forces involved. At this big show business briefing, we used big maps. The *real* briefing came later when we sat with the troops and crews and talked details. There was no way to cover everything with less than two days of planning and rehearsal. So we left lots of things for improvisation and common sense.

We took off at early afternoon using five airplanes—one was a spare. We landed at Sharm el Sheikh so that we could take off from the most southern airport and have more fuel to maneuver. We didn't have fuel for the round-trip. We planned to refuel either at Entebbe or Nairobi, Kenya, on the way back. We waited for the government to make a decision about when to execute the mission. We had to take off, to keep our time schedule, and if the government decided to cancel, they were to call us on the radio and say to come back. We took off at a temperature of 105 degrees Fahrenheit at over 180,000 pounds, which was more than 10,000 pounds heavier than the wartime maximum takeoff weight of the C-130. Maximum power, brakes off, taxi, and the aircraft did not accelerate, but there was no force in the world that could make us abort this mission. We prayed for every knot and took off just a few knots above stall speed. It was very difficult even to make the turn toward our course. We were a formation of four flying south in the middle of the Red Sea in full radio silence, one after the other. I didn't know if they were still behind me since I couldn't use the radio. Maybe number four hit the water because we flew just a few feet above the water to avoid radar detection by the

Saudi and Egyptian radars. The other pilots understood
the problem and, from time to time, they overtook me,
showed themselves, and then went back to their position.
We flew this way until Ethiopia. Then we climbed to
20,000 feet into the darkness. We flew in a loose
formation and used the radar to see each other and
avoid huge thunderstorms which were along the way.

We continued until the border of Kenya and Uganda
and then began to look for a bay which showed up well
on radar. It was here that we planned to have the three
airplanes hold for seven minutes while my plane
continued on. Unfortunately, over the bay, which was
our final navigation point, there was a huge African
thunderstorm with rain up to 50,000 feet or so. We had
to penetrate it in formation and it was hell inside—hail,
lots of lighting, noise, and wind. I just crossed it in five
minutes or so, but the other planes stayed in a holding
pattern in this terrible storm. This was one of the most
difficult parts of the mission. Remember, we were
overloaded, people and vehicles weren't strapped down.
It wasn't very pleasant.

I left them and pressed on. I saw the runway from
maybe twenty miles, light rain, overcast, but quite good
visibility below the clouds. I landed, of course,
completely dark, no external lights. I stopped the plane
in the middle of the runway and the doors were opened.
A few soldiers jumped from both side doors with
portable runway lights to mark the way for the other
three airplanes. We knew that once the shooting started,
the lights would go off. The job of these troops was to
take the control tower. I continued toward where the
hostages were and stopped. The other troops came out
with the Mercedes and the two Landrovers. They drove
to the terminal and ran in shouting in Hebrew and
English, "Everyone lie on the floor," and after a short bit
of fighting, all the terrorists were dead. Two of the
hostages were wounded also in the crossfire.

The other three aircraft came in to land and I
stayed on the side waiting, watching, in constant
communication. Then I heard that Yoni, commander of

the special forces, was hit outside of the terminal after the rescue. He was hit by a Ugandian soldier who was up in the old tower with a machine gun.

Number two landed without any problem; but when number three was just over the threshold, the Ugandians switched off the lights. He found that there was no runway beneath him so he flew on and made a hard landing on another runway about a mile ahead. Number four landed on the short runway with our portable lights. Then we were all on the ground, the terrorists were dead, and the Ugandians were shooting with tracers, not well aimed but a dangerous situation. We were trying to get some fuel from the tanks using an adapter we had brought with us to connect with their lines. The operation was successful, the hostages ready to go, the soldiers began to withdraw and return to the planes. Since the refueling process would take about an hour and the Ugandians were shooting in the area, we decided not to refuel and take any unnecessary risks. We taxied out onto the runway and one by one took off, heading toward Nairobi.

Before takeoff, the troops from my airplane shot up the Ugandian MiGs that were parked not far from the old terminal because there was a theoretical chance that they could chase us. We all knew that it was only a small possibility because they were MiG-17 day fighters and their level of training in night interception was low, but we took no chances. Anyway, Idi Amin was an S.O.B. and we hated MiGs as you know, so we eliminated them.

We taxied out onto the runway and one by one took off toward Nairobi. They let us land, the four of us. We got fuel and being on the ground was the first time we had time to go and see the hostages, which was a very emotional moment. It was a thing you remember forever, of course—some of them were shocked, some hysterical, laughter, none of them wanted to leave the airplane. They said we'll stay here until you bring us to Tel Aviv. The troops had their first chance to relax also. Eventually we got our fuel and took off for an eight-hour flight to Tel Aviv. About four hours before we landed, everyone in our country knew of the rescue because it was officially announced. Halfway up the Red Sea, we got an escort of F-4 Phantoms. It was a good feeling. And then landing, a short briefing, parties, and behaving wild. It was a great evening, but I didn't remember much because I hadn't slept well for six days.[3]

During the civil war in Lebanon, a sizable PLO force moved south to escape Christian and Syrian forces that were entrenched around Beirut. PLO units routinely clashed with Christian, Druze, and Shiite Muslim forces in southern Lebanon. Israel armed the Christian and Druze armies that contested the PLO infiltration.

In late 1977, Israel began to attack PLO positions with aircraft, artillery, ships, and ground troops to drive them away from the border area. Following a PLO rocket attack against Nahariya that killed three civilians in November, the IAF went into action. Israeli Phantom, Skyhawk, and—for the first time—Kfir fighter-bombers plastered over a dozen suspected PLO positions in southern Lebanon. This heavy series of retaliatory raids destroyed many PLO bases, but also caused numerous civilian casualties and generated an international public outcry.

In a bold move, in November 1977, Egyptian President Sadat called for a peace conference between Egypt and Israel. Prime Minister Begin welcomed the overture and invited Sadat to Israel. President Sadat traveled to Jerusalem and met with Prime Minister Begin and addressed the Israeli parliament. This set the stage for a peace initiative that after thirty years of hostility, ultimately led to an Egyptian/Israeli peace treaty.

David Ivry replaced Benjamin Peled as commander of the IAF in 1977. A quiet, cool fighter pilot, Lieutenant General Ivry inherited a force that had recovered from the 1973 conflict and was in the process of introducing a wide variety of advanced weaponry. The new air force commander soon had an opportunity to test many of these new systems in the skies over Lebanon.

The Egyptian/Israeli peace plan angered the PLO and the leaders of other Arab states, because Syrian and Jordanian territory captured in the 1967 war was still in Israeli hands and the

Palestinian question was still unresolved. As a result, terrorist attacks against Israel dramatically increased and Syria boosted its troop strength in Lebanon to more than thirty thousand. On March 11, 1978, a PLO terrorist team came ashore on the Israeli coast and captured a bus on the Tel Aviv–Haifa highway. Israeli forces assaulted the bus and killed the terrorists, but thirty-four civilians, including many women and children, were killed in the process. In response to this attack Israel launched Operation Latani. More than twenty-five thousand Israeli troops, supported by armor, artillery, and air strikes, assaulted Lebanon on March 15, 1978, with the goal of destroying PLO bases and driving out the terrorists. Israeli armored columns quickly moved north beyond the Litani River, killing more than 250 terrorists and capturing hundreds more.

During the operation, Israeli strike aircraft blasted dozens of suspected terrorist targets while fighters flew many patrol missions to deter Syrian planes. Reconnaissance aircraft, scout helicopters, and unmanned drones monitored the Israeli advance and identified the location of terrorist units and the activities of Syrian forces. The IAF's transport aircraft and helicopters contributed to the success of the operation through the movement of men and supplies and the evacuation of wounded Israeli troops.

Amir Yoeli, an Israeli pilot, commented on his participation in Operation Litani:

> I was flying the A-4 Skyhawk at the time and was still, as we say, "in my diapers." Pinpointing the targets was the most difficult part of the missions. At the time I was a junior member of the squadron so I had less of a responsibility in running the show up there but could concentrate on finding the target while the leader took care of the rest. Lebanon is a very beautiful country and flying over it gave me a feeling of tranquillity. The sights of our soldiers in there, the understanding of the guerillas, and their methods kept my targets at top priority. On one occasion I was given an artillery battery to locate and wipe out. We had prepared the flight very carefully and studied the target to the last detail. The leader questioned us until we started mumbling the

description. The planes were ready and we took off at 12:55 and the target was only twenty-eight minutes away.

All went well until we reached Sidon. A batch of clouds was serving as an anti-identification screen. The sun was behind us and the winds, according to the I.N.S. [inertial navigation system] were at 35 knots. It meant a long wait before some clearing up would enable us to locate the targets. After some radio discussions, we were given an alternate target—after all that work. The new target was a group of small-caliber antiaircraft guns. We spotted the site and headed for the drop. All my armament was ready and red ARM lights were on. Number one dove in and I followed close behind. As I was taking my eyes off him, I spotted black puffs ahead. We were both diving right into them. The dust from the ground identified the exact location of the guns and I was fixed onto the place where the dust was created. Sure enough, number one dropped his bombs and I mine. As we pulled out we looked back to see the hits, and they were on the money. The air pollution caused by the battery was gone and there was a warm feeling that there was one less antiaircraft site to worry about. As we headed back, we crossed a formation flying towards our initial target, we could see it clearly now, but it was their turn to play hide and seek. Our missions were far apart because it was a small area and everybody wanted a piece of the action.[4]

Israeli forces continued to hold a portion of southern Lebanon until June 1978, when a UN force took over. After Israeli units withdrew, the area near the border was controlled by a group of Christian militia armies. One led by Major Saad Haddad received considerable training and weaponry from Israel. Despite Israeli aid, the Christian armies were unable to halt PLO infiltration into southern Lebanon totally.

The United States fostered the peace negotiations between Egypt and Israel, and by late 1978 the two sides agreed to meet and work out the final details. President Sadat and Prime Minister Begin met with U.S. President Jimmy Carter at Camp David,

In the fall of 1969 the IAF received its first F-4E Phantom II. This aircraft could carry the same weapons load as four or more of the earlier aircraft then in service, and it could also defeat the latest MiGs in air combat.

A Mirage IIIC of the 101st Squadron lands after a mission. Note the empty air-to-air missile-launch rails under the wings. During the War of Attrition IAF fighter pilots increasingly used air-to-air missiles, like this Israeli-built Shafrir. Cannon and missiles each had their unique advantages; cannon were close-in weapons, up to 5,000 feet, while missiles had an effective range of 2,000 feet to 3 miles but had to be fired at the target aircraft's hot engine exhaust.

The strike camera of an IAF Phantom pilot took this unique photograph of his wing-man chasing an Egyptian MiG-17 low over the Sinai desert. Seconds after this photograph was taken, the MiG was shot down.

Wounded Israeli troops being evacuated by a UH-1 helicopter. Hundreds of Israeli soldiers were saved by helicopters, which rapidly transported them to trauma centers.

An A-4 Skyhawk over-flies a column of Israeli infantry while returning from a strike on the Golan Heights.

An Arab airfield under attack by IAF Phantoms. Heavy anti-aircraft defenses and Arab fighter patrols made this a dangerous mission. The results of these attacks were limited because aircraft and important facilities were protected by sand and concrete shelters.

IAF air-defense troops pose in front of a Hawk surface-to-air missile launcher in the Sinai. Air force controlled Hawk air-defense missiles and anti-aircraft guns protected army units during the 1973 War and downed more than forty Arab aircraft.

IAF Hercules C-130 transports played a vital part in the famous Entebbe hostage rescue mission. The C-130 is the IAF principal heavy-lift tactical transport, but the Hercules is also used to air-refuel F-4 Phantoms and A-4 Skyhawks.

IAF F-15 squadrons have the mission of defending Israeli airspace and achieving air superiority. Eagle pilots achieved more than sixty air-combat victories against Syrian aircraft in the skies over Lebanon.

An IAF F-16A Fighting Falcon. The F-16 was used by the IAF to bomb the Iraqi nuclear reactor near Baghdad in June 1981. The aircraft also engaged in air combat against Syrian aircraft and achieved more than forty victories.

The IAF used the Model 500 Defender attack helicopter in action during the Lebanon conflict.

In 1978 the IAF placed into service its first squadron of Kfir fighters. Built in Israel, these aircraft combined the J-79 turbo-jet engine from the Phantom with an upgraded Nesher (Mirage copy) airframe and Israeli-developed avionics. Israel aircraft industries produced over 200 Kfir aircraft and the fighter was used extensively during the Lebanon conflict.

A major contributor to the lopsided Israeli air combat kill ration was the E-2C Hawkeye command and control aircraft. Radar operators could detect incoming Syrian aircraft and vector IAF fighters to surprise them.

Maryland, in September 1978, to set an agenda for peace. Egypt agreed to recognize the State of Israel and sign a peace treaty, while Israel returned the Sinai to Egyptian control. Egypt, Israel, and other Middle East nations were offered military and economic aid in exchange for their support of the new peace initiatives. In June 1978, the U.S. Congress ratified a plan to supply sixty F-15 Eagle fighters to Saudi Arabia and fifty F-5E Tiger fighter-bombers to Egypt. Subsequently, Egypt received thirty-five F-4E Phantoms and forty F-16s in place of the F-5E fighters promised in the Camp David accords. The United States also agreed to provide Jordan with F-5E fighters, improved Hawk surface-to-air missiles, and other American weaponry.

Israeli military planners were concerned that modern Western tactical aircraft being supplied to Arab countries could upset the airpower balance in the Middle East. Maj. Gen. David Ivry, the IAF commander in 1978, stated, "We train all the time, but in every war we also train those who fly against us. And while we could afford adverse ratios of one to three, four, or even five when the Arabs were flying MiGs, we cannot accept those ratios when they fly the F-5E, much less the F-15."[5] As part of the peace plan, the United States agreed to provide an additional seventy-five F-16 fighter-bombers and fifteen F-15 fighters to Israel.

Terrorist attacks subsided for a time after Operation Latani. However, in the spring of 1979, the PLO intensified its efforts. In response to a particularly damaging attack at Nahariya on April 22, Israel changed its tactics from retaliating against terrorist attacks to preventing them. The IAF began flying regular reconnaissance missions over Lebanon, including the portions of the country under Syrian control. Terrorist training bases, headquarters, and artillery positions were blasted with bombs and naval gunfire or raided by commando units.

Israel unofficially agreed to refrain from directly confronting Syrian forces in Lebanon so long as they stayed in the northern part of the country and did not interfere with IAF reconnaissance and antiterrorist missions. However, aggressive Israeli air strikes against the terrorists prompted the Syrians to take action to support the PLO. On June 27, 1979, two flights of Syrian MiGs challenged an Israeli raid over Lebanon. Five Syrian MiG-21 fighters were shot down—four claimed by F-15 pilots and one destroyed by a Kfir pilot. This was the first air combat victory for both the F-15 and the Kfir and the most serious Israeli/Syrian air engagement since April 24, 1974.

The F-15 squadron leader tells the story of the combat:

We took off, fully armed for air-to-air combat, to cover the attacking aircraft. We linked up with the Kfirs on the way and climbed to 20,000 feet. Up there, the air is clear and there's no condensation. We patrolled the length and breadth of the "Battle Triangle," knowing all the time that we could run into MiGs at any moment. Over Sidon, we received orders to head north because enemy aircraft were heading for us at 15,000 feet.

The radar showed two MiG formations advancing on us—one attacking, one covering. The MiGs were no more than ten miles from our strike aircraft. Hitting the afterburners, we swooped down on them. They tried to break away when they saw what we were up to—but they never had much chance to do so: we had already locked onto most of them, splitting them up among us like wolves dividing their prey. "My" MiG was one of the second formation. The F-15 pilots hit the MiGs the moment they came within range. I wanted to make sure of my MiG and closed in, not waiting for him to approach me. By the time I got within firing range, three of the MiGs were already spiralling down. I slowed down, aimed, and fired a missile, and climbed above it— so my aircraft wouldn't be inadvertently damaged. My number two confirmed my kill. The fifth MiG was downed by a lone Kfir, which had finally joined us.[6]

This story recounts the Kfir pilot's part in the dogfight:

Captain S, a Kfir C-2 pilot, went into his first aerial combat with mixed feelings. He had been ordered on a combat patrol to cover attacking Phantoms on strike missions against PLO encampments in southern Lebanon; leading his number two at 12,000 feet at a speed of 400 knots, he received orders to engage Syrian Air Force MiGs approaching from the east with combat intentions. Releasing their drop tanks, the Kfirs vectored onto the Syrians.

But the faster F-15 Eagles were already engaging the MiGs, identified as MiG-21 PFMA(J)s, and one of them was already falling vertically, leaving a smoke steamer as it spun out of control, with the pilot ejecting. Another MiG had an Eagle sitting on its tail.

Captain S—covered by his wingman—maneuvered his Kfir onto two Syrian MiGs. Without hesitation, the young captain launched a Shafrir AAM [air-to-air missile] which exploded close to the number one of the Syrian Pair. Surprisingly, they maintained formation. S closed in and broke away to move himself into position once more. As he neared, he watched the Syrian MiG start ejecting white smoke and, immediately after, the pilot blew off his hood and bailed out. Without wasting time, the Kfir pilots closed in on the remaining MiG but, before they could open fire, the aircraft flew into a cloud bank and contact was lost.[7]

Israel continued to fly sorties over Lebanon, and on September 19, 1979, Syrian MiG-23 fighters attacked and fired on an IAF RF-4 but failed to hit it with their air-to-air missiles. Syrian aircraft again challenged Israeli air operations on September 24, and in the ensuing series of dogfights, IAF F-15s shot down four MiG-21 fighters. Tension between Israel and Syria remained high as a result of the air battles over Lebanon.

By late 1980, the IAF was receiving a steady stream of advanced F-15, F-16, and Kfir fighters and had a force of over forty Cobra and Defender attack helicopters. Aircraft such as the F-15, Kfir, E-2C Hawkeye, and prototype remotely piloted vehicles like the IAI Scout and Tadiran Mastiff had proven their utility in action over Lebanon. The IAF was also having several ex-airline Boeing 707 transports reworked into aerial-refueling tankers to support long-range attack operations. The withdrawal from the Sinai, which was agreed to in the Camp David Accord, had a dramatic impact on the IAF and its operations. Almost one-third of the operational strength of the force had been stationed in the Sinai. These aircraft were rapidly relocated to Israel. While the United States had agreed to build three new airfields in southern Israel, these bases would not be ready until the early 1980s. Particularly distressing was the loss of training airspace over the sparsely populated Sinai. Fixed-wing and helicopter training flights were increasingly flown over the Mediterranean Sea and the Negev Desert region.

Despite Syrian aerial opposition, Israeli forces continued to raid terrorist targets in Lebanon. During 1980 and early 1981 several air battles took place: four Syrian MiG-21 fighters were shot down, while no Israeli planes were lost. On April 28, 1981, the Syrians used transport helicopters to move troops into position to help the PLO defeat a Christian militia force fighting near Zahal, a town on the Beirut–Damascus highway. Prime Minister Begin authorized a strike against the helicopters to demonstrate his support for the Christian faction, which was fighting both the PLO and the Syrians in Lebanon. Israeli F-16 fighters attacked and shot down two Syrian Mi-8 helicopters.

Syria retaliated for this action by moving a number of SA-6 SAM batteries into the Bekaa Valley. Israel vigorously reacted to this escalation and threatened to attack the missile sites unless they were withdrawn. Dozens of drone aircraft were flown over the Bekaa Valley to test the defenses and collect intelligence. Several of these drones were shot down by the Syrians.

Terrorist raids and heavy shelling of Israeli border villages continued, and in April 1981, PLO raiders even tried to infiltrate Israel using a hot-air balloon. In response to terrorist attacks and Israeli frustration concerning the new Syrian SAMs in the Bekaa Valley, the IAF conducted an intense series of strikes against PLO targets in southern Lebanon. These attacks were soon answered by guerrilla artillery fire that hit towns and villages in northern Israel. As the cycle continued, Israel intensified its blows.

Then on June 7, 1981, Israel shocked the world when it announced that the IAF had bombed and destroyed the Iraqi Osirak nuclear reactor. If the Osirak reactor were to become operational, it would produce radioactive by-products that could be made into nuclear bombs or missile warheads. Israel was determined to prevent the reactor from coming into service.

The IAF had carefully planned and practiced the attack. Known as Operation Babylon, the risky raid was performed by fourteen hand-picked pilots, eight of whom flew F-16 fighter-bombers while the remaining six escorted the attackers in F-15s. Plans for the secret mission had been set well over a year earlier, after diplomatic efforts had failed to halt the construction of the Iraqi nuclear reactor. On two occasions the attack had been postponed. At 3:00 P.M. on June 7, 1981, the strike force took off from Etzion Air Base in the Sinai and headed toward Baghdad. The aircraft flew at low altitude on a path that skirted Arab military bases and villages and evaded Jordanian, Saudi, and Iraqi search radars. As the warplanes sped toward the target, they made several brief radio transmissions to report on their progress. Just prior to reaching the target, the F-15s broke into three groups and climbed to 25,000 feet to patrol near the important Iraqi fighter bases that surrounded Baghdad. One by one, the F-16s popped up, dived on the reactor complex, and released their bombs. After the bomb release, the Falcon pilots made a hard turn, dived to a lower altitude, and raced back toward Israel. Iraqi antiaircraft fire rose to meet the last few Israeli attackers but none were hit.

Sixteen bombs hit the target, and all but one of them exploded. The reactor dome was shattered and the building was reduced to smoking rubble. One French technician who was working late at the complex was killed.

In order to conserve fuel, the eight F-16s and six F-15s climbed to high altitude as they exited Iraqi territory. No fighters or missiles challenged the returning Israeli aircraft despite the fact they flew at high altitude over Saudi Arabia and Jordan. On the way home, they broke radio silence in order to inform headquarters of the successful mission and zero losses. Ninety minutes after the attack, the F-16 pilots were landing at Etzion, while the F-15 crews touched down at their home base.[8]

Operation Babylon destroyed the unfueled reactor and eliminated the Iraqi nuclear threat to Israel. The IAF had again demonstrated its capability to perform a surprise attack.

In response to continued shelling and raids from Lebanon, during June and July 1981, the IAF flew an intense series of air strikes against terrorist training bases, headquarters, and artillery positions throughout southern Lebanon. The PLO headquarters in Beirut was shattered by bombs on July 17 and hundreds of people were killed and wounded. The PLO responded with artillery, which grew so intense that Israel was forced to evacuate several border settlements. The U.S. special envoy Philip Habib arranged a cease-fire that took effect on July 24, 1981. Both sides honored the truce, but tension along the Israel/Lebanon border remained at a high level.

Israel refrained from striking Lebanese terrorist targets following the cease-fire but flew reconnaissance sorties to monitor Syrian and PLO activities. Syrian aircraft challenged these patrols on several occasions. In the dogfights that resulted, Syria lost a MiG-25 Foxbat on July 29, 1981, two MiG-23 Floggers in a battle on April 21, 1982, and two MiG-21s to IAF F-16s on May 26, 1982.

Terrorist activity against Israel's northern villages intensified during the spring of 1982—in May there were twenty-six separate incidents. Sustained shelling and the attempt on the life of Shalmo Argov, the Israeli ambassador in London, prompted Israel to conduct a series of air strikes against terrorist positions in Beirut and southern Lebanon. When the PLO responded with heavy artillery fire, Israel initiated an invasion of Lebanon that had long been planned by Defense Minister Ariel Sharon and other members of the Israeli government. The goal of this invasion, dubbed Peace for Galilee, was the elimination of the PLO and other terrorist groups that inhabited southern Labanon and the punishment of Syrian units.

The IAF played a major role in the Peace for Galilee operation. In a carefully orchestrated series of attacks, Israeli forces demolished the Syrian air defense network in the Bekaa Valley and scored a resounding aerial victory over the Syrians. When the Syrians threw their fighters into the fray, Israeli jets ambushed them. The result was some of the largest air battles ever witnessed in the Middle East. Over a four-day period, Israeli pilots shot down eighty-five Syrian aircraft and reportedly did not lose a single plane in air combat.

Some forty thousand troops with more than five hundred tanks and nearly one thousand other armored vehicles moved into Lebanon on June 6, 1982. Three division-sized task forces advanced north on different routes with the aim of quickly overrunning terrorist units before they could flee. Israeli landing craft put tanks and troops ashore south of Sidon to block the coast road escape route. Artillery, helicopter gunships, and air-craft blasted guerilla defenders.

Because of the surprise nature of the attack and the rapid advance, Israeli air and ground losses were small during the first few days of fighting. Aharon Ahiaz, a reserve pilot of a Skyhawk flying close air support for the invasion, had the mis-fortune of overflying a PLO antiaircraft training camp. His A-4 was hit by several SA-7 missiles and he spent seventy-five days as the prisoner of the PLO in Beirut before he was released. An IAF Cobra helicopter was also lost in action on the second day of fighting.[9]

Israeli pilots scored their first air combat victory of the Peace for Galilee operation on June 7 when a single Syrian MiG-23 was shot down. Israeli troops captured many terrorist camps and engaged in ground combat for the first time with Syrian forces near Jezzin on the second day of the invasion. On June 8, Israeli forces continued to drive north and met with heavy resistance from retreating PLO and Syrian commandos. Several air battles occurred over Lebanon when Syrian aircraft challenged Israeli planes, and seven MiGs were shot down.

One of the Israeli pilots gave his view of the action:

"During a sortie in which I was providing cover for our forces this morning [June 8], I received a message that two Syrian planes were closing in on us. Almost immediately, I spotted them on my screen. Judging by the MiGs' speed and direction, it was clear they had taken off on an attack mission," said the 25-year-old pilot who downed one of the two Syrian MiGs in a brief dogfight southeast of Beirut. The tall, slim captain said that this had been his first combat experience against enemy planes. "I attacked the MiG closest to me, while my partner, who flew the other plane that was with me on that mission, attacked the second MiG. I acted according to our combat doctrine, aware of the specific performance of my plane. I hit the MiG, it went into a spin, dropped and crashed. I did not see what happened to the pilots of the two MiGs," he added, "whether or not they managed to bail out after we hit their planes. We saw no parachutes."[10]

Worried by the quick Israeli capture of Southern Lebanon and the heavy losses suffered by PLO and Syrian units, President Assad ordered more SAM batteries to deploy into the Bekaa Valley and additional armored units to cross the border into Lebanon. Israeli air reconnaissance detected this buildup, and the IAF was given the authorization to attack the SAM defenses in the Bekaa Valley and to bomb the Syrian reinforcements. At dawn on June 9, Israeli tanks began moving north to flank the Syrians and drive directly into the Bekaa Valley. The IAF's CH-53 helicopters lifted troops into the Shouf mountains to block the Syrian retreat. Syrian and Israeli tanks fought several major battles during the day. The Syrians were forced to fall back, but both sides suffered heavy losses.

The events that led up to the Israeli air attacks in the Bekaa Valley were described by Brigadier General B, an IAF officer, who was unidentified for security reasons:

> As background, it was important to note that the missile batteries enabled the terrorists to fire at us from the Lebanese Bekaa Valley. The Syrians provided the terrorists with aircover and missile protection, which enabled them to operate freely. Two days prior to the IAF attack, Syrian missiles were launched from the Bekaa at our aircraft. These attempts to engage our forces could have hindered the IDF ground advance. Therefore, the Government of Israel decided that it would not be possible to simply shrug off the launching of missiles at our planes.[11]

The Syrians had moved an extensive air defense network into the Bekaa Valley in order to provide protection for their ground troops in Lebanon. This air defense shield included fifteen SA-6, two SA-3, and two SA-2 missile batteries with over two hundred ready-to-fire missiles and more than four hundred antiaircraft guns.

"The destruction of the missile batteries was the greatest test which the IAF has ever encountered," an IAF Colonel admitted. "Our aircraft had to face an advanced and concentrated array of missiles which were reinforced by the most sophisticated fighter aircraft in the eastern bloc. Moreover, strategic surprise was impossible under the circumstances. The Syrians were waiting for us."[12]

Lt. Gen. Rafael Eitan, Israeli chief of staff during the 1982 assault into Lebanon, explained how the Syrian SAM sites were destroyed:

> From the operational point of view I can say that we used the mini-RPVs, long before the war, to identify and locate all the Syrian missile batteries. We then used superior electronic devices which enabled us to "blind" or neutralize the missile sites' ground-to-air radar. We rendered them ineffective to take reliable fixes on our aircraft aloft. But in advance of direct aerial attacks, we used long-range artillery.[13]

Brigadier General B. continued his description of the attack against the SAMs in the Bekaa Valley on June 9:

> The incoming fire from all directions created confusion among Syrian ranks. The brunt of the operation called for a direct air attack upon the missile batteries. Most of the batteries were destroyed by iron bombs. The bulk of the Syrian deployment contained SA-6 missiles which, because of their mobility, are not dug in and were therefore relatively easy to identify. The remaining missiles were of the SA-2 and SA-3 type. The Syrians tried to hide the missiles beneath a smoke-screen. Yet, in spite of the smoke, or perhaps because of it, our pilots were able to detect all the targets. IAF planes swept in low and launched their Shrike missile at the Syrian batteries after target acquisition had been achieved. The Shrike anti-radiation, air-to-surface missile (which had been adapted and improved by Israeli technicians) homed in on the electromagnetic radiation emitted by the Soviet-built air defense radars. Diversionary devices were also camouflaged to resemble overflying aircraft in order to distract and confuse Syrian ground radar. Within a short span of time, the entire Syrian missile deployment began to crumble.[14]

"The operation lasted two hours," added Brigadeer General B.

Our attacking planes encountered about one hundred
MiG-21 and MiG-23 [Syrian] aircraft, which swooped
into the area, wave after wave. The MiG aircraft were
ostensibly dispatched to the area in order to protect the
missiles against IAF attack. This was an absurdity! Why
was it necessary to protect antiaircraft missile batteries?
The raison d'etre of the missile batteries is to down
aircraft.[15]

Captain G, an IAF pilot, recalled his part in the operation:

We were in the air at the climax of the large-scale attack
on the missile batteries; the air was filled with tension
due to the large number of enemy aircraft flying about
the area. We had to differentiate between our aircraft
and those of the enemy. We waited until we achieved
positive identification of the target while simultaneously
approaching two enemy aircraft, painted brown and
light yellow. We gave chase and when the aircraft
reached a routine launch mode, I fired and was able to
see the hit; immediately I turned to go for the other
aircraft but I was too slow. My number two had already
shot him down.[16]

With the IAF attack on the Syrian missile batteries in full
swing, Maj. R flew in a foursome of F-15s sent to cover the
attacking planes.

I will never forget that flight as long as I live. We were
flying over the Bakaa Valley, and the sun was sinking
into the sea. The radar caught sight of two MiG-21s
although we had trouble seeing them because the setting
sun was in our eyes.
   Both Number Four and I launched missiles, but
suddenly we found ourselves in an inferno of AA tracer
fire and rockets from the ground. I saw the approaching
rockets, and yelled to Number Three to get out.
   Meanwhile he downed one of the two MiGs. I followed

the second one northwards, and then I noticed something yellow under my left wing. I remember thinking, "Another MiG!"

The MiG I was chasing passed some 200 meters ahead of me. I looked at the pilot and he looked at me. I remember his white helmet clearly. He cut suddenly in an amazing turn that I would estimate at something like 8.5 G. He was getting in behind me. We were both flying very fast. I had to do something. At 800 meters I shot a missile and missed him. I shot a second and this time hit his tail. He continued flying and only gradually, gently crashed into the fields below.

I was hypnotized by the crash; suddenly the urgent command, "Cut! Cut!" was shouted over the radio. I had begun to cut when a great crash shook the plane. A missile had hit squarely on the exhaust of my right engine, and my tail was aflame.

"I will not bail out in Syrian territory," was the one thought that kept flashing through my mind. I had turned off my right engine and was rapidly losing power. If I could only make it out of AA fire range and cross the mountains. Meanwhile the other planes of my formation got in behind to cover me. Slowly, excruciatingly, I managed to climb and just barely scraped over the mountain ridges. I thought of flying out over the sea, where at least our navy was there to pick me up.

It took an enormous load off my mind that the other planes were covering for me. I had nothing to worry about except for the actual flying, which was difficult enough under the circumstances.

With each mile my mind became easier. I felt that I would be able to make it to an IAF base after all. My tail was still burning and only one engine was operational, but I did get to the Ramat David airfield. Landing was a tricky business, but somehow I got through it safely. The other planes had been behind me in the fullest sense of the word, ready to help out with suggestions and excellent flying advice.

I had always known that the F-15 was a dependable plane, but I had never before realized quite to what extent. Not only was my tail completely burnt and my right engine incapacitated, afterwards I saw that there had been a massive fuel leak, damage to the thermostat, and no fewer than four hundred bullet holes in the body of the plane. With all this, I managed to fly for twenty minutes after being hit and to land safely. If I had been flying any other type of plane, I don't think I would have come out of this alive.[17]

Lieutenant General Eitan discussed the Syrian response to the Israeli strikes:

The first reaction of the Syrians when we attacked their missiles was to scramble their air forces . . . any [Syrian fighter pilots] who crossed an imaginary line in the direction of our forces was destroyed, shot down. The imaginary line was actually the range of the missile batteries in Syria proper. The basic tactic of the Syrian air force is to take to the air and to cross this imaginary line, which brings them outside the protective range of their home-based missiles. They do what they can, then run back for cover.[18]

An IAF Phantom squadron commander summed up the operation: "The success of the operation was not only in that the mission was accomplished in the best possible manner, but that all our pilots returned home safely. . . . From an aviation and military viewpoint, we made history. I am certain that this operation will have broad repercussions upon all the world's air forces."[19]

Certainly the Soviet Union, supplier of the Syrian-manned SAM batteries and MiG fighters, took notice. Col. Gen. Yensery S. Yuvarov, deputy commander of the Soviet Air Defense Force, and a team of Russian military experts were promptly dispatched to Syria to investigate what had happened.

Of the nineteen Syrian SAM sights in the Bekaa Valley, ten were put out of action almost immediately and seventeen had been damaged or destroyed by the end of the day. The IAF had studied the lessons of the 1973 war and was now well prepared to deal with air defense systems. First, the search and fire control radars of the Syrian air defense network were jammed and many drones and decoys were flown over the Bekaa Valley in order to confuse the defenses. Then Israeli artillery, rockets, Shrike antiradar missiles, and other weapons blasted the Syrian command centers and radars, blinding the defenses. Dozens of F-16s, Phantoms, Kfirs, and Skyhawks then rolled in and bombed the Syrian SA-2 and SA-3 missile sites, SA-6 vehicles, and antiaircraft guns. Israeli jets delivered their bombs from medium altitude so that they remained above the effective range of light antiaircraft fire. The attacking aircraft also spewed out hundreds of flares, which confused and neutralized the seekers of SA-7 infrared-homing missiles.

The IAF had E-2C airborne warning and control aircraft in the air using their long-range radar to scan Syrian airspace for warning of an attack by Syrian fighter aircraft. Israeli RPVs were probably circling over the major Syrian fighter bases, giving the Israelis warning that Syrian MiGs were moving to take off. The Israelis undoubtedly jammed the radio and data link communications between aircraft and control centers, depriving the Syrian pilots of an accurate picture of the tactical situation. Flights of F-15s and F-16s were vectored in to ambush each successive wave of Syrian fighters. At one point during the operation, there were reportedly ninety Israeli aircraft and sixty Syrian jets airborne over the battle area. This was one of the biggest aerial confrontations since World War II. With the advantages of accurate situation awareness and better aircraft, weapons, and pilots, it is easy to understand how Israeli pilots were able to shoot down dozens of Syrian jets.

On June 10, Israeli armed columns continued their drive north toward Beirut and into central Lebanon, resulting in several major ground battles between Israeli, Syrian, and PLO forces. Israeli fighter-bombers again bombed SAM batteries in the Bekaa Valley and hit Syrian reinforcements that were moving into Lebanon. A series of major air battles erupted as waves of Syrian Air Force aircraft few into Lebanon to challenge Israeli jets and ground forces. Syrian fighters and Gazelle attack helicopters armed with HOT antitank missiles hit a number of Israeli vehicles and caused many casualties. However, the Syrians paid a heavy price: twenty-six Syrian fighters and three helicopters were shot down by a combination of Israeli jets and antiaircraft fire during this fifth day of Peace for Galilee.[20]

Maj. Gen. David Ivry, the IAF commander in 1982, summarized the air situation during a press conference held just after the war on the celebration of the thirty-fourth Israeli Air Force Day:

It took them [the Syrians] time to evaluate what was happening in the air battles. By Friday morning [June 11] they already understood the situation. We had already shot down 60 of their aircraft. Nevertheless, they continued to scramble them. I believe that what happened then was already the result of a psychological pressure of "let's make a last effort to shoot down several Israeli aircraft." And this was already a reaction of impulse and less of consideration. I cannot say for certain that this is what happened. This is a feeling. What is interesting is that when we began to attack on Friday, June 4, the Syrians did not react despite the fact that we were attacking Beirut, and, as a rule in the past, when we attacked terrorist targets in the Beirut area, the Syrians would react. In my opinion, the cumulative effect of the last three years was a factor here. In the three years before the war we became a significant deterrent factor in the air. We had shot down 24 Syrian planes [including 2 Mi-8 helicopters] without losing a single aircraft. On Monday, June 7, 1982, they began to intercept us. In the beginning they thought twice. On Monday a MiG-23 was shot down. On Tuesday [June 8] a few more began to come. Seven were shot down. And with the attack on the missiles there began a massive intercept effort.[21]

By June 11, the sixth day of the conflict, Israeli forces reached the outskirts of Beirut and threatened to cut off the main road between the city and the Bekaa Valley. Israeli armored units rushed forward and called for heavy air support in order to capture additional terrain before a UN-arranged cease-fire took effect at noon.

Amir Yoeli, an IAF pilot who served with a Kfir C2 squadron, flew a ground attack mission in support of this battle:

> I was given a ground support mission to hit a target near the road that led east from Beirut. We came in from the east because we wanted the sun behind us, and since there was very little SAM activity at the time, there wasn't a problem. As we approached our target, we communicated with our forces on the ground and tried to get the exact location of their vehicles. The sky was constantly disturbed by black puffs at about 10,000 feet, but the forces underneath were living through a shelling attack. It was very hard to get an exact location from them. We circled around the approximate point but could not identify any of our troops. At last I spotted some heavy artillery with help from a guiding voice of an officer on the ground. All systems were go and we dove for a positive identification of the target. After verifying with some local groups that we are not going against our own troops, we went in. I dropped first, and my wingman a few seconds after me. It was a hit. Another pair of Kfirs joined in on the channel and I directed them to another battery a bit west of the one we had just hit. Since there were explosions still going on the ground, it was easy for them to come in after us and destroy their target. It did not take more than thirty seconds before we heard the ground forces cheer on the radio. Whether or not both batteries were aiming at our troops or only one, I still don't know, but it doesn't make much of a difference. Our targets were always difficult and we had to use extreme caution being most of the time over hostile territory.[22]

On June 11, 1982, large numbers of Syrian aircraft again took to the air and tried to attack Israeli jets and ground forces. Israeli fighters pounced on the attackers and eighteen Syrian aircraft were shot down by the Israelis. The cease-fire brought the fighting to an end late in the day on June 11. During a week of heavy fighting, the IAF had shot down more than eighty Syrian aircraft, knocked out twenty SAM batteries in the Bekaa

Valley, and destroyed hundreds of Syrian and terrorist vehicles and fortifications. Terrorist groups and Syrian units fought back aggressively against the massive Israeli ground assault and caused many casualties. However, the weight of numbers, air superiority, and the mobility and firepower of Israeli forces overwhelmed the defenders.

The cease-fire broke down on June 13, and heavy fighting resumed between Israeli, Syrian, and terrorist units. Israeli forces continued their drive north in an attempt to link up with the Christian Phalangists to trap PLO and Syrian units in Beirut. By late June, the Israelis had indeed linked up with the Christian forces and had closed the trap. Fighter-bombers pounded terrorist and Syrian positions blocking the path of the Israeli advance and hammered resupply convoys.

Israeli and Syrian fighters again clashed on June 24 and two MiG-23 aircraft were shot down in a brief dogfight. Syrian forces pushed additional SA-6 batteries into the Bekaa Valley to rebuild their defenses. Israeli reconnaissance patrols quickly detected this move. Air strikes put one battery out of action on June 24 and blasted several other Syrian air defense units in the Bekaa Valley two days later.

Israeli forces began the siege of Beirut on July 1 with a massive overflight of fighters at dusk. The IAF jets made mock bombing runs and blasted the city with sonic booms from high-speed passes. Ground forces clashed daily, and heavy artillery fire chewed up the city. Initially the IAF played only a limited role in the siege. However, in response to a heavy PLO counterattack on July 22, Israeli tanks, artillery, and fighter-bombers hammered guerrilla strongpoints throughout Beirut. These were the first direct strikes made against Syrian fortifications since June 25. The Syrians moved a battery of SA-8 mobile SAMs into the Bekaa Valley during the night of July 24. The latest Soviet-built tactical air defense weapon, the radar-guided SA-8 missile, could hit aircraft from a range of more than six miles and reach an altitude of over four miles. Israeli reconnaissance spotted this deployment, and fighter-bombers destroyed three of the four vehicles of the battery. The remaining SA-8 launcher exacted revenge late in the afternoon of July 25 by shooting down an Israeli F-4 Phantom.

The IAF played a major role in Peace for Galilee and the siege of Beirut. During the initial period of action, which lasted from June 6 to 11, IAF aircraft flew more than two thousand sorties. Israeli jets, helicopters, and transports flew several thousand sorties in support of later operations.

In air-to-air combat, the IAF accounted for eighty-five Syrian aircraft. Some forty-four of these fell to pilots flying the F-16 Falcon, while F-15 crews were credited with forty victories. One Syrian aircraft was downed by an F-4 Phantom crew. Most Syrian losses were MiG-21 and MiG-23 fighters, but some SU-22 fighter-bombers and helicopters were also shot down.[23] Most of these victories were attributed to short-range infrared-guided missiles, including the late-model AIM-9L, earlier versions of the Sidewinder, the Rafael Shafrir 2 and the new Rafael Python. A number of Syrian jets were destroyed by AIM-7F missiles fired from IAF F-15s but only about six aircraft fell to Israeli aircraft cannons. The need for positive visual identification—because of the crowded skies—prompted Israeli pilots to rely primarily on short-range dogfight missiles.

An IAF F-16 pilot who fought during the 1982 conflict commented, "The weapons system has shortened the duration of air battles." He added, "Once we used to shoot them down with guns at a range of 100–300 meters from behind. To reach such relatively short range, you need time—several minutes. The improvement of the weapons systems permits shooting them down at a longer range, and reduces the risk."[24]

The pilot continued, "The Syrian pilots in some instances showed greater boldness than usual, and they tried to fight. . . . One should bear in mind that Syrian pilots had combat experience from battles they fought with us in the past, and they did apply some of the things they had learned. But the gap is still wide."[25] He concluded, "While the downing of many MiGs brought great satisfaction and honor, the attack on the missiles is one of the great achievements of the air force and will be long remembered."[26]

During the Lebanon conflict, the IAF demonstrated that it had integrated the hard lessons of the 1973 war through its destruction of the Syrian air defense umbrella in the Bekaa Valley. Israeli pilots then concentrated their attention on stopping Syrian reinforcements from reaching the battle area and on destroying PLO strongpoints and fortifications. Accurate intelligence, the advanced weapons delivery systems fitted to Israeli fighter-bombers, and intensified training enabled Israeli pilots to bomb targets with pinpoint accuracy. Israeli aircrew and aircraft losses were kept to a minimum through the heavy use of ECM, decoy flares, and weapons delivery tactics that kept aircraft above the range of most antiaircraft fire.

"The war of the helicopters," said Major General Irvy, "was extremely dangerous this time. They flew over an area where it was difficult to determine the location of the concealed danger. At times, an area at the front was already mopped up, but in the rear of the front line there were still terrorists who fired at the helicopters."[27]

Helicopters and transport aircraft played a vital role in helping to ensure the success of Israeli operations in Lebanon. Transport and helicopter crews braved heavy fire to evacuate wounded troops and move vital supplies to the front line. Transport helicopters evacuated more than one thousand wounded to hospitals in Israel. During the assault of Beaufort Castle, a helicopter flew up to the fort and evacuated wounded even as the battle raged. A Bell 212 helicopter was shot down in the process of flying one of these important medical rescue missions. Also, C-130 transports served to evacuate injured soldiers. Fixed- and rotor-wing transports brought ammunition, food, and supplies to the front line and moved captured PLO war materiel back to Israel.

The IAF AH-1 Cobras and MD-500 Defenders flew hundreds of scout and attack sorties during the conflict. In attacks against Syrian and PLO forces, attack helicopters fired 137 TOW wire-guided missiles. Ninety-nine of these hit home, resulting in the destruction of twenty-nine tanks, fifty-six other vehicles, four radar sites, one Syrian Gazelle helicopter, and several additional targets.[28]

Four Israeli helicopters were lost in action, two of which were shot down by friendly antiaircraft fire.[29] Several effective attacks by Syrian Gazelle attack helicopters scared Israeli ground troops, and, as a result, army units sometimes fired on IAF helicopters. The IAF has the responsibility of providing air defense for the Israeli army. During the Lebanon conflict, IAF antiaircraft units worked closely with the army. Their antiaircraft systems downed several Syrian aircraft and helicopters with gun and missile fire. Army commanders liked the Vulcan air defense system because the cannon was also highly effective against ground targets.

The success of the IAF in the 1982 Lebanon conflict can be attributed to effective equipment, well-trained personnel, and a flexible tactical doctrine that coordinated air force, army, and navy operations. Israeli battle commanders benefited from the efficient command and control network that was developed following the 1973 war. This system could integrate information from many sources, including real-time intelligence from RPVs and AWACS aircraft.

The Israeli siege of Beirut ended in late August. As part of the cease-fire agreement, a multinational force composed of soldiers from the United States, France, Italy, and Great Britain took control of Beirut to oversee the withdrawal of PLO forces. Even after the multinational force took control of Beirut, a large force of Israeli troops continued to garrison southern Lebanon. The IAF provided support for this occupation force. Helicopters and transports flew in and out of Lebanon with supplies, while reconnaissance and fighter aircraft patrolled over the northern part of the country to keep tabs on the Syrians and Lebanese factions.

Following the Lebanon war, Israel continued to strengthen the IAF. An additional seventy-five F-16 Falcon fighter-bombers were ordered. These new jets were improved versions of the F-16C/D Fighting Falcons, which featured the high-thrust General Electric F110 turbofan engine and a significant amount of Israeli-built avionics equipment. At the same time, Israeli companies initiated development of a new home-built fighter. Known as the Lavi, this new jet was to succeed the Kfir on the Israel Aircraft Industries assembly line. In 1982, Lt. Gen. Amos Lapidot, Lavi program manager, assumed command of the IAF.

In January 1983, Israel disclosed that the Soviet Union had supplied Syria with several batteries of long-range SA-5 anti-aircraft missiles. With a range of over 150 miles against high-flying targets, the SA-5 could threaten IAF aircraft over Lebanon and much of northern Israel. Israeli planners viewed the SA-5 deployment as a provocative act. However, since the missile sites were located on Syrian territory and none were fired at

Israeli planes, only diplomatic efforts were used to challenge the new threat.

Israel continued its reconnaissance missions over Lebanon, and when buildups of terrorist forces were detected, Israeli aircraft bombed their positions. On November 20, 1983, a Kfir was lost to antiaircraft fire during a strike against targets in the Shouf mountains of Lebanon. An IAF pilot described the situation:

> We easily found the area—it was already covered with smoke and debris from previous attacks, with bomb craters clearly visible in the dark ground. We entered the attack, but were immediately faced by dense antiaircraft fire; the gunners were expecting us. On releasing my bombs, I saw the aircraft of my companion leaving behind white trails of fuel. He reported over the radio that he had been hit. I tried to locate and report on the damage, but he said that he was having difficulty in controlling the Kfir. I told him to try and keep altitude in order to gain distance, but he entered into a wide spin pointing toward the ground. He ejected at the last moment, his parachute opening just before the Kfir hit the ground.[30] The Israeli pilot was rescued by Lebanese Christian forces and returned to Israel.

The UN peacekeeping forces in Lebanon used their airpower on several occasions to hit back at Syrian and Lebanese artillery. In September, October, and November 1983, French Navy Super Etendard fighter-bombers blasted Druze gun batteries and other positions. On December 4, U.S. Navy carrier-based A-6 and A-7 attack aircraft bombed gun positions that had been pounding the U.S. Marine positions around the Beirut airport. During the series of strikes, an A-6 and an A-7 were lost to missile fire. The skies of Lebanon were dangerous because of the presence of the Syrians and the various Lebanese factions, which were armed with a variety of advanced Soviet-supplied antiaircraft weapons.

Israel continued to occupy a portion of southern Lebanon until 1985. After the Israeli withdrawal from Lebanon, the IAF assumed prime responsibility for reconnaissance and attack of terrorist targets.

After the PLO withdrawal from Lebanon in 1982, its members settled in several Arab countries. A major PLO base was set up in Tunis, Tunisia, and from here many international terrorist activities were coordinated. In response to a terrorist attack against a yacht in Cyprus that left three Israelis dead, the IAF was again called into action. On October 1, 1985, IAF F-15s flew 1,500 miles across the Mediterranean Sea and bombed the PLO headquarters in Tunisia. The raid destroyed several buildings and killed seventy-three people. An Israeli pilot who flew on the attack said,

> After I pulled out of the dive, I saw the bombs hitting the target accurately. A lot of smoke curled up. From the bird's view you don't see much detail. The picture is not as you see it afterwards on television. You only see that you hit those houses you wanted to hit. We assembled again and started on our way home. After this there is the release of tension which is huge. I myself gave an enormous shout in the cockpit to get rid of the tension. The feeling is mixed: you see the huge destruction you left behind, but with the knowledge that we carried out the task perfectly, just as we wanted to do it.[31]

The IAF F-15 Eagle fighter-bombers that performed the mission flew a five-hour round-trip mission and refueled several times from Boeing 707 tankers. While several aircraft swooped in to deliver their bombs, other F-15s patrolled overhead to defend against air attack by Tunisian fighters. An E-2C Hawkeye radar-warning plane escorted the strike group. Israeli Defense Minister Yitzak Rabin said that the raid was flown to demonstrate to the PLO that "the long arm of Israeli retribution will reach them wherever they are."[32]

Following the Israeli raid on Tunisia, Syrian planes began challenging Israeli reconnaissance missions over Lebanon. On November 20, 1985, IAF F-15 Eagle fighters engaged and shot down two Syrian MiG-23s that had attempted to ambush an Israeli reconnaissance plane. The IAF's commander, Maj. Gen. Amos Lapidot, commented about the event in an interview:

They are not very happy about us carrying out routine
reconnaissance over Lebanon, and they attempt to
interfere with us from time to time. During the past
weeks they stepped up these actions and have provoked
dangerous situations. There were several occasions in the
past weeks when we were forced to abort our missions in
order not to heat up the situation too much.

Today a situation developed to which we could not
avoid reacting. Their approach was made in such a
threatening posture and at such a range that we were
forced to abort the patrol. We had to defend our
reconnaissance planes with additional combat aircraft
that were there for that purpose.

We operate with the intention of keeping the Syrian
planes at arm's length and not provoking a confrontation, so that we can carry out our reconnaissance as
usual.

Today, for some reason, the Syrians continued
threatening our planes, reaching such close range that
we were forced to engage them.

One has to remember that modern combat aircraft are
armed with missiles that have ranges of 20 kilometers or
more. Therefore the danger to our planes begins when
the Syrian planes are still in their own airspace. And
when we react, we can do so while still in Lebanese
airspace.[33]

This was the first Israeli–Syrian dogfight since 1983. The IAF
had flown many sorties over Lebanon and struck targets thirteen times since the 1982 conflict, but Syrian aircraft stayed
well clear of those bombing missions.

In spite of the Syrian challenge, the IAF continued its reconnaissance and bombing attacks in Lebanon. In October 1986,
and IAF F-4E Phantom was lost near Sidon, Lebanon, during an
attack against a terrorist base. The pilot and navigator of the
Phantom successfully ejected. The pilot of the aircraft clung to
the skid of an IAF Cobra attack helicopter and was carried
through heavy antiaircraft fire to safety, but the navigator was
captured by a Lebanese military force. The IAF has routinely
flown reconnaissance aircraft and unmanned RPV drones over

Lebanon to monitor Syrian and terrorist activities. Terrorist targets detected by these reconnaissance operations have been struck on a frequent basis.

As the IAF moved into its fourth decade, the air arm had to face a new set of economic, political, and military challenges. The IAF inventory now included a large force of F-15, F-16, F-4, Kfir, and A-4 tactical aircraft, plus hundreds of support systems ranging from advanced radar networks to trainers. All of the famed Mirage/Nesher fighters were gone, having been sold to Argentina or retired, and A-4 Skyhawks were also rapidly being retired from service. Early-model Kfir jets were also gone, having been placed in storage or sold. For several years, two dozen Kfirs were leased to the U.S. Navy and Marine Corps and used as adversary aircraft to simulate enemy jets. During the early 1980s, the Israeli government supported the development of a new Israeli-built fighter. Known as the Lavi, this new aircraft was to be the replacement for aging Israeli Skyhawk, Kfir, and Phantom fighter-bombers. The Lavi was also to serve as the IAF's new advanced trainer aircraft. Israel Aircraft Industries had already refurbished the IAF's fleet of Fouga Magister primary jet trainers.

The IAF flies many specialized surveillance aircraft, including E-2C Hawkeye radar planes and (according to the U.S. Congressional Record) Boeing 707, OV-1D Mohawk, and Beech RU-21 aircraft fitted with specialized sensors. The air force has over two dozen Boeing 707 and C-130 aircraft, and these transports serve in both refueling and logistics roles. The famous C-47 Dakotas still fly with the IAF, and small numbers of Israeli-built Arava transports are in use. The helicopter component was upgraded through the addition of a small number of Aerospatiale SA-366 Dauphin helicopters. The IAF plans to purchase AH-64 Apache attack helicopters, and UH-60 Blackhawk transport helicopters.

Israeli air superiority was challenged by a number of developments in the late 1980s. First, the air arms of its potential opponents were receiving an infusion of advanced aircraft. Syria now has the Soviet-built MiG-29, which is similar to the West's latest fighters; Saudi Arabia has purchased dozens of Tornado and F-15 fighters; while Jordan has bought the French

Mirage 2000. The qualitative improvement in Arab aircraft, weapons, and pilot experience has diminished Israel's margin of superiority.

The introduction of advanced short- and medium-range surface-to-surface missiles into the armed forces of Syria, Iraq, Saudi Arabia, and other neighboring Arab countries has created a new threat to Israel. The fighters and Hawk surface-to-air missiles of the IAF have almost no capability to intercept these high-speed weapons. This is not a new threat. During the 1973 war, Syria fired a number of FROG rockets at Israeli targets, but the weapon had limited range and poor accuracy. Modern Soviet- and Chinese-produced SS-12, SS-21, CSS2 and similar western-designed missiles have much greater reach, improved accuracy, and can be armed with conventional, chemical, or even nuclear warheads. These missiles could damage and/or destroy Israeli airfields and army formations, and threaten civilian population centers as well. The Israeli military and civilian leadership has made it known that it would not tolerate an attack by surface-to-surface missiles and would retaliate with all means at its disposal, including the use of special weapons if necessary. At the same time, Israel has initiated a sizable civil defense effort and a program to develop and field air defense missiles capable of shooting down tactical ballistic missiles. The selection of several Israeli firms to participate in the U.S. Strategic Defense Initiative (Star Wars) indicates that progress has been made toward this goal. In addition, Israel demonstrated its capability to produce long range ballistic missiles on September 21, 1988, with the launching of Offeq (Horizon) 1, the country's first satellite. This launch made Israel the eighth nation to place a satellite in space.

The peace treaty with Egypt and budget cutbacks have had a significant impact on the IAF. In August 1987, the Israeli cabinet decided to cancel the Lavi fighter. In addition, the IAF has been forced to streamline its operations in order to save money. Major General Lapidot transferred command of the IAF to Maj. Gen. Avihu Ben-Nun in September 1987. Major General Ben-Nun was the commander of one of the IAF's first Phantom squadrons, commander of two air bases, and head of military planning.

As the IAF moves into the 1990s, it will increasingly need to focus on quality rather than quantity. In the wake of the Lavi cancellation, additional F-16s have been ordered. These new fighters will be supported by Phantoms, which are being upgraded by Israel Aircraft Industries, and declining numbers of Skyhawks and Kfirs. Advanced avionics and ECM systems developed for the Lavi will be fitted to IAF aircraft and new stand-off weapons and guided missiles put into service. Innovative doctrine and tactics, developed through thousands of hours of combat and training, would be used by IAF personnel should they have to fight. Intensified training and higher standards have been instituted to ensure that all IAF personnel remain ready for action. This is a vital necessity because with each passing year more combat-experienced pilots, maintenance personnel, ordnance handlers, and other veterans retire from the force. Speaking about air force strategy, Major General Ben-Nun has stated, "We must keep the balance of quality in our favor. We don't have an answer to everything. Avionics and advanced weapons are only one kind of answer. Keeping and attracting good people is our single biggest problem—though we still do it better than anyone else."[34]

The IAF has a proud heritage. In the event of a future call to action, the personnel of the force will do their best to ensure victory. Members of the IAF, the fighter pilots, the mechanics, and the air defense missile battery commanders know that they are Israel's first line of defense and that the safety of the country rests in their hands.

# _Appendix_

## IAF Aircraft

| Aircraft | Crew | Wing Span (ft.) | Length (ft.) | Loaded Weight (lb.) | Engines | Engine Thrust (HP or lb.) | Maximum Speed (MPH) | Range (mi.) | Ceiling (ft.) | Weapons |
|---|---|---|---|---|---|---|---|---|---|---|
| Airspeed Consul | 2 | 53.4 | 35.4 | 8,300 | 2 Armstrong Siddeley Cheetah | 365 HP each | 190 | 900 | 19,000 | — |
| Auster AOP5 | 2/3 | 36 | 22.4 | 1,990 | 1 Lycoming 0-290 | 130 HP | 130 | 250 | 15,000 | Grenades & bombs |
| Avia S199 | 1 | 32.5 | 29.7 | 7,700 | 1 Junkers Jumo 211F | 1,350 HP | 367 | 528 | 31,000 | 2 20-mm cannons 2 13-mm machine guns |
| Avro Anson | 2 | 56.5 | 42.2 | 9,770 | 2 Armstong Siddeley Cheetah | 420 HP | 190 | 700 | 19,200 | — |
| Beechcraft Bonanza, Model 35 | 4 | 32.8 | 25.2 | 2,650 | 1 Continental E185 | 185 HP | 184 | 750 | 17,000 | Bombs, 1 machine gun |
| Beechcraft Queen Air | 2 | 50.2 | 35.5 | 8,800 | 2 Lycoming 1-650-540 | 380 HP each | 248 | 1,560 | 26,800 | — |
| Beechcraft RU-21 | 2/4 | 45.9 | 35.5 | 9,650 | 2 Pratt & Whitney T74CP | 550 HP each | 249 | 1,170 | 25,500 | ECM equipment |
| Boeing B-17G | 10 | 103.7 | 74.4 | 44,560 | 4 Wright R-1820 | 1200 HP each | 287 | 1,800 | 35,000 | 13 12.7-mm machine guns |
| Boeing C-97 Stratocruiser | 4 | 141.2 | 110.3 | 153,000 | 4 Pratt & Whitney R4360 | 3500 HP each | 375 | 4,300 | 35,000 | — |
| Boeing Stearman PT-17 | 2 | 32.1 | 25 | 2,717 | 1 Continental W670 | 220 HP | 124 | 505 | 11,300 | — |

| Aircraft | No. | Length | Span | Weight | Engine | Power | Speed | Range | Ceiling | Armament |
|---|---|---|---|---|---|---|---|---|---|---|
| Boeing 707-320 | 3/5 | 145.7 | 152.9 | 328,000 | 4 Pratt & Whitney JT3D | 18,000 lb. each | 615 | 5,735 | 39,000 | — |
| Bristol Beaufighter | 2 | 57.9 | 42.8 | 21,000 | 2 Bristol Hercules | 1670 HP each | 312 | 1,480 | 26,000 | 4 20-mm cannons, 6 0.303-in. machine guns |
| Britten-Norman Islander | 2 | 49 | 39.5 | 6,300 | 2 Lycoming 0-540-54C5 | 260 HP each | 170 | 1,263 | 14,600 | — |
| Cessna Skywagon | 1 | 36 | 25.9 | 2,800 | 1 Teledyne Continental 0-470U | 230 HP | 170 | 1,163 | 17,700 | |
| Cessna Super Skywagon | 1 | 36.6 | 27.6 | 3,300 | 1 Teledyne Continental | 285 HP | 173 | 1,275 | 16,100 | |
| Consolidated PBY-5 Catalina | 2 | 104 | 63.9 | 34,000 | 2 Pratt & Whitney R1820 | 1200 HP each | 196 | 2,520 | 15,800 | — |
| Curtis C-46 Commando | 2 | 108.1 | 76.4 | 45,000 | 2 Pratt & Whitney R2800 | 2,000 HP each | 234 | 1,200 | 24,500 | — |
| Dassault Ouragan | 1 | 40.2 | 35.2 | 13,646 | 1 Hispano Suiza Nene 104B | 5,000 lb. | 584 | 520 | 42,500 | 4 20-mm cannons, 2,000 lb. of weapons |
| Dassault Mirage IIIC | 1 | 26.9 | 38.4 | 18,600 | 1 Snecma ATAR B | 9,370 lb., 13,378 lb. afterburner | 386 | 400 | 59,000 | 2 30-mm cannons, 2,000 lb. of weapons, 2 AAMs |
| Dassault Mystere IVA | 1 | 36.5 | 42.1 | 16,530 | 1 Hispano Suiza Verdon 350 | 7,716 lb. | 696 | 572 | 49,200 | 2 30-mm cannons, 2,000 lb. of weapons |

## IAF Aircraft *(continued)*

| Aircraft | Crew | Wing Span (ft.) | Length (ft.) | Loaded Weight (lb.) | Engines | Engine Thrust (HP or lb.) | Maximum Speed (MPH) | Range (mi.) | Ceiling (ft.) | Weapons |
|---|---|---|---|---|---|---|---|---|---|---|
| Dassault Super Mystere B2 | 1 | 34.5 | 46.1 | 19,840 | 1 Snecma ATAR 101G | 7,495 dry, 9,920 afterburner | 783 | 540 | 55,700 | 2 30-mm cannons, 2,000 lb. of weapons |
| De Havilland Tiger Moth | 2 | 29.4 | 23.9 | 1,770 | 1 De Havilland Gypsy | 130 HP | 109 | 201 | 13,600 | — |
| De Havilland Dragon Rapide | 2 | 48 | 34.5 | 6,000 | 2 De Havilland Gypsy | 200 HP each | 150 | 520 | 16,000 | — |
| De Havilland Chipmunk | 2 | 34.4 | 25.4 | 2,000 | 1 Bristol Siddeley Gypsy Major | 140 HP | 138 | 300 | 16,000 | — |
| De Havilland Mosquito FB6 | 2 | 54.1 | 40.5 | 22,300 | 2 Rolls Royce Merlin | 1,230 HP each | 380 | 1,200 | 36,000 | 4 20-mm cannons, 4 0.303-in. machine guns, bombs, rockets |
| Dornier DO27 | 1 | 39.4 | 31.6 | 4,000 | 1 Lycoming 650-480 | 274 HP | 174 | 685 | 20,800 | — |
| Dornier DO28 | 2 | 51.9 | 37.5 | 8,000 | 2 Lycoming 10,540 | 290 HP each | 184 | 768 | 19,400 | — |
| Douglas C-47 Dakota | 2 | 95 | 64.5 | 26,000 | 2 Pratt & Whitney R1830 | 1,200 HP each | 229 | 1,500 | 23,000 | Bombs |
| Douglas C-54 | 3 | 117.5 | 93.9 | 7,300 | 4 Pratt & Whitney R2000 | 1,350 HP each | 274 | 3,300 | 22,500 | — |

| Aircraft | | | | Engine | Power | | | | Armament |
|---|---|---|---|---|---|---|---|---|---|
| Douglas DC-5 | 3 | 78 | 62.2 | 20,000 | 2 Wright GR-1320 | 900 HP each | 230 | 1,600 | 23,700 | — |
| Fairchild F-24 | 1 | 36.3 | 24.9 | 2,500 | 1 Ranger G-410B2 | 165 HP | 132 | 640 | 16,800 | Bombs, machine gun |
| Fokker S11 | 2 | 36.1 | 26.8 | 2,425 | 1 Lycoming 0435 | 190 HP | 130 | 400 | 12,630 | — |
| Fouga Magister | 2 | 37 | 33.6 | 6,978 | 2 Turbomeca Marbore | 836 lb. each | 440 | 576 | 40,000 | 2 machine guns, rockets, bombs |
| General Dynamics F-16A/B | 1/2 | 31 | 49.5 | 24,000 | 1 Pratt & Whitney F100 | 14,670 dry 23,800 afterburner | 1,350 | 500 | 50,000 | 1 20-mm cannon, 6 AAMs 12,000 lb. of weapons |
| General Dynamics F-16C/D | 1/2 | 31 | 49.5 | 27,000 | 1 General Electric F110 | 16,000 dry 27,000 afterburner | 1,360 | 600 | 50,000 | 1 20-mm cannon, 6 AAMs 12,000 lb. of weapons |
| Gloster Meteor F.8 | 1 | 37.1 | 44.6 | 15,700 | 2 Rolls Royce Derwent | 3,500 lb. each | 592 | 600 | 40,000 | 4 20-mm cannons, rockets, bombs |
| Grumman E-2C | 5 | 80.7 | 57.6 | 50,000 | 2 Allison T-56 | 4,900 HP each | 374 | 1,600 | 30,000 | — |
| Grumman OV-1D | 2 | 48 | 41 | 18,000 | 2 Avco Lycoming T56 | 1,160 HP each | 285 | 900 | 25,000 | — |
| Grumman Widgeon | 2 | 40 | 31.1 | 4,528 | 2 Ranger L-440 | 200 HP each | 153 | 920 | 14,600 | — |
| IAI Arava | 2 | 68.5 | 42.5 | 15,000 | 1 Pratt & Whitney PT-6 | 780 HP | 203 | 650 | 24,000 | 3 machine guns |
| IAI Nesher | 1 | 26.9 | 49.2 | 20,000 | 1 Snecma ATAR 9C | 9,500 lb. dry, 14,110 lb. afterburner | 1,320 | 650 | 45,000 | 2 30-mm cannons, 2 AAMs, 4,000 lb. of weapons |

## IAF Aircraft (continued)

| Aircraft | Crew | Wing Span (ft.) | Length (ft.) | Loaded Weight (lb.) | Engines | Engine Thrust (HP or lb.) | Maximum Speed (MPH) | Range (mi.) | Ceiling (ft.) | Weapons |
|---|---|---|---|---|---|---|---|---|---|---|
| IAI Kfir | 1 | 26.9 | 50.8 | 23,000 | 1 General Electric J79 | 11,870 lb. dry, 17,900 lb. afterburner | 1,320 | 650 | 50,000 | 2 30-mm cannons, 6,000 lb. of weapons |
| IAI Westwind | 2 | 44.8 | 52.1 | 20,000 | 2 General Electric CJ 010 | 3,100 lb. each | 541 | 2,120 | 45,000 | — |
| Lockheed C-130 H | 4 | 132.6 | 97.7 | 155,000 | 4 Allison T-56 | 4,050 HP each | 384 | 4,700 | 23,000 | — |
| Lockheed Hudson | 2 | 65.5 | 44.3 | 18,500 | 2 Wright Cyclone | 1,200 HP each | 250 | 2,160 | 24,500 | — |
| Lockheed Lode Star | 3 | 65.5 | 49.8 | 18,500 | 2 Wright Cyclone | 1,200 HP each | 271 | 1,600 | 3,000 | — |
| Lockheed Constellation | 3 | 123 | 95.1 | 72,000 | 4 Wright R 3350 | 2,200 HP each | 330 | 2,400 | 25,000 | — |
| McDonnell Douglas A-4H Skyhawk | 1 | 27.5 | 40.3 | 18,000 | 1 Pratt & Whitney J-52 P8 | 9,300 lb. | 675 | 600 | 47,000 | 2 30-mm cannons, 6,000 lb. of weapons |
| McDonnell Douglas A-4N Skyhawk | 1 | 27.5 | 42.6 | 20,000 | 1 Pratt & Whitney J52 P408 | 11,200 lb. | 685 | 606 | 47,000 | 2 30-mm cannons, 8,200 lb. of weapons |
| McDonnell Douglas F-4E Phantom | 2 | 38.2 | 62.9 | 56,000 | 2 General Electric J79-GE-17 | 11,820 dry, 17,900 afterburner | 1,500 | 800 | 58,700 | 1 20-mm cannon, 8 AAMs, 12,000 lb. of weapons |

| Aircraft | No. | | | Weight (lb.) | Engine | Power | Speed (mph) | Range (mi.) | Ceiling (ft.) | Armament |
|---|---|---|---|---|---|---|---|---|---|---|
| McDonnell Douglas F-15A Eagle | 1 | 42.7 | 63.8 | 42,000 | 2 Pratt & Whitney F100 | 14,670 dry, 23,800 afterburner | 1,650 | 800 | 60,000 | 1 20-mm cannon, 8 AAMs, 12,000 lb. of weapons |
| Miles Gemini | 2 | 50 | 36 | 5,300 | 2 Cirrus Blackburn | 100 HP each | 145 | 820 | 13,500 | — |
| Norduyn Norseman | 2 | 51.7 | 32.4 | 7,400 | 1 Pratt & Whitney WASP | 600 HP | 155 | 442 | 17,000 | — |
| Nord Morecrin | 2 | 33.6 | 23.6 | 2,300 | 1 Regnier 460 | 135 HP | 174 | 560 | 16,400 | — |
| Nord Noratlas | 4 | 106.8 | 72.1 | 45,400 | 2 Bristol 1738 | 2,040 HP | 252 | 1,740 | 28,200 | — |
| North American AT-6 | 2 | 42 | 29.5 | 5,000 | 1 Pratt & Whitney R1340 | 550 HP | 210 | 630 | 24,000 | Machine guns, bombs |
| North American P-51D Mustang | 1 | 37 | 32.2 | 11,600 | 1 Packard V 1650 | 1,450 HP | 437 | 950 | 41,900 | 6 12.7-mm machine guns, rockets, bombs |
| Pilatus PC-6 | 1 | 49.9 | 36.1 | 4,400 | 1 Turbo Mecca Astazov | 532 HP | 174 | 500 | 28,000 | — |
| Piper Cub | 2 | 35.2 | 22 | 1,400 | 1 Lycoming | 125 HP | 110 | 500 | 9,500 | Bombs |
| Republic Seabee | 2 | 37.6 | 27.9 | 3,000 | 1 Franklin 6A8-215 | 215 HP | 120 | 560 | 11,700 | — |
| RWD-13 | 1 | 37.7 | 25.6 | 1,958 | PZI Junior | 120 HP | 135 | 500 | 19,500 | — |
| Socata Ralley E | 1 | 31.3 | 22.7 | 874 | Continental 0-300 | 145 HP | 136 | 550 | 11,800 | — |
| Sud Aviation Vautour IIA | 1 | 49.5 | 54.1 | 33,000 | 2 Snecma ATAR 101 | 7,716 HP each | 690 | 1,000 | 49,000 | 4 30-mm cannons, 5,300 lb. of weapons |

# IAF Aircraft (continued)

| Aircraft | Crew | Wing Span (ft.) | Length (ft.) | Loaded Weight (lb.) | Engines | Engine Thrust (HP or lb.) | Maximum Speed (MPH) | Range (mi.) | Ceiling (ft.) | Weapons |
|---|---|---|---|---|---|---|---|---|---|---|
| Supermarine Spitfire Mk 9 | 1 | 36.9 | 31.2 | 7,300 | 1 Rolls Royce Merlin | 1,710 HP | 404 | 434 | 42,000 | 2 20-mm cannons, 4 0.303-in. machine guns, 1,000 lb. of weapons |
| Taylor-craft C | 1 | 36 | 22 | 1,200 | 1 Lycoming 0-145 | 55 HP | 105 | 275 | 17,000 | — |
| Temco Buckaroo | 1 | 29.1 | 21.7 | 1,840 | 1 Continental C145 | 145 HP | 160 | 400 | 14,000 | — |
| Vultee BT-13 | 2 | 42 | 28.6 | 3,981 | 1 Pratt & Whitney T2B2 | 450 HP | 182 | 800 | 21,000 | — |

# IAF Helicopters

| Aircraft | Crew | Rotor Diameter (in.) | Length (ft.) | Loaded Weight (lb.) | Engines | Engine Thrust (HP) | Maximum Speed (MPH) | Range (mi.) | Ceiling (ft.) | Weapons |
|---|---|---|---|---|---|---|---|---|---|---|
| Aerospatiale Frelon SA 321K | 2 | 62 | 63.6 | 27,550 | 3 Turbomecca Turmo | 1,550 each | 149 | 404 | 7,300 | — |

| | | | | | | | | | | Armament |
|---|---|---|---|---|---|---|---|---|---|---|
| Bell AH-IS Cobra | 2 | 44 | 44.4 | 9,500 | 1 Avco Lycoming T55 | 1,800 | 172 | 357 | 11,400 | 1 20-mm cannon, 8 TOW missiles, 38 rockets |
| Bell 476 | 2 | 37.1 | 32.5 | 2,850 | 1 Lycoming VO 435 | 270 | 105 | 250 | 17,600 | — |
| Bell 206 Set Ranger | 2 | 33.3 | 31.1 | 3,000 | 1 Allison 250-C18 | 317 | 133 | 362 | 18,500 | — |
| Bell UH-1D (Augusta 205) | 2 | 48 | 41.9 | 9,500 | 1 Avco Lycoming T53 | 1,250 | 138 | 360 | 11,000 | — |
| Bell 212 | 2 | 48.1 | 57.2 | 11,200 | 1 Pratt & Whitney PT 6T | 1,800 | 161 | 261 | 14,200 | — |
| Hiller VH-12E | 2 | 35.4 | 27.9 | 2,700 | 1 Franklin 6V4 | 200 | 95 | 500 | 5,200 | |
| McDonnell Douglas Model 500 | 2 | 26.3 | 23 | 2,550 | 1 Allison 250-C20 | 420 | 152 | 366 | 14,400 | Guns, 4 TOW missiles |
| McDonnell Douglas AH-64 | 2 | 48 | 58.2 | 16,000 | 2 6E T700 | 1,800 | 185 | 400 | 18,000 | 1 30-mm cannon, 16 Hellfire rockets |
| Sikorsky S-55 | 2 | 53 | 42.2 | 7,900 | 1 Wright R-1300 | 800 | 112 | 360 | 8,600 | — |
| Sikorsky S-58 | 2 | 56 | 56.8 | 13,000 | 1 Wright Cyclone | 1,525 | 122 | 248 | 9,100 | — |
| Sikorsky CH-53 | 2 | 72.2 | 67.1 | 42,000 | 3 General Electric T64 | 3,925 each | 196 | 251 | 21,000 | — |
| Sikorsky UH-60 | 2 | 53.6 | 64.9 | 18,000 | 2 6E T700 | 1,800 | 155 | 400 | 18,000 | — |

## IAF Helicopters (continued)

| Aircraft | Crew | Wing Span (ft.) | Length (ft.) | Loaded Weight (lb.) | Engines | Engine Thrust (HP or lb.) | Maximum Speed (MPH) | Range (mi.) | Ceiling (ft.) | Weapons |
|---|---|---|---|---|---|---|---|---|---|---|
| Black Hawk Sud Aviation Alouette | 2 | 33.4 | 31.9 | 3,527 | 1 Turbo-Artouste IIC | 530 | 115 | 350 | 7,050 | — |

## IAF/Arab Air Forces Exchange Ratio

### Aircraft Loss Breakdown

| | Total Arab losses | In air combat | On the ground | From air defense weapons | Unknown, fracticide and maneuvering suicide | IAF combat losses (ACM losses) |
|---|---|---|---|---|---|---|
| 1948 | 57 | 23 | 30 | 4 | 2 | 8 (2) |
| 1948–56 | 3 | 3 | | | | 0 (0) |
| 1956 | 9 | 7 | | | 2 | 15 (1) |
| 1956–67 | 13 | 12 | | | 1 | 0 (0) |
| June 1967 War | 451 | 60 | 378 | 3 | 10 | 48 (10) |
| War of attrition (June 1967–August 1970) | 150 | 113 | — | 25 | 12 | 38 (4) |
| August 1970–October 1973 | 39 | 34 | — | ~4 | 1 | 8 (2) |
| Yom Kippur War October 1973 | 447 | 277 | 22 | 43 | 105 | 109 (11) |

| | | | | | |
|---|---|---|---|---|---|
| November 1973–June 1979 | 6 | 6 | — | — | 2 (0) |
| June 1979–June 1982 | 25 | 22 | — | 3 | 0 (0) |
| Lebanon, June 1982 | 95 | 85 | — | 7 | 3 | 6 (0) |
| Since June 1982 | 5 | 3 | — | 1 | 1 | 2 (0) |
| Total | 1300 | 644 | 430 | 87 | 140 | 236 (30) |

Overall exchange ratio in air-to-air combat: 21.5 to 1; overall conflict exchange ratio: 5.5 to 1. The IAF does not recognize "ace" status. However, many pilots have achieved more than five air-to-air victories and one individual has seventeen kills to his credit.
Table prepared from IAFs sources; Dick Pawloski, "Changes in Soviet Air Combat Doctrine and Force Structure," *General Dynamics Publication* (July 1987): II–129; and material from numerous books and periodicals.

# IAF Air-to-Air Victories

**1948 Total: 23   Cannon: 100%**
  15  Spitfire
   6  Avia
   2  Mustang (est.)

**1948–56 Total: 3   Cannon: 100%**
   2  Meteor
   1  Ouragon

**1956 Total: 7   Cannon: 100%**
   7  Mystere IV

**1956–67 Total: 12   Cannon: 93%   Missile: 7%**
   1  Mystere IV
  11  Mirage

**1967 Total: 60   Cannon: 100%**
  50  Mirage
   5  Super Mystere
   3  Mystere IV
   1  Ouragon
   1  Vautour

**War of Attrition Total: 113   Cannon: 70%   Missile: 30%**
 105  Mirage
   5  Phantom
   2  Skyhawk

**1970–73 Total: 34   Cannon: 70%   Missile: 30%**
  14  Mirage/Nesher
  20  Phantom (est.)

**Yom Kippur War Total: 277   Cannon: 30%   Missile: 70%**
 183  Mirage/Nesher
  94  Phantom (est.)

**1973–79 Total: 6   Cannon: 20%   Missile: 80%**
   3  Phantom
   3  Mirage/Nesher (est.)

**1979–82 Total: 22   Cannon: 10%   Missile: 90%**
  14  F-15
   7  F-16
   1  Kfir

**Lebanon, 1982 Total: 85   Cannon: 7%   Missile: 93%**
  40  F-15
  44  F-16
   1  Phantom

**Since June 1982 Total: 3   Missile: 100%**
   3  F-15
  Total: 644

## Breakdown of IAF Victories by Fighter Type

|  | Approximate Victories | Percent of Totals |
|---|---|---|
| Mirage, Nesher, Kfir | 367 | 56.99 |
| F-4 Phantom | 123 | 19.10 |
| F-15 Eagle | 57 | 8.85 |
| F-16 Falcon | 51 | 7.92 |
| Spitfire | 15 | 2.33 |
| Mystere IV | 11 | 1.70 |
| Avia | 6 | 0.93 |
| Super Mystere B2 | 5 | 0.78 |
| Meteor | 2 | 0.31 |
| Ouragon | 2 | 0.31 |
| A-4 Skyhawk | 2 | 0.31 |
| P-51 Mustang | 2 | 0.31 |
| Vautour | 1 | 0.16 |
| Totals | 644 | 100.00 |

### Approximate breakdown of victories by weapon type

| | | |
|---|---|---|
| Cannon | (20-mm, 30-mm) | 45 |
| Missile | (AIM-9 Sidewinder, Shafrir, Python, Matra 530, AIM-7 Sparrow) | 55 |

# Notes

## Chapter 1. War of Independence

1. J. N. Westwood, *The History of the Middle East Wars* (Greenwich, CT: Bison Books, 1984), 8.

2. Ze'ev Schiff, *A History of the Israeli Army* (New York: Macmillan, 1985), 15.

3. Westwood, *History of Middle East Wars*, 10.

4. "A Short History of the Israeli Air Force," *Aerospace Historian* (March 1972): 11.

5. William Gunston, *An Illustrated Guide to the Israeli Air Force* (New York: Arco Books, 1982), 16–17.

6. Trevor N. Dupuy, *Elusive Victory: The Arab-Israeli Wars, 1947–1974*, (New York: Harper & Row, 1978) 12–19.

7. Westwood, *History of Middle East Wars*, 13.

8. David J. Bercuson, *The Secret Army* (New York: Stein & Day, 1984), 20–21.

9. Richard Goldman and Murray Rubenstein, *Shield of David* (Englewood Cliffs, NJ: Prentice-Hall, 1978), 29.

10. Robert Jackson, *The Israel Air Force Story* (London: Tandem Books, 1970), 31.

11. Gunston, *Illustrated Guide*, 34–38.

12. Goldman and Rubenstein, *Shield of David*, 42–43.

13. Benjamin Kegan, *The Secret Battle for Israel* (Cleveland, OH: World, 1966), 55.

14. Lou Lenart, interview with author, Los Angeles, May 22, 1988.

15. Bercuson, *Secret Army*, 130.

16. Gunston, *Illustrated Guide*, 38–39.

17. Nathaniel Linch, *Edge of the Sword* (New York: Putnam, 1962), 316.

18. Rudolph Augarten, interview with author, Los Angeles, June 22, 1988.

19. Bercuson, *Secret Army*, 188.

20. Jackson, *Israel Air Force Story*, 43.

21. Goldman and Rubenstein, *Shield of David*, 47.

22. Ibid., 50.

23. Rudolph Augarten, interview with author, Los Angeles, June 22, 1988.

24. Ibid.

25. Linch, *Edge of the Sword*, 364–65.

26. "Mosquito," *Born in Battle Magazine*, #19 (Eshel Dramit, Ltd., 1981): 26–28.

27. Rudolph Augarten, interview with author, Los Angeles, June 22, 1988.

28. Goldman and Rubenstein, *Shield of David*, 54–55.

29. Ezer Weizman, *On Eagles' Wings* (New York: Macmillan, 1976), 80–82.

30. "A Short History of the Israel Air Force," *Aerospace Historian* (March 1972): 13.

## CHAPTER 2. THE EARLY YEARS

1. Benjamin Kegan, *The Secret Battle for Israel* (Cleveland, OH: World, 1966), 179–82.

2. William Gunston, *An Illustrated Guide to the Israeli Air Force* (New York: Arco Books, 1982), 42–43.

3. "Expansion to 1956," *Born in Battle Magazine* #2 (Eshel Dramit, Ltd., 1978): 18–19.

4. Robert Jackson, *The Israel Air Force Story* (London: Tandem Books, 1970), 65–68.

5. Ibid., 65.

6. Kegan, *Secret Battle*, 204.

7. Kenneth Munson, *Dassault MP 450 Ouragon* (Windsor: Profile Publications Ltd., 1979), 132–145.

8. Gunston, *Illustrated Guide*, 62–63.

9. Aharon Yoeli, interview with author, Tel Aviv, November 17, 1988.

10. Richard Goldman and Murray Rubenstein, *Shield of David* (Englewood Cliffs, NJ: Prentice-Hall, 1978), 72.

## CHAPTER 3. THE SINAI CONFLICT

1. S.L.A. Marshall, *Sinai Victory* (Nashville, TN: Battery Press, 1968), 33.

2. J. N. Westwood, *The History of the Middle East Wars* (Greenwich, CT: Bison Books, 1984), 35.

3. Moshe Dayan, *Diary of the Sinai Campaign* (New York: Harper & Row, 1966), 33.

4. Trevor N. Dupuy, *Elusive Victory: The Arab-Israeli Wars, 1947–1974* (New York: Harper & Row, 1978), 138–43.

5. Ibid., 146–47.

6. Sidney Bisk and David Larcombe, "We Trained Nasser's Air Force," *Royal Air Force Flying Review* (January 1957): 25–26.

7. Alfred Goldberg, *"Air Operations in the Sinai Campaign"* (Maxwell Air Force Base, AL: Air War College, Air University, November, 1959), 5.

8. Dayan, *Diary*, 218.

9. Goldberg, *Sinai Campaign*, 5–7.

10. Patrick Falcon, "Thirty Years Later—Review of the French Air Force Contribution to the Suez Victory," *Air Fan* (November 1986): 68–77.

11. Chaim Herzog, *The Arab-Israeli Wars* (New York: Random House, 1982), 118–20.

12. Marshall, *Sinai Victory*, 45.

13. Guy Rimon, "Pride of Place," *Israel Air Force Magazine* (1989) 58.

14. Vic Flintman, "The Suez Campaign 1956," *Scale Aircraft Modeling* (November 1986): 54–75.

15. "History of the IAF 101 Squadron," *Born In Battle Defense Update* #75 (September 1986): 42–45.

16. Marshall, *Sinai Victory*, 69.

17. Yallo Shavit, interview with author, Tel Aviv, Israel, November 17, 1987.

18. Robert Henriques, *One Hundred Hours to the Suez* (New York: Collins, 1957), 196–99.

19. Eliezer Cohen, interview with author, Tel Aviv, Israel, November 15, 1987.

20. Charles Christienne and Pierre Lissarague, *The History of French Military Aviation* (Washington, DC: Smithsonian Institution Press, 1986), 473.

21. "IAF 101 Squadron," p. 44.

22. Glen Ashley, "Suez Crisis," *Scale Models International* (September 1984): 493.

23. Flintman, *Suez Campaign 1956*, 59.

24. Dupuy, *Elusive Victory*, 211.

25. Marshall, *Sinai Victory*, 141–165.

26. Alan W. Hall, "Republic F-84 Thunderstreak," *Scale Aircraft Modeling*, (March 1987): 250–83.

27. Vic Flintman, "Suez 1956, a Lesson in Airpower," *Air Pictorial* (August–September 1965): 270.

28. Dupuy, *Elusive Victory*, 212.

29. Flintman, *Suez Campaign, 1956*, 66.

30. Ze'ev Schiff, *A History of the Israeli Army* (New York: Macmillan, 149.

31. Ibid.

32. Christienne and Lissarague, *French Military Aviation*, 473.

33. Schiff, *Israeli Army*, 149.

## Chapter 4. Modernization

1. William Gunston, *An Illustrated Guide to the Israeli Air Force* (New York: Arco Books, 1982) 60–65.

2. J. A. Cook, *Quantity or Quality? An Analysis of Current UPT Philosophy*, Professional Study No. 4544 (Maxwell Air Force Base, AL: Air War College, Air University, January, 1972). This study provides an overview of the Israeli pilot training philosophy.

3. Ezer Weizman, *On Eagles' Wings* (New York: Macmillan, 1976), 173–98.

4. "Egypt's Aviation Industry," *Interavia* (November 1966): 1796–98.

5. Gunston, *Illustrated Guide*, 72–73.

6. "Dassault Mirage III," *Born in Battle Magazine* #13 (Eshel Dramit, Ltd., 1981): 4–5.

7. Richard Goldman and Murray Rubenstein, *Shield of David* (Englewood Cliffs, NJ: Prentice-Hall, 1978), 78.

8. Thomas J. Marshall, "Israeli Helicopter Forces, Organization and Tactics," *Military Review* (May 1972): 94–99.

9. Robert Jackson, *The Israel Air Force Story* (London: Tandem Books, 1970), 127.

10. Edward Luttwak and David Horowitz, *The Israeli Army* (New York: A. Lane Publishers, 1975), 223.

11. Ibid., 187.

12. Guy Rimon, "Pride of Place," *Israel Air Force Magazine* (1989 Annual Edition): 59.

13. "Dassault Mirage III," 24.

14. A. J. Barker, *Six-Day War* (New York: Ballantine Books, 1974), 39.

15. Gunther E. Rothenberg, *The Anatomy of the Israeli Army* (New York: Hippocrene Books, 1979), 132.

## Chapter 5. The Six Day War

1. Ze'ev Schiff, *A History of the Israeli Army* (New York: Macmillan, 1985), 155.

2. "The Six-Day War," *Born in Battle Magazine* #6 (Eshel Dramit, Ltd., 1979): 22.

3. Yallo Shavit, interview with author, Tel Aviv, November 17, 1987.

4. Edgar O'Ballance, *The Third Arab-Israeli War* (Hamden, CT: Anchor Books, 1970), 70.

5. "Airfield Attack, Lessons of Middle East Wars," *Born in Battle Magazine* #37 (Eshel Dramit, Ltd., 1984): 13.

6. Warren Wetmore, "Israelis' Air Punch Major Factor in War," *Aviation Week & Space Technology* (July 3, 1967): 18–23.

7. David Horowitz and Edward Luttwak, *The Israeli Army* (1975), 227.

8. David Eshel and Stanley M. Ulanoff, *The Fighting Israeli Air Force* (New York: Arco Books, 1985), 54–60.

9. D. K. Palit, *Return to the Sinai* (New Delhi: Palit & Palit, 1974), 23.

10. Chaim Herzog, *The Arab-Israeli Wars*, (New York: Random House, 1982), 197.

11. Eliezer Cohen, interview with author, Tel Aviv, November 15, 1987.

12. Wetmore, "Israelis' Air Punch," 19.

13. Guy Rimon, "Pride of Place," *Israel Air Force Magazine* (1989 Annual Edition): 60.

14. Wetmore, "Israelis' Air Punch," 23.

15. Trevor Dupuy, *Elusive Victory: The Arab-Israeli Wars, 1947–1974* (New York: Harper & Row, 1978), 315.

16. "Massive Resupply Narrows Israeli Margin," *Aviation Week & Space Technology* (June 19, 1967): 16.

17. A retired senior IAF officer, interview with author, Tel Aviv, November 17, 1987.

18. Dupuy, *Elusive Victory*, 279.

19. Gunther E. Rothenberg, *The Anatomy of the Israeli Army* (New York: Hippocrene Books, 1979), 146–47.

20. Dupuy, *Elusive Victory*, 326.

21. Schiff, *Israeli Army*, 156.

22. Ibid.

23. "Six-Day War," 21.

24. Major General B. Peled (Ret.), interview with author, Tel Aviv, June 18, 1978.

## CHAPTER 6. THE WAR OF ATTRITION

1. *Military Balance* (London: International Institute for Strategic Studies, 1968–69), 45.

2. D. Eshel, Ed., "From Mirage to Kfir," *War Data*, No. 2 (Eshel-Dramit, Ltd., 1979): 10.

3. Kenneth Munson, "Skyhawk," *War Data*, No. 7 (Eshel Dramit, Ltd., 1980): 12.

4. *Military Balance*, 44.

5. Ibid., 46.

6. Eliezer Cohen, interview with author, Tel Aviv, November 1987.

7. "Airborne & Commando Raids," *Born in Battle*, #5 (Eshel Dramit, Ltd., 1979): 56.

8. James Feron, "Dayan Ridicules Claims of Arabs on Israeli Toll," *The New York Times* (April 18, 1969): 7.

9. James Feron, "Israeli Jets Attack UAR" *The New York Times* (July 21, 1969): 1.

10. S. Gilboa, interview with author, Tel Aviv, November 17, 1987.

11. James Feron, "Israeli Reports Downing 11 Jets in Suez Clashes," *The New York Times* (September 12, 1969): 1.

12. James Feron, "Israelis Maintain Pressure on UAR in New Airstrike," *The New York Times* (September 14, 1969): 1.

13. Hirsh Goodman, "Reliable Veteran," *The Jerusalem Post Magazine* (October 19, 1984): 4–5.

14. "A Talk with General Bar Lev," *Newsweek* (November 24, 1969): 52.

15. John Bentley, "Inside Israel's Air Force," *Flight International* (March 19, 1970): 427.

16. Yallo Shavit, interview with author, Tel Aviv, November 17, 1987.

17. John Bentley, "Inside Israel's Air Force Part 2—The Enemy We Face," *Flight International* (April 23, 1970): 669.

18. Ibid., 668.

19. "Mrs. Meir Declares Israeli Air Raids Show that Nasser Is a Failure," *The New York Times* (February 6, 1970): 11.

20. Edgar O'Ballance, *The Electronic War in the Middle East: 1968–70* (London: Faber & Faber, 1974), 107.

21. Peter Grosse, "Nasser Concedes that Israelis Have Air Superiority in Mideast," *The New York Times* (February 8, 1970): 6.

22. "Israeli Planes Seek to Thwart SAM-3s," *The New York Times* (March 25, 1970): 8.

23. James Feron, "Israelis Report Downing 5 MiGs Over Suez Canal," *The New York Times* (March 28, 1970): 4.

24. "Middle East: Other Fronts," *Newsweek* (April 13, 1970): 39.

25. Munson, "Skyhawk," 38–40.

26. Lawrence Whetlen, "June 1967–June 1971: Four Years of Canal War Reconsidered," *New Middle East* (June 1971): 19.

27. *Military Balance*, 32.

28. Richard Eder, "Israelis Report Russians Fire Rockets," *The New York Times* (July, 1970): 6.

29. O'Ballance, *Electronic War in the Middle East*, 114.

30. "The Air War in the Middle East: Israel's Air Force," *Born In Battle Magazine*, #2 (Eshel Dramit, Ltd., 1978): 50.

31. Ibid.

32. Ze'ev Schiff, "The Israel Air Force," *Air Force Magazine* (August 1976): 36.

33. Eshel, "From Mirage to Kfir," 12–13.

34. *Military Balance* (London: International Institute for Strategic Studies, 1971–1972): 29.

## CHAPTER 7. THE YOM KIPPUR WAR

1. *Military Balance* (London: International Institute of Strategic Studies, 1973–74), 33.

2. "Yom Kippur Arab-Israeli War," *Warplane* #93 (1983): 1841–45.

3. *Military Balance*, 36.

4. IAF Wing Commander, interview with author, Ramat David Air Base, Israel, November 15, 1987.

5. "Air Defense—Evolution of the Air Defense Missile Threat," *Born in Battle* #78 (Eshel Dramit, Ltd., December 1986): 18–29.

6. James M. Loop and Steven J. Zaloga, *Soviet Tanks and Combat Vehicles 1946–The Present* (Dorset: Arms & Armour Press, 1988), 216–21.

7. Ibid., 201–8.

8. Major A.J.C. Cavalle, ed., *Airpower and the Spring*, (Washing-

ton, DC: Invasion USAF Southeast Asia Monogram Series (1982), 44.

9. "The War in the Air," *Born in Battle Defense Update* #42, Yom Kippur Special (Eshel Dramit, Ltd., 1983): 18.

10. Yallo Shavit, interview with author, Tel Aviv, November 17, 1987.

11. John F. Kreis, *Air Warfare and Air Base Defense*, USAF Special Studies (Washington, DC: Office of Air Force History, 1988), 338.

12. N. Merchavi, interview with author, Tel Aviv, November 19, 1987.

13. Senate Committee of Armed Services, Subcommittee on Tactical Air Power, Hearings, March 11–21, 1974, 4306–18.

14. Mike Gaines, "Pilotless over the Battlefield," *Flight International* (December 1979): 1837.

15. "The War of the Day of Judgment," *Newsweek* (October 22, 1973): 28–29.

16. "Israel's Phantoms," *Born in Battle*, F-4 Phantom II Special Issue (Eshel Dramit, Ltd., 1981): 45.

17. "Selected Readings in Tactics," *The 1973 Middle East War*, U.S. Army Command and General Staff College Publication RB 100-2 (Ft. Leavenworth, KS: August 1976), 5–9.

18. N. Merchavi, interview.

19. "Israel's Phantoms," 44.

20. Ze'ev Schiff, *A History of the Israeli Army* (New York: Macmillan, 1985), 161.

21. IAF Wing Commander, interview.

22. Senate Committee of Armed Services, Hearings, Department of Defense Appropriations Fiscal Year 1977, Book 5, 440.

23. Terrance Smith, "Tel Aviv Says Attack Destroys Artillery and Missile Sites," *The New York Times* (October 19, 1973): 1.

24. Henry Kamm, "Two Top Generals Foresee Sinai Triumph," *The New York Times* (October 21, 1973): 6.

25. N. Merchavi, interview.

26. Trevor Dupuy, *Elusive Victory: The Arab-Israeli Wars, 1947–1974* (New York: Harper & Row, 1978), 609.

27. *Military Balance* (London: International Institute of Strategic Studies, 1972–73), 33.

28. Charles W. Corddry, "The Yom Kippur War Lessons New and Old," *National Defense* (May–June 1974): 509.

29. "The War in The Air," 22.

30. Senate Committee of Armed Services, 4249.

31. "Air Defense Equipment in Israel," *Born in Battle* #23, (Eshel Dramit, Ltd., 1982): 23.

32. Corddry, "Yom Kippur War," 508.

33. "The War in the Air," 19–20.

34. Corddry, "Yom Kippur War," 508.

35. Ibid.

36. Dupuy, *Elusive Victory*, 609.

37. "Yom Kippur War," 1845.

## Chapter 8. Unending Conflict

1. Benjamin Peled, Notes from the International Symposium on Military Aspects of the Arab–Israeli Conflict, October 12–17, 1975, Jerusalem.

2. "From Kfir to Lavi," *Defense Update* #55 (Eshel Dramit, Ltd., 1984): 20.

3. Brigadier General Joshua Shani, interview with author, Washington, DC, May 13, 1988.

4. Amir Yoeli, interview with author, New York, January 20, 1988.

5. Bonner Day, "New Role for the Israeli Air Force" *Air Force Magazine* (August 1978): 35.

6. "Eagle vs. MiG," *Born in Battle Magazine* #13 (Eshel Dramit, Ltd., 1980): 37.

7. "Kfir in Combat," *Born in Battle Magazine* #14, (Eshel Dramit, Ltd., 1980): 37.

8. Dan McKinnon, *Bullseye One Reactor* (San Diego, CA: House of Hits Publishing, 1987), 108–175.

9. "Interview with Captured Pilot," *The Jerusalem Post* (July 4–10, 1982): 7.

10. Major Moshe Fogel, "The Syrian Missiles, Peace for Galilee Combat Reports," *IDF Journal* (December 1982): 43.

11. Ibid.

12. Ibid.

13. Paul S. Cutler, " 'We Learned both Tactical and Strategic Lessons in Lebanon,' Lt. Gen. Rafael Eitan," *Military Electronics Countermeasures* (February 1983): 100.

14. Fogel, "Syrian Missiles," 43.

15. Ibid.

16. Ibid.

17. Guy Rimon, "My F-15 Was on Fire," *Israel Air Force Magazine* (October 1988): 13.

18. Cutler, "We Learned Lessons," 100.

19. Fogel, "Syrian Missiles," 43.

20. "Israel Reveals Lebanon War Victories," *Flight International* (April 9, 1983): 979.

21. Yoram Inspector, "Complete Air Superiority," *Bamahane (Hebrew)* #42 (July 21, 1982): 10–11.

22. Yoeli interview.

23. "U.S. Arms Used in Lebanon War Outstrip Soviets," *Wall Street Journal* (August 5, 1982): 4.

24. Tzvi Gutman, "The Magic Formula of the F-16 Pilots," *Bita 'on Heyl Ha' Avir* (Hebrew) #28 (July 1982): 6.

25. Ibid.

26. Ibid.

27. Inspector, "Complete Air Superiority," 10–11.

28. Karl Schnell, "Experiences of the Lebanon War," *Military Technology* (July 1984): 30.

29. Ibid.

30. "From Kfir to Lavi," 20.

31. "Bombing Raid at the Heart of the PLO," *Israel Air Force Magazine* (November 1985): 12–13.

32. "Targeting the PLO," *Newsweek* (October 14, 1985): 52.

33. "Syrian Air Force Much More Aggressive: Interview with IAF Commander Lapidot," *The Jerusalem Post* (November 21, 1985): 19.

34. Merov Halperin, "General Avihu Ben-Nun, Incoming IAF Commander," *Israel Air Force Magazine* (September 1987): 46.

# Index